Adult Intentions, Student Perceptions

A volume in
Educational Leadership for Social Justice
Jeffrey S. Brooks, *Series Editor*

Adult Intentions, Student Perceptions

How Restorative Justice is Used
in Schools to Control and to Engage

Kristin E. Reimer
Monash University, Australia

INFORMATION AGE PUBLISHING, INC.
Charlotte, NC • www.infoagepub.com

Library of Congress Cataloging-in-Publication Data

A CIP record for this book is available from the Library of Congress
http://www.loc.gov

ISBN: 978-1-64113-504-7 (Paperback)
       978-1-64113-505-4 (Hardcover)
       978-1-64113-506-1 (ebook)

Printed in the United States of America

Contents

Series Editor's Preface.. vii
    Jeffrey S. Brooks

Foreword... xi
    Joel Westheimer

Acknowledgments... xvii

1 Introduction: The Rise of Restorative Justice in Schools.............. 1
    My Own Restorative Justice journey... 4
    Restorative Justice—An Introduction 5
    A Question of Language 7
    Moving Through the Book 8

2 The Tensions Within Restorative Justice: A Continuum
    of Understandings 11
    Affirmative Restorative Justice... 12
    Transformative Restorative Justice 14
    Social Control or Social Engagement 17

3 Listening to the Voices in the Schools 29
    Scotland... 30
    Canada... 30
    Data Collection 31
    Learning Circles 34
    Notes 40

4 **Rocky Creek: The Canadian School Story**................................**41**

Alberta... 42

Notes... 67

5 **Rocky Creek Public School: Educator Intentions**.....................**69**

Educator Intentions.. 69

Note... 79

6 **Rocky Creek Public School: Student Perceptions**....................**81**

Conclusion... 95

7 **Royal Mills High School: The Scottish School Story**..................**97**

National.. 97

Regional... 107

Royal Mills High School....................................... 112

Notes... 124

8 **Royal Mills High School: Educator Intentions**.........................**125**

Educator Intentions.. 125

9 **Royal Mills High School: Pupil Perceptions**............................**135**

Pupil Perceptions.. 135

Conclusion... 148

Notes... 148

10 **Holding the Studies Side by Side**...**149**

Scottish Summary: The Reality of Both/And........... 150

Canadian Summary: Individual Commitment......... 152

Holding the Studies Side by Side.......................... 154

Intentions versus Perceptions.............................. 154

The Real Question: Social Control or Social Engagement?...... 160

Conclusion: Restorative Justice as Window............ 161

11 **Restorative Justice as a Window Into Relationships**..................**163**

Summary of Study.. 163

The Lens and the Window.................................... 164

Implications... 165

Final Words... 170

References...**173**

Series Editor's Preface

Jeffrey S. Brooks

I am pleased to serve as series editor for this book series, *Educational Leadership for Social Justice*, with Information Age Publishing. The idea for this series grew out of the work of a committed group of leadership for scholars associated with the American Educational Research Association's (AERA) Leadership for Social Justice Special Interest Group (LSJ SIG). This group existed for many years before being officially affiliated with AERA, and has benefited greatly from the ongoing leadership, support, and counsel of Dr. Catherine Marshall (University of North Carolina–Chapel Hill). It is also important to acknowledge the contributions of the LSJ SIG's first Chair, Dr. Ernestine Enomoto (University of Hawaii at Manoa), whose wisdom, stewardship, and guidance helped ease a transition into AERA's more formal organizational structures. This organizational change was at times difficult to reconcile with scholars who largely identified as nontraditional thinkers and push toward innovation rather than accept the status quo. As the second chair of the LSJ SIG, I appreciate all of Ernestine's hard work and friendship. Moreover, I also thank Drs. Gaetane Jean-Marie (University of Northern Iowa) and Whitney Sherman Newcomb, the third and fourth chairs of the LSJ SIG, for their visionary leadership, steadfast commitment to high standards, and collaborative scholarship and friendship.

Adult Intentions, Student Perceptions, pages vii–ix
Copyright © 2019 by Information Age Publishing
All rights of reproduction in any form reserved.

I am particularly indebted to my colleagues on the LSJ SIG's first publications committee, which I chaired from 2005–2007: Dr. Denise Armstrong, Brock University; Dr. Ira Bogotch, Florida Atlantic University; Dr. Sandra Harris, Lamar University; Dr. Whitney Sherman, Virginia Commonwealth University; and Dr. George Theoharis, Syracuse University. This committee was a joy to work with and I am pleased we have found many more ways to collaborate—now as my fellow series editors of this book series—as we seek to provide publication opportunities for scholarship in the area of leadership for social justice.

This book, *Adult Intentions, Student Perceptions: How Restorative Justice is Used in Schools to Control and to Engage* by Kristin E. Reimer is the 23rd in the series. The book makes an important contribution in that it is an in-depth exploration of restorative justice in schools. The book is based on a fascinating cross-national comparative research project. Chapters are engaging and grounded in the words of participants.

Again, welcome to this twenty-third book in this Information Age Publishing series, *Educational Leadership for Social Justice.* You can learn more about the series at our web site (http://www.infoagepub.com/series/Educational-Leadership-for-Social-Justice). I invite you to contribute your own work on equity and influence to the series. We look forward to you joining the conversation.

—**Professor Jeffrey S. Brooks**
RMIT University

Other Books in the Educational Leadership for Social Justice Book Series

Anthony H. Normore, Editor (2008). *Leadership for social justice: Promoting equity and excellence through inquiry and reflective practice.*

Tema Okun (2010). *The emperor has no clothes: Teaching about race and racism to people who don't want to know.*[1]

Autumn K. Cypres and Christa Boske, Editors (2010). *Bridge leadership: Connecting educational leadership and social justice to improve schools.*

Dymaneke D. Mitchell (2012). *Crises of identifying: Negotiating and mediating race, gender, and disability within family and schools.*

Cynthia Gerstl-Pepin and Judith A. Aiken (2012). *Defining social justice leadership in a global context: The changing face of educational supervision.*

Brian D. Fitch and Anthony H. Normore, Editors (2012). *Education-based incarceration and recidivism: The ultimate social justice crime-fighting tool.*

Christa Boske, Editor (2012). *Educational leadership: Building bridges between ideas, schools and nations.*

Jo Bennett (2012). *Profiles of care: At the intersection of social justice, leadership, & the ethic of care.*

Elizabeth Murakami-Ramalho and Anita Pankake (2012). *Educational leaders encouraging the intellectual and professional capacity of others: A social justice agenda.*

Jeffrey S. Brooks and Noelle Witherspoon Arnold, Editors (2013). *Antiracist school leadership: Toward equity in education for America's students.*

Jeffrey S. Brooks and Noelle Witherspoon Arnold, Editors (2013). *Confronting racism in higher education: Problems and possibilities for fighting ignorance, bigotry and isolation.*

Mary Green (2014). *Caring leadership in turbulent times: Tackling neoliberal education reform.*

Carol Mullen (2014). *Shifting to fit: The politics of black and white identity in school leadership.*

Anthony H. Normore and Jeffrey S. Brooks, Editors (2014). *Educational leadership for ethics and social justice: Views from the social sciences.*

Whitney N. Sherman and Katherine Mansfield, Editors (2014). *Women interrupting, disrupting, and revolutionizing educational policy and practice.*

Carlos McCray and Floyd Beachum (2014). *School leadership in a diverse society: Helping schools to prepare all students for success.*

M. C. Kate Esposito and Anthony H. Normore, Editors (2015). *Inclusive practices for special populations in urban settings: The need for social justice leadership.*

Jeffrey S. Brooks and Melanie C. Brooks, Editors (2015). *Urban educational leadership for social justice: International perspectives.*

Natasha Croom and Tyson Marsh (2016). *Envisioning Critical Race Praxis in Higher Education through Counter-Storytelling.*

Tyson Marsh and Natasha Croom (2016). *Envisioning a Critical Race Praxis in K–12 Leadership through Counter-Storytelling.*

William DeJean and Jeff Sapp (2016). *Dear Gay, Lesbian, Bisexual, and Transgender Teacher: Letters of Advice to Help You Find Your Way.*

Note

1. Winner of the American Educational Studies Association 2011 Critics Choice Award

Foreword

It was the middle of the week—Wednesday morning—when state education officials, district superintendents, school administrators and teachers across the country received a letter from government officials. "Dear Colleague," it began, and then moved quickly to the purpose of the communiqué. Federal law, the letter informed its recipients, requires that public schools "administer student discipline without discriminating on the basis of race, color, or national origin." It went on to note that the law "prohibits public school districts from discriminating in the administration of student discipline based on certain personal characteristics."[1]

Whether you are reading this from Canada, the United States, or elsewhere, it would be reasonable to assume that this letter hails from half a century ago, perhaps immediately following the passage of the historic U.S. Civil Rights Act of 1964 or the many instances of human rights legislation that swept through Canada in the 1960s and '70s. But that assumption would be wrong. On January 8, 2014, the U.S. Department of Justice's Civil Rights Division and the U.S. Department of Education's Office for Civil Rights issued this "Dear Colleague" letter in an effort to end official Federal support for "zero tolerance" policies in schools. Study after study had found that zero tolerance policies (mandated predetermined punishments for students who commit certain specified offenses) had resulted in a dramatic increase in discrimination against racial minority children and children with disabilities (Alexander, 2010; Ayers, Ayers, & Dohrn, 2002). Studies also found that rather than improving the school climate for

Adult Intentions, Student Perceptions, pages xi–xvi
Copyright © 2019 by Information Age Publishing
All rights of reproduction in any form reserved.

non-offending students, zero-tolerance policies instead sowed distrust and divisiveness, damaging relationships among and between both students and teachers (APA Task Force, 2008; Lustick, 2017).

The most comprehensive and censorious U.S. report on zero tolerance policies in education came from Harvard 14 years before the "Dear Colleague" letter. *Opportunities Suspended: The Devastating Consequences of Zero Tolerance and School Discipline Policies* (Harvard Civil Rights Project, 2000) strongly condemned the disproportionate impact and ineffectiveness of zero tolerance policies and called for their withdrawal or modification. African-American students, the report found, were more than three times as likely as their White peers to be expelled or suspended. Although African-American students represent 15% of students, they made up 35% of students suspended once, 44% of those suspended more than once, and 36% of students expelled. Zero tolerance policies also led to an increase in police involvement in often routine disciplinary matters. More than half of the students who were involved in school-related arrests were Hispanic or African-American.

Although Canada's first official zero tolerance policy was adopted by Ontario's Scarborough Board of Education in 1993 (Bhattacharjee, 2003), it was not until 2000 that Ontario passed the Safe Schools Act followed quickly by Ontario's first Code of Conduct. These pieces of legislation mirrored many of the U.S. zero tolerance policies but allowed for school administrators to consider "mitigating circumstances" before implementing the mandatory punishments. Whether the laws allowed for the consideration of mitigating circumstances or not, overall, the outcomes were striking. In 2000–2001, the year before the Safe Schools Act was implemented, 113,778 students were suspended; by 2003–2004, the number of students suspended rose by 34% to 152,626. This number now represented 7.2 percent of all Ontario students. (In Ontario's Grand Erie District School Board, fully 1 in 10 students was suspended that year at least once). Expulsions increased 1,700% from 106 students to 1908.

As a result, in 2005 the Ontario Human Rights Commission (OHRC) launched a complaint against the Ministry of Education and the Toronto District School Board, charging discrimination against racialized students and students with disabilities. Similar concerns were raised in other provinces. By 2007, Ontario and most of the rest of Canada had abandoned the foray into U.S.-style zero tolerance in school discipline.[2] Several years before the "Dear Colleague" letter in the United States, Ministries of Education in Ontario and a number of other provinces had already made clear to education officials and school leaders that they now believed that zero tolerance policies did not reduce violence or increase safety in schools; that there are long-term detrimental consequences for children who are suspended or expelled; and that it was possible through other means to create "a safe environment with a low number of disciplinary referrals" (Bhattacharjee, 2003, p. iv).

Discipline by Other Means: Restorative Justice in Schools

The turn against zero tolerance policies meant that other means were needed to create a safe and respectful school environment. "Politically, zero tolerance looks good," wrote Vicky Mather, Director of the Alberta Teachers Association's Safe and Caring School project, but what we really need is to focus on building relationships over exacting punishment; what we need "is a place where these students feel they belong" (Macdonald, 1997). Rather than discriminatory policies that threatened punishment, education officials began to talk about creating positive and inclusive school communities (Hermanns, 2018). Now, even the highest education officials such as U.S. Secretary of Education Arne Duncan argued that "zero tolerance policies...should be replaced by locally tailored approaches" that aim to create a positive school climate (Pullman & Comley LLC, 2014). But what did these locally-tailored approaches look like? In both Canada and the United States, schools experimented with alternatives: parent meetings, peer mediation, community councils, and behavioral support for at-risk students.

One approach to non-punitive discipline showed an especially marked gain in popularity. Restorative justice approaches to dealing with school disciplinary infractions had been around for decades, but a turn in school reform towards the importance of school community and healthy school cultures coupled with the turn away from zero-tolerance policies made restorative justice one of the most attractive new reforms.

Against this backdrop, Kristin Reimer conducted the careful case studies of restorative justice practices in the two schools described in this book, one in Alberta, Canada, and the other in Scotland. Reimer spent enough time in both schools to produce two rich and insightful portraits that challenge both critics and advocates alike. The research Reimer conducts represents a detailed exploration of the cultures of both schools, how and why they have chosen to use restorative justice for disciplinary problems, and the challenges and successes they face. She finds that restorative justice represents a set of tools that engender not one idea about schooling but many. Do restorative practices lead to transformation or stasis? To social engagement or social control? To meaningful and authentic relationships or to coercive ones?

Her examination is also rooted in her own experiences as a student and practitioner of restorative justice. For more than fifteen years, the author has worked in a variety of settings including juvenile justice facilities, schools, and a teacher education program. These experiences provide a unique lens through which she focuses our attention on the challenges and possibilities teachers, administrators, and scholars face in adopting and researching restorative justice approaches.

Restorative justice, Reimer argues, should transform the way we think about violations of community norms. Its central principle is that transgressions of behavior are not violations of rules but rather violations of relationships. Yet if a school's ethos privileges individual achievement over community, then the relationships on which restorative justice depends become purely instrumental. She finds that restorative justice, depending on the specifics of its implementation and the school context, can be used to pursue compliance as easily as to cultivate community. It can be used to reify hierarchy and authority or to foreground relationships. It can be aimed at managing individual student behavior or at transforming the school culture. Most often, it is doing many of these at once. Without a broader focus on the school, district, and even national context, a central goal of many restorative justice advocates—valuing and fostering strong relationships and classroom and school community—can easily be bypassed. In those kinds of implementations, restorative justice practices lose their transformative power.

Reimer came to this research as a passionate advocate for restorative justice in schools and continues to see its transformative promise. Yet what I most admire about this book is that where she ends up in the final pages is not where she started her journey. It is this ability to critically examine and re-examine her own assumptions that make this book fascinating and tremendously useful.

—**Joel Westheimer**
University of Ottawa

Notes

1. I would like to thank Carl Hermanns, professor of education at Arizona State University for his generosity of time during an extended conversation in which he educated me about the history of zero tolerance policies in the United States and associated controversies.
2. Two outliers are worthy of mention here. As early as 1999, the newly elected Progressive Conservative government in Nova Scotia formed a School Conduct Committee made up of a broad range of stakeholders in the education field. Despite promises to incorporate school-based zero tolerance policies in the

campaign leading up to the election, the Committee recommended that a zero tolerance policy not be adopted for use in Nova Scotia and the government accepted the recommendation. One of the Committee's specific concerns was that zero tolerance policies have a disproportionate impact on poor, minority, and special needs students (Nova Scotia School Code of Conduct Committee, 2000; Progressive Conservative Party, 1999). By contrast, although restorative discipline approaches had been in use in Alberta for many years, Alberta's Ministry of Education formally rejected the use of zero tolerance policies only in 2015. The amended Safe Schools Act indicated "a move away from 'zero tolerance' policies which have been proven ineffective" and specified that the code of conduct "must ensure that support is provided for students who are impacted by inappropriate behaviour as well as for students who engage in inappropriate behaviour" (Alberta School Boards Association, 2015, p. 2).

References

Alexander, M. (2010). The New Jim Crow: Mass incarceration in the age of colorblindness. New York, NY: The New Press.

Alberta School Boards Association. (April 2015). *Alberta's amended school act: Welcoming, caring, respectful and safe learning environments. Series on Alberta's Amended School Act.* Edmonton, Canada: Safe and Caring Schools & Communities.

American Psychological Association Task Force. (2008). Are zero tolerance policies effective in the schools? An evidentiary review and recommendations. *American Psychologist, 63,* 852–862.

Ayers, W., Ayers, R., & Dohrn, B. (2002). Introduction: Resisting zero tolerance. In W. Ayers, B. Dohrn & R. Ayers (Eds.), *Zero tolerance: Resisting the drive for punishment in our schools* (pp. xi–xvi). New York, NY: New Press.

Bhattacharjee, K. (2003). *The Ontario Safe Schools Act: School Discipline and Discrimination.* Toronto, Canada: Ontario Human Rights Commission.

Harvard Civil Rights Project. (2000). *Opportunities suspended: The devastating consequences of zero tolerance and school discipline policies.* Boston, MA: Harvard University.

Freiberg, H. J., & Lapointe, J. M. (2006). Research-based programs for preventing and solving discipline problems. In C. M. Evertson & C. S. Weinstein (Eds.), *Handbook of classroom management* (pp. 735–786). Mahwah, NJ: Erlbaum.

Lustick, H. (2017). "Restorative justice" or restoring order? Restorative school discipline practices in urban public schools. *Urban Education.* 10.1177/0042085917741725.

Macdonald, K. (1997). Safe and caring schools project: Zero tolerance. *ATA News, 31*(8).

Nova Scotia School Code of Conduct Committee. (December 2000). *Report on school conduct code.* Retrieved from http://www.ohrc.on.ca/en/ontario

-safe-schools-act-school-discipline-and-discrimination/vi-disproportionate
-impact-other-jurisdictions#fn110

Progressive Conservative Party. (1999). John Hamm's plan for Nova Scotia: Strong leadership . . . a clear course. Halifax: Nova Scotia. 25. Retrieved from https://www.poltext.org/sites/poltext.org/files/plateformes/ns1999pc _plt._26122008_112055.pdf

Pullman & Comley, LLC. (2014). *School Law Alert—Dear Colleague Letter Firmly Urges Districts to Abandon "Zero Tolerance" in Student Discipline Policies.* Available at http://www.pullcom.com/news-publications-483.html.

U.S. Department of Education. (2014). *Dear colleague letter: Nondiscriminatory administration of school discipline.* Available at https://www2.ed.gov/about/ offices/list/ocr/letters/colleague-201401-title-vi.pdf.

Acknowledgments

Any research, any writing, any human endeavor happens collectively. I am deeply grateful to all who have walked with me, supporting, challenging and being in relationship with me as I make sense of the journey.

To my participants: Thank you for sharing freely your thoughts, insights, time and energy.

> *To the students:* You are inspiring in your capacity to live so fully in the moment. Thank you for giving me a window into your dynamic, spirited lives.
>
> *To the educators:* Thank you for your honesty, your engagement, and your passion. Your desire to do well by your students is admirable.
>
> *To the management teams:* Thank you for opening the doors to your schools. Each one truly has been transformed, in large part due to your own personal commitment to the students' wellbeing.

To my PhD supervisor, Dr. Lorna McLean: It was a true gift to be your student. You are an exceptional mentor, academic, researcher, educator, and person.

To other RJ scholars: I am grateful that your work exists, carefully considered and often passionately expressed. I am honored to join in community with you, to offer my own thoughts.

To the Educational Leadership for Social Justice series editor, Dr. Jeffrey Brooks: Thank you for your leadership in this series and for your support and encouragement to enter into this conversation.

Adult Intentions, Student Perceptions, pages xvii–xviii
Copyright © 2019 by Information Age Publishing

To my family, especially my parents: Thank you for supporting me with your love, prayers and your time as you cared for Oscar. Your support made this possible.

To my love and partner, Louis: Thank you for continuing to believe in me unreasonably. You convinced me to start this journey, supported me through it, and insisted that I finish it with integrity.

To my dear son, Oscar: You came to be in the midst of this study. You made completing it much more difficult and yet also made it, and everything else, much more delightful and meaningful. May your own school experiences be full of engagement, challenge, support, and coherence.

Portions of this book were previously published in the *Journal of Peace Education* and the *Australian Educational Researcher*.

Reimer, K. (2018). Relationships of control and relationships of engagement: Student experiences of restorative justice. *Journal of Peace Education.*

Reimer, K. (2018). "The kids do a better job of it than we do": A Canadian case study of teachers addressing the hypocritical application of restorative justice in their school. *The Australian Educational Researcher.*

1

Introduction

The Rise of Restorative Justice in Schools

Restorative justice (RJ) is an idea whose time may have finally arrived. Although the concept has ancient roots and the term has existed in Western societies since the 1970s, only recently has it gained general public recognition. In schools, RJ's popularity appears to be rising worldwide. As anecdotal evidence of this increasing popularity, Google Alerts daily fill my inbox with news stories about RJ in schools. In fact, schools are the fastest growing area for the practice of RJ.

For an approach that has long been on the fringes, considered countercultural, this recent public attention has generated unease among some RJ advocates. Many advocates understand RJ to be radically different from mainstream ways of approaching such issues as crime and anti-social behavior (Sullivan & Tifft, 2001; Zehr & Toews, 2004). These advocates claim that RJ, in its ideal, is transformative: Beyond being simply an alternative, perhaps innocuous, approach, using RJ raises fundamental questions about how our societies are structured and how our relationships are experienced (Bargen, 2011; Elliott, 2011; Lockhart & Zammit, 2005; Woolford, 2009). As

Adult Intentions, Student Perceptions, pages 1–9
Copyright © 2019 by Information Age Publishing

1

RJ is embraced by mainstream society, some advocates wonder if what is embraced is the same version of RJ that they support and understand. Mainstream attention raises the questions, asked by advocates since the birth of RJ as a social movement: "What do people involved in RJ (practitioners, state agencies, stakeholders, community members, educators, students) actually understand RJ to be?" and "What do they see as its broader goals?"

It is difficult to answer these questions as there is no universal definition of RJ (Clamp, 2016; Johnstone & Van Ness, 2007; Woolford, 2009); "restorative justice has come to mean all things to all people" (McCold, 2000, p. 358). Despite an increasing number of schools embracing the approach, it is not clear what school leaders who implement RJ are trying to achieve. The differences in understanding are dramatic. For some, RJ is about creating an environment of and for student engagement that challenges traditional systems of discipline while at the same time facilitating deep learning. For others, RJ is an effective disciplinary tool, used to solidify compliance and mete out punishment, albeit in a kinder, gentler way.

McCluskey et al. (2008a) draw examples of these vastly different understandings from a Scottish pilot project. In some pilot project schools, staff understood RJ to challenge taken-for-granted structures and systems of discipline and control in schools; in these schools, the head teachers advocated for abandoning punishment completely and focused on creating and sustaining positive relationships. In other schools, staff members viewed RJ as simply another tool in the toolbox alongside disciplinary practices that emphasized compliance and punishment; in these schools, obedience was sought through both RJ and other measures. As McCluskey et al. (2008a) show, RJ can be used either to disrupt the status quo and transform a school's ethos or to maintain the status quo, reinforcing compliance and obedience.

This book is grounded in a study in which I explored these various understandings of RJ—through both the eyes of those implementing their understandings of RJ (school leaders and educators) and through the eyes of those on the receiving end of the understandings (students). This study illuminates the intersection between how educators view and use RJ and how students experience RJ. I examined the use and experience of RJ in two schools, set in different contexts; one school was in Scotland and one in Canada.

RJ in these countries emerged from differing contexts and differing discourses. RJ has deep roots in Canada, tied to both the traditions of Canada's First Nations people and to early efforts within the mainstream criminal justice system (Eagle, 2011; Elliott, 2011; Vaandering, 2009). In Canada,

RJ has been applied in schools since the 1990s (Drewery & Winslade, 2003; Morrison, 2007b). Scotland, in contrast, introduced its first school-based RJ pilot project in 2004 (Hendry, 2009; McCluskey et al., 2008b). Scottish practitioners drew on the experience of other countries to gather information, using previously developed ideas to build their own specific Scottish model (Hendry, 2009). By studying RJ in schools in these two different settings (Scotland and Canada), I was able to see how understandings and experiences of RJ are shaped by context and culture.

My study focused on the intersection between adult intentions and student perceptions. While it is important to understand the intentions of educators in using RJ in schools, those aims must be examined against the actual impact that such practices have on students if their efficacy is to be understood. Thus, the research was guided by two central questions that speak to this intersection: "How did students in two different schools experience RJ?" and "For what purposes were educators and school leaders implementing RJ in these Scottish and Canadian schools?"

Qualitative studies of RJ in schools in general tend to focus on the adult experience of implementing an approach for students (Cronin-Lampe & Cronin-Lampe, 2010; Karp & Breslin, 2001; Reimer, 2009; Vaandering, 2009; Zulfa, 2015). Student voice, although touted as key to the practice of RJ, has been historically missing from much of the research. More recent studies, however, are working to intentionally create space for student voice in RJ research (Cavanagh, Vigil, & Garcia, 2014; Duncan, 2015). This book is part of that recent trend, prioritizing the student experience and asking students to offer their expertise as to the effect RJ has on themselves and their schools. Their voice and experience, however, must be understood in concert with the actions and intentions of the educators and school leaders implementing RJ. Only then can we develop an accurate picture of the impact the adult views and understandings have on student experiences.

Drawing on the insights of the research on student voice, my approach was premised on the convictions as articulated by Cook-Sather (2006): "that young people have unique perspectives on learning, teaching and schooling; that their insights warrant not only the attention but also the responses of adults; and, that they should be afforded opportunities to actively shape their education" (p. 359). Viewing students as experts of their own realities and providing opportunities for them to engage in an inquiry into their realities, builds our body of knowledge while at the same time enriching the experience of those students who participate in studies. As a product, the research community gains knowledge in order to understand the complexities of school; as a process, the students involved have their voices and experiences validated. In this study, student co-researchers were invaluable to understanding the actual impact of RJ on students—rather than the one intended by adults.

My Own Restorative Justice Journey

I come to this research as an RJ practitioner and advocate. I first received training in the field in 1999 in Ontario, Canada as a volunteer with a victim–offender mediation center. Subsequently, I worked and studied in the United States for 6 years in the fields of conflict transformation and RJ. My RJ work included, as part of an incredible team, facilitating meetings between juvenile offenders and their victims, working with victims and perpetrators of crimes of severe violence, assisting churches to think through restorative responses to harm, helping to facilitate restorative circles in schools to deal with incidents of harm, and training volunteer facilitators in RJ philosophy and process. More recently I volunteered with several Canadian RJ organizations facilitating victim–offender meetings; supporting a long-term sex offender in living safely within the community; and as part of a local restorative justice network, a group that seeks to expand RJ services and public awareness.

As a teacher educator, I designed a course currently offered to teacher candidates at the University of Ottawa in Canada on employing restorative philosophy in the classroom. In this course, teacher candidates are encouraged to ask difficult questions about the structure of schools and to use RJ to transform the school ethos rather than as a kinder, gentler way to punish. In all my current teaching in the Faculty of Education at Monash University in Australia, I use restorative circles and relational pedagogy to connect my students to their own knowledge, to one another, to the content of the class, and to the world. Thus, as is true for all researchers, I do not approach my research from a neutral position.

I entered into this research not to substantiate my own beliefs, but to understand as fully as possible how educators view RJ, how students experience RJ, and what that experience reveals about the state of RJ in schools. I was not interested in confirming my belief that RJ was the panacea that would transform conflict, people, schools, and societal conditions; I wanted to know if transformation was indeed the experience—or part of the experience—of students. I embarked on the study with a curiosity born of my own personal commitment to a transformative vision of RJ. This curiosity assisted me in asking questions of people, contexts, and discourses so as to substantially understand the politics of RJ in the schools studied in Scotland and Canada. Indeed, this curiosity led me to answers I never expected, answers that deeply impact my own experience of RJ, and my own current understandings.

Restorative Justice—An Introduction

Advocates of RJ, aligning with most faith, cultural, and humanistic traditions, assert that all people are interconnected. In broad terms, in RJ, harm is viewed as a violation of individuals and relationships rather than as a violation of rules or laws (Zehr, 2002). The centrality of people and relationships makes RJ relevant not only to the justice system, but to most social units, organizations, or institutions—from neighborhoods and families to places of worship and schools.

There is nothing radically new about RJ. Elliott (2011) lists among its many roots: alternative dispute resolution, teachings and circle processes of indigenous peoples around the world, faith-based approaches, victimology, therapeutic discourses, peacemaking criminology, and penal abolitionism. While its exact origins may be disputed (Daly, 2002), and the term has only been articulated in Western society since the early 1970s, there is no doubt that RJ's inherent values resonate with many traditions and communities (Sawatsky, 2001). People intimately understand that harm is a violation of people and relationships, not only laws.

Restorative Justice in Schools

While RJ has been used broadly within and as an alternative to the criminal justice system, its popularity and practice in education is relatively recent worldwide (Bargen, 2010; Drewery, 2004; Morrison & Vaandering, 2012). Nevertheless, it appears to be rising in popularity in schools in North America and around the world (Fronius, Persson, Guckenburg, Hurley & Petrosino, 2016; Mayworm, Sharkey, Hunnicutt, & Schiedel, 2016). The motives behind the expansion of RJ depend on the schools involved: desires to lower suspension and expulsion rates (Vaandering, 2009); realizations that punitive discipline is ineffective for long-term change (Morrison, 2007a; Stinchcomb, Bazemore, & Riestenberg, 2006); and calls to find substantive solutions for student disengagement, discipline issues, bullying, conflict, and violence (Bargen, 2010; McCluskey et al., 2008b; Morrison, 2007a; Smith, 2006).

In schools, framing problems as violations of relationships rather than of institutional rules requires a significant shift from a traditional approach to discipline where a broken rule leads to set punishments determined by an authority figure. Some schools focus their use of RJ on responding to student behavior or harm, viewing RJ as an alternative behavior management tool; others view RJ as a comprehensive approach affecting all school relationships, policies, and practices, a way to nurture healthy school communities (Evans & Vaandering, 2016; Morrison, 2015).

Evans and Vaandering (2016) take the comprehensive approach, offering a holistic definition of RJ in schools as "facilitating learning communities that nurture the capacity of people to engage with one another and their environment in a manner that supports and respects the inherent dignity and worth of all" (p. 8). For educators in these schools, RJ is a philosophical and pedagogic approach that addresses the individual needs of students in the social context of their relationships with each other, as well as with teachers, administrators, and others. Hendry (2009) states that RJ in schools is fundamentally about proactively building, maintaining, and repairing relationships. RJ—philosophically and in practice—directs participants into the complex social, cultural, ethical, and historical realities that form and inform classroom environments and the students within them.

With this comprehensive, relational approach, RJ attempts to understand the needs and purposes behind harmful behavior by involving all those affected and giving voice to the multiple and complex narratives that comprise an incident (Amstutz & Mullet, 2005; Drewery, 2004; Kecskemeti & Winslade, 2016). Ultimately, RJ seeks to address underlying individual and collective needs and strengthen relationships, thus making school safe and engaging for all its members (Hendry, 2009; Hopkins, 2011).

In schools, comprehensive RJ is actualized through such practices (among others) as classroom circles, peer mediation, and multi-party restorative conferences that encompass both proactive measures that build interpersonal skills and relationships as well as responsive ones that deal with incidents of harm (Amstutz & Mullet, 2005; Hopkins, 2011; Morrison, 2007b). Common to all practices is a focus on dialogue and understanding the perspective of others (Hendry, 2009; Hopkins, 2011). The practice of comprehensive RJ is guided by empathy, where a better understanding of each other can lead to mutually supportive environments and robust, equitable learning communities.

In practice, however, the comprehensive approach is not dominant; RJ is more often used to attend to individual student misbehavior rather than whole school culture (McCluskey, 2013). North American schools that first adopted RJ, in the 1990s and early 2000s, identified the damage that suspensions could inflict on individuals and school communities and implemented RJ as an alternative to suspensions and other exclusionary discipline measures (Evans & Vaandering, 2016; Morrison, 2015). RJ, in many of these schools, was used as a response to student behavior or student harm; it was—and often still is—predominantly used as an alternative behavior management tool.

Although definitely an improvement on purely punitive measures, behavior management RJ contrasts sharply with comprehensive RJ. While its nominal practice might employ the same or similar techniques, the philosophical objectives are narrower: to promote positive change in individual student behavior. Success is usually measured by reduced expulsion rates, fewer visits to the principal's office, and/or increases in attendance (Jain, Bassey, Brown, & Kalra, 2014; Lewis, 2009; Wachtel, 2012). For the most part, RJ is seen as effective for eliciting positive change in individual student behavior (Educational Institute of Scotland, 2013; Stinchcomb et al., 2006; Youth Justice Board, 2004). However, Vaandering (2013) points out that this narrow focus on behavior and discipline (perhaps inadvertently) redirects attention back to rules and blame, and away from relationships and social engagement. What is lost in that redirection, advocates would say, is the creation of a school culture in which people and relationships form the cornerstone of safety, belonging, and learning (Boyes-Watson & Pranis, 2014; Riestenberg, 2012; Vaandering, 2013).

In short, the same words and similar practices are used by schools implementing RJ. And yet, RJ can look and feel quite different from one school to another (McCluskey et al, 2008a; Vaandering, 2014).

A Question of Language

Intentional choices have been made in this book in regards to language. The first involves my choice to use the term, *restorative justice,* throughout most of the book. Some who apply restorative philosophy in schools tend to replace the term *justice* with restorative *approaches,* restorative *practices,* restorative *discipline* or restorative *schools* to distance it from its criminal justice connotations (Amstutz & Mullet, 2005; Morrison, 2007b; Vaandering, 2011). Indeed, the Scottish school in this study consciously chose to use the term *restorative approaches* or *RA* to encompass their broad understanding of the approach. The Canadian school, however, used a mixture of terms—from RJ to RA to simply *restorative.* I have chosen to use the term RJ as the default term in this book. I do this for two reasons: first, to eliminate any confusion that excessive switching between various terms might produce; second, and more fundamentally, to align with Vaandering's (2011) argument that the use of "restorative" paired with "justice" is significant, and serves as a "compass needle guiding proponents in the field to their desired destinations" (p. 308) in a way that *practice* or *approach* cannot. Vaandering explores in depth the two concepts (restorative and justice) and concludes that when justice is understood as "honoring the worth of the other through relationship" (p. 324) then the pairing of the terms accurately describes restorative processes, outcomes, and philosophy. Thus, using the term RJ is not a narrowing of restorative ideas to the criminal justice setting, but rather an expansion of what constitutes justice in all settings.

In an attempt, however, to honor the intentions of the Scottish school, provide an accurate description of the Scottish setting, and reflect its actual use, I use the term RA instead of RJ when discussing the Scottish region and school. Other language choices are necessitated by the multi-site case study being set in two different countries where differing words are used to describe the same concept. Relevant for this study, *pupils* in Scotland are referred to as *students* in Canada; *principals* in Canada are referred to as *head teachers* in Scotland. I have chosen to use the term most common to the country to which I am referring. My choice to switch between terms is driven by a desire to provide the reader with an authentic view of the context in which the cases are set, staying true to the language the reader would hear when immersed in the setting. When writing about both cases or more generally, however, I default to the term most common to Canada, the land from which I originate.

Moving Through the Book

The book begins with a discussion of RJ, drawing on the literature to explore the tensions that exist within RJ: different forms of implementation and philosophical understandings. I then provide a description of the design of the research upon which this book is based. Against this background, I tell the stories of the two schools; first, Canada, then Scotland. In the telling, I identify the lessons revealed about adult intentions for using RJ and the student experience of it. In the discussion section, I explore what the findings reveal about the intersection between educator intentions for the use of RJ and the experience of students. It is here that the importance of attending to school relationships starts to emerge.

Each stage of this study raised complex questions about the intended purposes of RJ in schools and definition(s) of RJ. This study challenges a common assumption of some RJ advocates that implementing RJ necessarily creates a classroom environment of social engagement (where students are empowered to engage with one another and think critically, and school relationships and hierarchies are transformed). The student experience in this study shows that RJ can as readily be mobilized to create classroom environments of social control (where students are taught obedience and compliance, and authority and hierarchy are reinforced).

This study eventually determined that the key element is not the implementation of different forms of RJ, but, in fact, the predominant relational objectives in a school. Some relational objectives in schools skew toward controlling students; others toward engaging students. RJ can as readily be implemented for either. The real strength of RJ, as seen in this book, is for its insight into the quality and character of school relationships.

2

The Tensions Within Restorative Justice

A Continuum of Understandings

It is clear by now that there is no monolith that is RJ. A universally accepted understanding of RJ simply does not exist. To understand different implementations of RJ in schools, we must dig into the philosophical tensions that exist within the field (Aertsen, Parmentier, Vanfraechem, Walgrave, & Zinsstag, 2013; Johnstone & Van Ness, 2007; MacAllister, 2013).

Woolford (2009), calling upon Nancy Fraser's (1997, 2000) theory of justice, suggests all responses to injustice can be understood as either affirmative or transformative. Affirmative responses typically deal with individual behavior without challenging the systemic roots of injustice. An affirmative understanding of RJ focuses on addressing isolated incidents of harm and changing individual behavior—similar to the behavior management RJ introduced in Chapter 1. Affirmative practice of RJ might, for example, bring together disruptive students where, through dialogue, the hope is a change in individual behavior and the restoration of previous order to the classroom. Scholars advocating affirmative RJ (among them: Daly, 2000; Duff, 2003; London,

11

2011; MacAllister, 2013; Tonry, 2011; Wheeldon, 2009) believe the benefit of RJ is that it improves upon—but does not dismantle—existing systems.

The transformative view, on the other hand, understands RJ as a radical paradigm shift with a profound potential to address societal injustices and power imbalances (Llewellyn, 2011a; Lyubansky & Shpungin, 2016; Sullivan & Tifft, 2001; Zehr, 1990). Its advocates see RJ as a worldview, and not just a technique for addressing behavior management and disciplinary issues in isolation (Bargen, 2011; Eagle, 2011; Hendry, 2009; Umbreit & Armour, 2010; Zehr, 2010). Woolford (2009) describes transformative RJ as "fostering opportunities for individuals and collectives to evaluate their lives and their worlds, and to initiate attempts to bring change into these arenas: to address injustice and to improve the lives of the many" (p. 17).

In the practice of transformative RJ, students, teachers, and other relevant school community members work together, through dialogue, to address the wellbeing of all involved, build school relationships, and meet everyone's identified needs. This is similar to the comprehensive RJ introduced in Chapter 1. Responsive to the actual context and classroom environment, a dialogue could, for example, involve questions addressing and making all the parties aware of: specific harms, relational issues, classroom inequities, unfair processes, hierarchies, and power relationships. Disruptive behavior, while not the primary focus, will likely change by giving voice to and effectively addressing bigger issues which may lie at the root of the behavior. Elliott (2011) succinctly sums up this transformative understanding of RJ: "In philosophy and practice, restorative justice asks what is necessary to live collectively and as our 'best selves'" (p. 5).

While the different understandings of RJ—transformative versus affirmative—are philosophically distinct, it is important to note that both in the actual practice and implementation of RJ in classrooms, as well as in the scholarly writings of its theorists, the distinction between transformative and affirmative is often blurred. These ideas exist on a continuum. Setting out each end of this continuum helps us better understand what lies on the spectrum between each ideal and to parse out the limitations of each, even when in combination. Examining the extreme ends also helps us to dig into the purposes underpinning the use of transformative and affirmative RJ in classrooms: a tension between wanting to engage students (transformative) and control them (affirmative).

Affirmative Restorative Justice

Woolford (2009), a transformative RJ advocate, insists, "anything less than a transformative approach to injustice tends to only scratch the surface of the problem, ignoring its deeper cultural, structural, and political roots" (p. 153). Those who advocate for an affirmative understanding of RJ, however, claim that they are not ignoring these deeper roots, but are rather being pragmatic. By focusing on individual behavior, these scholars assert that the likelihood is increased that institutions will actually adopt RJ (London, 2011; MacAllister, 2013; Wheeldon, 2009). Institutions are unlikely to adopt RJ if it is presented as boundless, or a "way of life" (Llewellyn, 2011b). Llewellyn (2011b), although embracing many aspects of transformative RJ, advocates for limiting RJ's scope to issues of wrongdoing, rather than a more open-ended approach. MacAllister (2013), writing about the role of RJ in schools, concurs, suggesting that RJ is more relevant if proponents restrict themselves to modest, specific claims about RJ's educational potential.

RJ is seen to be more relevant to institutions if presented with a narrow scope; some scholars also show how RJ is often only allowed to operate within institutions—criminal justice or schools—if it does not challenge core elements of the system (Elliott, 2011). Vaandering (2009), in her research into the implementation of RJ in two Canadian elementary schools, observed the tendency of institutions to avoid challenge, finding that schools were open to dialogue until the analysis was turned on their own structures. In her research into conflict resolution initiatives in schools, Bickmore (1998) found that initiatives such as peer mediation were limited in scope to student conflict. These initiatives were not given the latitude to address adult conflict; neither could they challenge broader patterns of discipline and control or attend to policies and practices that exacerbated conflict in schools (Bickmore, 1998). Vaandering and Bickmore critique what they see as only partial implementation of such initiatives. Affirmative advocates would see their studies as confirmation that a focus on individual student behavior allows RJ and conflict resolution initiatives to be accepted by schools, a better outcome than no RJ whatsoever.

The increasing popularity of RJ in schools seems to attest to successful engagement between RJ and conventional education systems. Most research in schools is conducted from an affirmative RJ stance, focusing on the effectiveness of RJ to attend to individual misbehavior (McCluskey, 2013). And, for the most part, measuring affirmative outcomes casts RJ in a favorable light. Over five years of RJ implementation, a school in Baltimore found an overall decrease of 26% in the number of detentions, coinciding with a 25% increase in enrollment (Wachtel, 2012). The Youth Justice Board for England and Wales, in an evaluation of school-wide restorative practices across 26 schools, found that restorative conferences usually led to successful resolutions and that teachers perceived an improvement in student behavior compared to non-restorative schools (Youth Justice Board,

2004). Given these positive results—working within the system and focusing on individual behavior—affirmative RJ advocates suggest that it is counterproductive and distracting to use RJ for broader systemic transformation.

In this context, RJ is framed as innocuous to fit within the school system. Educators are encouraged to view RJ as one more tool—along with others—to deal with behavior issues, where the emphasis is on compliance and punishment (Bargen, 2010; McCluskey, 2013; McCluskey et al., 2008a; Vaandering, 2009). Indeed, teachers are assured that RJ is simply another way of thinking about what they are already doing, rather than an idea based on a radically different paradigm (Vaandering, 2009).

What they are already doing, tends to be focusing on individual behavior as separate from systemic issues. Educators, McCluskey et al. (2008b) critique, often fixate on an individual as a troublemaker, rather than consider how particular students—due to differences of class, race, gender—become identified more often as troublemakers or disruptive students. McCluskey et al. (2008b) write that when educators use RJ to focus only on an individual's behavior, "restorative justice cannot fully respond to essential questions of power, class and gender" (p. 206).

Affirmative RJ advocates wonder, however, whether it is possible—and therefore productive—to even attempt to fully respond to those *essential questions.* Llewellyn (2011b) bridges the divide between transformative and affirmative scholars, suggesting that even if RJ cannot fully address such questions, RJ can open the conversation. Sullivan and Tifft (2001), transformative RJ advocates, counter that opening the conversation is not sufficient; it is irresponsible for RJ to deal with individual harmful acts without examining the unjust structures in which those acts occur, as well as our own complicity with those structures. These transformative-affirmative arguments are ongoing within the RJ field (Aertsen et al., 2013). Enns and Myers (2009) summarize the tension: "In the end, however, restorative justice advocates must determine whether (or to what degree) they are seeking to represent a transforming *alternative* to the system's core philosophy of retribution, or merely a subsidiary *complement* that attempts to make the criminal justice system a little kinder and gentler where and when possible" (p. 24, emphasis in original). From an affirmative point of view, RJ as complement to the system is a worthwhile goal.

Transformative Restorative Justice

From a transformative point of view, making the system kinder and gentler is not enough. RJ—in philosophy and practice—is a critique of society in terms of taken-for-granted assumptions, power dynamics, and structural injustice. Some transformative RJ advocates suggest that if people are sufficiently grounded in principles and values of transformative RJ, they will inevitably attend to issues of social injustice and power dynamics (Bargen, 2011; Conrad & Unger, 2011; Elliott, 2011). Enns and Myers (2009) strongly support this, showing how holistic peacemaking—a broader framework into which transformative RJ fits—identifies both the particularities of the harmful act, as well as the influence of larger discourses or forces. They employ Camara's (1971) *spiral of violence* model which reveals how structural injustice is usually invisible, woven into the fabric of society and accepted as normal; what is visible is the rage that erupts from people who have been victim to invisible, structural violence. Similarly, Conrad and Unger (2011) draw upon Bourdieu and Passeron (1990) to tie interpersonal violence at school to the violence of schooling, a symbolic, structural, taken-for-granted violence. Although RJ allows for attention to both the specific and the structural wrongdoing (Llewellyn, 2011b), Enns and Myers (2009) claim that RJ often responds to the visible violence without acknowledging the structural violence. To be transformative, they argue, it is necessary to attend to both. Vaandering (2009) agrees, holding to a vision of not simply restoring a school community to its same taken-for-granted structures but "transforming it to what it could be—a place characterized by possibility, relationship, hope, and justice" (p. 39).

Yet radical change is difficult for both individuals and institutions. Social institutions shape and reinforce the norms by which we live; it is an immense task to even recognize our underlying assumptions, let alone challenge them. Worldviews are not easily dismissed. As Vaandering (2009) points out, RJ often gets shaped to serve the dominant worldview. In schools, for instance, there are inherent tensions between values that underpin transformative RJ and those that underpin more common approaches based on behavioral theories (Hendry, 2009; McCluskey et al., 2008a; Morrison, 2007a; Morrison & Vaandering, 2012; Reimer, 2009) and even teachers who are committed to RJ often maintain or revert to prevailing authoritarian, punitive approaches (Thorsborne, 2013; Vaandering, 2009). Inertia within systems and societies are barriers to the implementation of transformative RJ.

Some RJ advocates argue that resistance to transformative RJ is more deliberate than pure inertia. Institutions often have little interest in opening themselves to critique (Illich, 1971/1983). As Elliott (2011) charges, "the needs of these institutions are viewed as more important than the needs of the people they were meant to serve" (p. 169). The transformative message of RJ is sometimes intentionally altered so as to minimize its potential and strengthen existing structures. Zehr warned in 2010: "Change efforts are often first ignored, then resisted, then likely to be co-opted. Indeed, there are ample signs of the latter already in the field" (p. viii). Woolford (2009) alerts us to the fact that RJ can be used to "create individual citizens who are non-combative and peaceable resolvers of conflict. Such individuals are obviously appealing to governments that would like to have a passive citizenry more apt to engage in talk than to protest and undertake acts of civil disobedience" (p. 86). Some RJ scholars, too, have pointed out that governments tend to re-package old practices under the name of RJ, simply modifying RJ principles to fit a more retributive agenda (Daly, 2002; Pawlychka, 2012; Sullivan & Tifft, 2001) and to make harsher aspects of that agenda more palatable (Cunneen, 2012). RJ—at least transformative RJ—is actively resisted and co-opted.

Although the idea of transformation is celebrated by many RJ advocates, research is scarce. In schools, research tends to focus on the effectiveness of RJ (Arnott, 2007; Chmelynski, 2005; Lewis, 2009; Porter, 2007) and on identifying best practices for implementation (Cavanagh, 2010; Karp & Breslin, 2001; Morrison, 2007a; Reimer, 2009; Riestenberg, 2003; Wearmouth, McKinney, & Glynn, 2007). Some themes of transformation and affirmation do emerge within the research into implementation of RJ: Schools need to first ask whether the values of RJ fit their school culture (Hendry, 2009; Wearmouth et al., 2007); principals, teachers, and other staff members are socialized in a retributive culture and their reluctance (or inability) to abandon that culture could be a major obstacle for implementing RJ (Karp & Breslin, 2001; Thorsborne, 2013; Vaandering, 2009); and tensions are evident between existing philosophies and discipline practices and the philosophy of RJ (McCluskey et al., 2008a; Riestenberg, 2003; Thorsborne, 2013).

Understanding the distinction between transformative and affirmative RJ and the continuum between them is useful for illustrating that RJ is not a philosophical monolith. There are clearly some very different, even contradictory, ideas and objectives at play in the discussion and practice of RJ in classrooms. Exploring these distinctions can, possibly, help us better understand how RJ can be applied to either incite systemic change, preserve the status quo, or some overlapping combination. The distinction brings clarity, of a sort, where RJ advocates can better understand just what is occurring in classrooms where RJ is being applied.

This study had two prongs: It was undertaken to understand what perspective was being utilized in the classrooms and, *also*, to understand what drove the use of a particular perspective. While knowing the distinction between transformative and affirmative helps identify what is occurring, my study suggests that this, in isolation, does little to answer why an approach is being used. To understand this we need another step, beyond mere taxonomy of RJ, that examines what actually underpins the purpose of RJ in schools. That step is to attempt to determine which desire the educator, administrators, and institutions aspire to, a desire for social engagement or a desire for social control.

Social Control or Social Engagement

Morrison and Vaandering (2012) draw upon Elliott (2011), Morrison (2011), and Zehr (2005) to write that institutions that embrace RJ experience a paradigm change characterized "as a shift away from being a rule-based institution to a relationship-based institution, or from being an institution whose purpose is social control to being an institution that nurtures social engagement" (Morrison & Vaandering, 2012, p. 145). I would argue that this difference in purpose—social control or social engagement—also describes that which underpins affirmative RJ and transformative RJ, respectively.

Affirmative RJ as Social Control
Compliance, Order, Management

School staff face both external and internal pressure to achieve a variety of often competing goals—academic, pedagogic, social, and cultural. As McCluskey (2013) writes, it is hardly surprising that, in the face of such pressure, "school leaders and teachers may come to see compliant students as good students, a quiet class as a good class, and a good school as one where there is no conflict" (p. 135). Teachers rarely identify compliant students as an end goal of education. Yet, varied educational studies have shown that even caring teachers committed to inclusive, participatory ideals find that the reality and stress of the job (e.g., large class sizes, student disinterest, hierarchical schooling structure) lead them to resort to authoritarian, controlling measures (Cavanagh, 2011; Herr & Anderson, 2003; Porter, 1996; Raby, 2012; Vaandering, 2013). Many educators view compliance and order as prerequisites for learning; this view opens the potential for compliance and order to become ends in themselves (Thorsborne, 2013). The assertion that order is a prerequisite for learning, a cornerstone of most theories of classroom management, is linked to beliefs about how learning should look—quiet, disciplined, and predictable (Raby, 2012). Interrelated is the view that compliance and order are independent goods, teaching submission to authority and preparing students for hierarchy and power imbalances present in greater society (Raby, 2012).

Views of compliance as essential to learning and life do not occur within a vacuum. Staff members who take this view are both reflecting and affirming similar discourses within educational culture and society as a whole. In reference to the inclination in secondary schools to obedience-oriented discipline, Raby (2012) writes, "Dominant beliefs about teenagers as needing containment, concern with losing order, and fears regarding classroom safety may shape this institutional culture" (p. 83). Raby's writing concurs with that of Foucault (1979) who identified similarities between schools and prisons, both founded as disciplinary bodies. Foucault's (1991) governmentality shows how individuals become constituted as objects of power through institutionalized practices. Some educational scholars see this objectification happening in schools where the purposes of control and compliance are embedded and difficult to change (Harber & Sakade, 2009; Kohn, 1996). Most scholars who conduct research in schools agree that an educational focus on control and compliance teaches students to obey authority; these scholars differ, however, on whether this is a positive or negative outcome (Cavanagh, 2011; Raby, 2012).

RJ is usually not explicitly stated to be an authoritarian approach, such as those outlined above. Yet if order is indeed accepted as a prerequisite for learning, the allure of RJ as a technique to accomplish this order becomes apparent. Teachers are often told that RJ will "help them *manage* student behaviour and that working WITH students is for the purpose of regulation and social order, not relationship" (Vaandering, 2013, p. 322, emphasis in original). This understanding of RJ—what I have identified as affirmative RJ—is critiqued by Vaandering (2013) as being narrowly focused on behavior and discipline and thus focuses attention on rules, blame, and punishment, and away from relationships.

Rules

As Vaandering (2013) points out, emphasis on compliance, order, and management often leads to discussion about the role of rules in enforcing such order. A common societal view is that rules are necessary for people to co-exist successfully. Raby (2012) agrees with this, but also problematizes the usual view of rules as common sense; she points out that rules reflect deep beliefs about human nature and about what is acceptable behavior. Drawing from her own study of three Canadian secondary schools, Raby (2012) identifies values and assumptions commonly underpinning school rules: acceptance of authority, particularly in preparation for work; construction of certain kinds of workers and citizens, those who are "obedient, punctual and restrained in dress, rather than innovative, independent, or defiant in the face of inequality" (p. 27); and reflection and production of dominant culture morality.

Nucci (2001) explored how children distinguish between moral, conventional, and personal domains. Building on this work, Raby (2012) categorizes school rules into these three domains: Moral rules refer to actions innately seen as wrong, whether a rule exists or not; conventional rules are contextual and supported through consensus or authority; and personal rules cover individual choice within cultural parameters. Raby's (2012) study found that most students appreciated moral rules (e.g., no bullying, no theft) and accepted conventional rules (e.g., no smoking, follow dress code) as long as they did not encroach on their personal domain. School behavior codes tend to not distinguish between moral and conventional codes leading to conflict between staff and students (Goodman, 2006; Raby, 2012; Rowe, 2006). Teachers might view lateness as a moral issue of order and respect; students often view it as contextual and distinct from morality. When conventional rules are ascribed moral status, Goodman (2006) refers to this as "derivatively moral." Adding to this confusing mix of rules and morality, codes of conduct most often express expectations for student behavior, with no mention of staff behavior (Raby, 2012). The ability for adults to ascribe rules with morality, as well as the primary attention given to student behavior, points to the role of rules in maintaining student compliance and social order.

Behavior and Punishment

In order for rules to be effective in maintaining order in schools and classrooms, the rules need to be enforced, usually through attention to student behavior. As a tidy cyclical relationship, behavior management approaches tend to reinforce social control and education as compliance (Morrison & Vaandering, 2012). RJ brought into schools in an affirmative sense is seen as a behavior management practice, another tool to deal with student disruption (McCluskey, 2013). The focus of RJ, if brought in as such a tool, is on changing student behavior to better fit teacher and school expectations.

To change student behavior so that rules are followed, social order is maintained, and learning can occur, the most common method is one of punishment and consequences. McCluskey et al. (2013) found that although students felt that behavioral change could be best accomplished through rewards and recognition, teachers were more likely to rely on punishments and sanctions. Again, the reliance on punishment fits into a broad societal view that values punishment as both necessary and effective (London, 2011; Thorsborne, 2013). Punishment is an ambiguous, rarely defined term, yet it evokes strong feelings (Pawlychka, 2012). Many schools shy away from using the term *punishment*, preferring instead the language of *consequences*, which connote a guiding of students to learn appropriate future behavior (Raby, 2012). Yet Kohn (1996) sees little distinction between *punishments* and *consequences* from the student point of view—regardless of the word used, students either choose to behave or suffer penalties. Raby (2012), too, found that only a minority of participants in her study—staff or students—identified a difference between punishments and consequences.

RJ, often framed as an alternative to punishment, would not seem to sit comfortably with such a practice and focus. However, as Morrison and Vaandering (2012) assert, "while educators readily embrace the RJ premise that relationship is more important than the behavioral incident, they are reluctant to let go of the option to punish and exclude" (p. 148). In this sense, RJ needs to be understood within a wide societal framework that is increasingly comfortable with punitive measures (Cunneen, 2012). Indeed, one of the tensions between affirmative and transformative RJ centers on the role of punishment. Critiquing RJ from a transformative perspective, Cunneen (2012) writes, RJ "has not been a counterweight to increased punitiveness, nor has it grown in isolation from these broader trends in penalty" (p. 21). For affirmative advocates, the alignment of RJ with punishment is not a problem; Tonry (2011) identifies RJ as one of the "new paradigms of punishment" (p. 22). As a new paradigm of punishment, the purpose of punishment is seen as moral reparation (Duff, 2001) and restoration of belief in a just and orderly world (London, 2011). According to London (2011), studies do not prove that restorative measures alone are more conducive to healing and the restoration of social trust than punishment. In his view, the ideal RJ combination would be appropriate punishment, sincere apology, and a form of restitution (London, 2011).

A Focus on the Individual

Underlying all aspects of social control in schools is a neoliberal conception of the individual as rational, independent, and distinct from a network of relationships (Llewellyn, 2011b; Llewellyn & Llewellyn, 2015; Meyers, 1997). In this conception, even if relationships are discussed, Llewellyn (2011b) contends that they are appreciated only for how they can be useful to the individual.

In schools, the effort to control behavior as detailed above is reinforced by a focus on individuals and specific incidents (McCluskey, 2008b; Morrison & Vaandering, 2012). Schools focusing on behavior will define the child or culture as deviant or deficient, without shedding light on larger social inequalities that might also play a role (Morris, 2005; Raby, 2012).

Raby (2012) illustrates this phenomenon through a look at *repeat offenders* in schools. Students who repeatedly break school rules are characterized as defiant, conflating conventional rule violations into moral ones. She found that minority, working-class, or otherwise marginalized students were more likely to have their actions noticed and recorded and, therefore, more likely to be defined as defiant (Raby, 2012). Seen only as individuals, responsible for their own failure to comply with rules, systemic and structural inequalities are ignored.

Affirmative RJ also takes an individualistic perspective, focusing on specific incidents decontextualized from wider societal conditions and the complexity of relationships (Cunneen, 2012; McCluskey, 2013). One consequence of such an individualized view is that a distinction is made between *good* students who might benefit from an RJ process and *bad* students who are deemed to present too great a risk for RJ (Cunneen, 2012; Raby, 2012). As in the previous repeat offender example, most marginalized groups are seen to present the greatest risk and are often subjected to punishment without an RJ process (Cunneen, 2012).

Affirmative RJ and Social Control

Cunneen (2012) identifies what he calls the paradox of RJ: "It promotes a more socially responsible and emancipatory approach to criminal justice and penalty, yet it is an approach that fits with at least some of the values that predominate within more punitive law-and-order politics" (p. 3). I would argue that this assertion is particularly true for affirmative understandings of RJ, driven by a purpose of social control.

As pointed out, RJ has emerged within societal discourses that uphold the individual as more important than the collective, view order and compliance as prerequisites to learning and as goods in and of themselves, and utilize external rules and punishment to control behavior and reinforce social order. In many ways, RJ practices and theories have been "unwittingly influenced by a liberal individualistic approach" (Llewellyn, 2011b, p. 100); RJ is limited by the structures within which it operates (Llewellyn & Llewellyn, 2015). RJ has come, in an affirmative sense, to mirror the very structures it claims to critique.

The International Institute for Restorative Practices (IIRP) is an international not-for-profit organization and prolific RJ training center (Llewellyn & Llewellyn, 2015). Vaandering (2013), in an examination of one of IIRP's main training components, the social discipline window (McCold & Wachtel, 2003), points out that the language of dominance (terms such as *authority, regulation of behavior, maintaining social order,* and *social control*) takes precedence in this model over the language of relationships. Vaandering (2013) argues that juxtaposing words such as behavior and social order with concepts of relationships and people result in confusion and diluted (or, I would say, affirmative) versions of RJ. Besides its main campus in the United States, IIRP has ten international offices or affiliates (IIRP, 2013). Although exact numbers are not available, anecdotally the influence of IIRP and its presentation of an affirmative-leaning version of RJ is significant. Both schools in my study, for example, mentioned at least minimal connection to IIRP. IIRP, it should be noted, is diverse in its practices and also engages in work at other points along the affirmative-transformative continuum.

Affirmative RJ, undertaken for the purpose of social control in schools, fits comfortably within schools, reinforcing existing structures and programs that encourage compliance through a focus on rules, individual behavior, and punishment. Morrison and Vaandering (2012) warn against an increasing trend in Canadian schools to align RJ with safe school initiatives that, while having some similar traits to RJ, are behavioral approaches that focus on social control. Cunneen (2012) laments that, for the most part, RJ has taken its place in the world smoothly, without significant challenge to the values underpinning that world order. This smooth transition, however, only applies to affirmative RJ and is not the case for transformative RJ.

Transformative RJ as Social Engagement

Relationships

Contrary to a view of students as individuals to be managed, transformative RJ is grounded in the idea that humans are relational and thrive in contexts of social engagement rather than social control (Morrison & Vaandering, 2012). The understanding of life as built upon social connections and interactivity is consistent with most lived experiences and social and individual realities. Yet given the individualistic conception—largely neoliberal—in which much social science, public policy, and political narrative is steeped, a conceptual shift is required to assert the primacy and reality of relationships. Educators experience this tension in schools, feeling the need to control students while at the same time recognizing that they, as teachers, are "in the business of relationships" (Thorsborne, 2013, p. 48). Cavanagh (2011) pushes this idea further: "Relationships are at the core of who we are and what we are in schools" (p. 139). Social engagement shifts the focus from managing behavior to honoring the dignity and humanity of all members of the school community (Morrison & Vaandering, 2012).

Relational theory claims that humans are fundamentally relational and relations must be carefully understood and developed (Bingham &

Sidorkin, 2004; Llewellyn & Llewellyn, 2015). The theory is both an old and relatively recent idea, drawing on such thinkers as Buber, Noddings, Bakhtin, Dewey, Gadamer, Heidegger, Gilligan, and Freire to put forward a cohesive frame of reference "based on the assumption that relations have primacy over isolated self" (Bingham & Sidorkin, 2004, p. 2). Relational theorists offer an account of the self as constituted in and through relationship with others (Llewellyn & Llewellyn, 2015). This understanding of self does not deny the meaningful existence of individuals, but challenges the conception of individuals as distinct and apart from relationship. According to Bingham and Sidorkin (2004), "The self is a knot in the web of multiple intersecting relations; pull relations out of the web, and find no self. We do not have relations; relations have us" (p. 6). Several RJ writers in recent years have placed RJ within the framework of relational theory (Llewellyn, 2011b; Llewellyn & Llewellyn, 2015; Morrison & Vaandering, 2012). Although relationships have always been central to an understanding of RJ, they have often been couched in religious or spiritual terms (Llewellyn, 2011b) or co-opted for the purpose of social control. When focusing on the individual, such as in affirmative RJ, relationships are seen to be in service to the individual, who exists regardless of relationships; in contrast, a relational view claims that relationships are essential to the imagining, understanding and constituting of an individual. The self does not exist in isolation.

Relationships, though crucial, are not inherently good. A relational view is fundamentally concerned with the character and conditions of relationships (Llewellyn, 2011b); this concern extends not only to interpersonal relationships, but to the full range of relationships—personal and public—in which humans exist and are constituted (Llewellyn & Llewellyn, 2015). In a study focused on Maori students, Bishop, Ladwig, and Berryman (2014), learned that the quality of in-class relationships and interactions with teachers were the main influence on the students' educational achievements. Within those relationships, most teachers reproduced society-wide power imbalances and demonstrated low expectations for students; students reciprocated with low educational achievements (Bishop et al., 2014). In contrast, students thrived in classrooms characterized by caring relationships and high expectations (Bishop et al., 2014). The Manifesto of Relational Pedagogy found in Bingham and Sidorkin's (2004) book, *No Education Without Relation,* states, "Human relationality is not an ethical value. Domination is as relational as love" (p. 7). Given the profound impact that relations have in human lives, it is imperative that attention be paid to the nature of those relations.

Llewellyn (2011b) sees potential in employing relational theory to both challenge affirmative RJ and develop transformative RJ. Morrison and Vaandering (2012) call for RJ to be grounded in relational pedagogy, describing how RJ "honors individual self-worth, but also nurtures relational, classroom ecologies that provide spaces for students to gain appropriate status within a web of relationships that exists amongst all participants in a school community" (p. 151). In this transformative sense, the success of RJ is not measured in behavior modification, but by the change in the quality of social relationships that result (Llewellyn & Llewellyn, 2015).

Mutuality

In order for social engagement to be fully enacted, the character and conditions of relationships need to be further explored. According to Llewellyn (2011b), what is ultimately sought is relational justice that "aims at realizing the conditions of relationships required for well-being and flourishing" and is characterized by "equality of relationships" (p. 91). Equality is contextual and grounded in lived relationships, underpinned by mutual respect, concern, and dignity (Llewellyn, 2011b). She elaborates on these three essential qualities: respect, rooted in a context of concern for others, recognizes the rights and needs of others; concern emerges out of knowledge of another's needs, aims and positions, and is revealed through interconnectedness; and dignity resides not solely within an individual but within those interconnections. Thus, relational justice is realized as these qualities are experienced in different contexts.

In schools, equality of relationships is experienced when adults view students as humans to be engaged with rather than as "objects to be controlled" (Morrison & Vaandering, 2012, p. 145). This view shifts the onus from adults who control the decisions and choices to mutual decision-making and sense-making, whether in pedagogy or other aspects of schooling. Equality of relationships means that expectations and support can be given and received by any individual of any age (Morrison, 2011). In its purest form, equality of relationships would result in radically different schooling experiences than those found in most mainstream western schools. Writing about implementing effective relational pedagogy for Maori students, Bishop et al. (2014) recommend a classroom where power is shared and teachers relate to and interact with students so that new knowledge is co-created. "Such a classroom will generate totally different power relationships, interaction patterns, and educational outcomes" (Bishop et al., 2014, p. 210).

Noddings (2004) concurs, highlighting how mutually enhanced learning for teachers and students is a product of relational pedagogy. Genuine student participation—such as when students are involved in meaningful mutual decision-making and sense-making—both erodes the gap that usually exists between teachers and students and fosters democratic citizenship (Noddings, 2004; Raby, 2012).

Affirmative RJ tends to focus primarily on modifying student behavior and attitudes. In acknowledgement of the mutuality required for equality of relationships, transformative RJ advocates call attention to the necessity for adults, too, to be open to asking questions of their own relationships and behaviors. Vaandering (2013) suggests that adults in schools need to commit to living restoratively with each other before or at the same time that students are introduced to RJ. Thorsborne (2013) agrees, calling for RJ values to be seen as equally important for adults as for students. The call for RJ to be seen as relevant to adults as to students refers both to how specific incidents of harm are dealt with, as well as broader implications.

Beyond Harm

A focus on equality of relationships creates space to respond not only to incidents of harm, but to all relationships, policy decisions, pedagogy, curriculum, professional development, and institutional development (Conrad & Unger, 2011; Morrison & Vaandering, 2012). Cavanagh (2011) refers to this encompassing vision as creating a culture of care. He outlines three domains of this culture: being in relationship (situating relationships at the core of schooling), living in relationships (creating a sense of community in schools which includes using RJ to respond to harm), and learning in relationships (viewing relationships and interactions as central to learning).

When relationships and interactions are viewed as central to learning, both the content of lessons and pedagogical choices are affected (Noddings, 2004; Vaandering, 2013). Interconnectivity becomes key to engaged teaching and learning (Llewellyn & Llewellyn, 2015). Often students are asked to separate school from their personal and cultural space; relational pedagogy opens up ideas about what a learning classroom looks like, inviting students to make connections between their identities and relationships and classroom content (Raby, 2012). For Llewellyn and Llewellyn (2015), this interconnectivity in the classroom is the basis for critical thinking and good judgment. While such attributes and skills are often portrayed as individual traits, Llewellyn and Llewellyn (2015) understand them as emerging from the community. They draw on Haraway (1990) who asserts that relational critical thinking does not equate with mindless consensus; rather, classrooms need to be seen as spaces for contradictory standpoints and embodied realities that provide for "transgressive boundaries, potent fusions, and dangerous possibilities" (p. 198).

Attention to Power Relations

When students and teachers focus on the connectedness of people, one of the *dangerous possibilities* is that power relations become more visible and contested (Llewellyn and Llewellyn, 2015). To create a culture of care built on equality of relationships requires attention to social injustices, dominating and hierarchical systems of power in schools, disparities, and symbolic violence (Cavanagh, 2011; Conrad & Unger, 2011). It is not enough to attend to injustice in interpersonal relations if there are broader injustices underpinning those relations. Relational equality is concerned with addressing those broader injustices in social relations (Llewellyn, 2011b). Relational equality seeks the broader realignment of power.

Bishop et al. (2014) provide an example of what this realignment of power could look like in the context of education with Maori students. They envision pedagogies rooted in Maori epistemological terms that address ongoing power imbalances and racism and "would create a context that would reorder the relationships between teachers and students in classrooms and mainstream/public schools" (p. 190). What is required in this instance is the combination of a culturally responsive approach with broad critical, sociocultural approaches to learning (Bishop et al., 2014).

Genuine engagement between students and teachers, based on equality of relationships, could raise questions about the organization of schools and their focus on rules, competition, and individualism (Raby, 2012). Students and staff have the potential, to varying degrees, to replicate such discourses and/or transform them; they are "thoroughly enmeshed in the social fabric, both reproducing and disrupting it" (Raby, 2012, p. 204). Although some educational scholars feel it is misleading to encourage students to play a role in altering unequal structures of schooling given how entrenched these systems are, others feel that the only way to break collective disenfranchisement is for students to become more equipped in engaging in such actions (Raby, 2012). Raby (2012) concludes that student participation in schools is ultimately desirable and beneficial for democracy, but tempers this assertion by insisting that school staff need to be genuinely open to potential, possibly radical, changes resulting from student participation. Llewellyn and Llewellyn (2015) elaborate, writing that it is not enough to simply make people feel included, inquiry "must be undertaken with a genuine appreciation for what is said and not said, and in that the 'answers' might make a difference to the outcome" (p. 16). This is what McCluskey (2013) refers to as a "radical re-imagining" of school relationships and school structures.

Transformative RJ and Social Engagement

Transformative RJ, underpinned by social engagement and not by social control, is "attentive to the range of private and public relationships that support, or potentially thwart, human flourishing" (Llewellyn & Llewellyn, 2015). Transformative RJ is not committed to preserving existing relations or restoring relations to a prior state, but, rather, attends to the current conditions and characteristics of relations so that they can be transformed to the ideal of equality of relationship (Llewellyn, 2011b). This understanding of RJ entails a future orientation, assessing current conditions and relations to understand how best to create or sustain conditions of equal relationship in the future (Llewellyn & Llewellyn, 2015).

As a concrete example of RJ as social engagement, Vaandering (2013) has taken McCold and Wachtel's (2003) social discipline window, critiqued as a social control and affirmative RJ model, and modified it to become a relationship window. The relationship window identifies interactions that either diminish or nurture one's inherent worth as a human being. She shifts the focus from managing behavior to honoring connections, dignity and humanity. McCluskey (2013) also offers specific recommendations for how to live out social engagement or what she names a *strong* version of RJ, including: openness to challenge and risk; monitoring the effect of disadvantage and the impact of inequality and discrimination; seeing school as a community, not an institution; pedagogy and curriculum influenced by restorative principles; and adults who model positive ways of working and communicating (pp. 135–136). According to McCluskey (2013) the most convincing sign that a school has embraced a strong version of RJ is that members of that school community continually insist that the school is not restorative enough; transformative RJ is dynamic and contextual, requiring continual reflection and action.

Transformative RJ, as outlined here, is based on social engagement, holding relationships at its core and insisting that those relationships are grounded in mutuality, encompass all aspects of schooling and attend to structural and power imbalances. Transformative RJ seeks to disrupt the usual discourses that value individuals, order, compliance, rules, behavior, and social control. Disrupting these discourses is much more difficult than aligning oneself with them, as affirmative RJ often does. Yet, transformative RJ advocates would insist that disruption is required if we are, as Elliott (2011) puts it, to live collectively as our best selves.

3

Listening to the Voices in the Schools

Researching an approach such as RJ, with its focus on people and relationships, calls for careful attention not only to *what* you are researching, but *how* you are conducting that research. I sought to align the *how* with the values and principles of RJ, following the practices of other restorative researchers (Umbreit & Armour, 2010; Vaandering, 2009; Zehr, 2005). In a 2006 conference presentation, Howard Zehr, often referred to as the grandfather of RJ, identified what he believed were the three most important values upon which to ground all RJ work: respect, humility, and awe. Elaborating, he wrote that we need to profoundly respect the perspectives, needs and worth of all involved; embrace a humility that recognizes the limitations of what we know; and to approach the world with awe, appreciating the mystery, ambiguity and contradictions within the lives of those we meet (Zehr, 2006, pp. 12–13).

Since my focus was on the intersection between adult intentions and student experience, I shaped my research so as to, as best I could, respect the perspective of educators and students, recognize my own limitations in understanding their realities, and appreciate the ambiguities and

Adult Intentions, Student Perceptions, pages 29–40
Copyright © 2019 by Information Age Publishing
All rights of reproduction in any form reserved.

paradoxes that exist in their lives. In short, I wanted to engage with school leaders, educators, and students in such a way that they taught me about their understandings of and experiences with RJ.

Based on restorative values, I conducted a qualitative case study that explored the adult understandings and student experiences at two schools, one in Canada (Rocky Creek[1]) and one in Scotland (Royal Mills). The schools were selected for similarities in the age of students and length of time the schools had been involved with RJ. Orum, Feagin, and Sjoberg (1991) discuss how case studies allow people to tell their stories, which is "simply to remain most authentic to the form in which people often experience their own lives" (p. 21). I explored the contexts, stories, and discourses, as discovered in documents and individual and collective experiences. I immersed myself in the settings of the two schools in order to learn about the daily lives of the educators and students, both the group ethos and particular experiences. Recognizing my limitations as an adult participant observer to be privy to student experiences, I also engaged students as my co-researchers, greatly enhancing my understanding of their daily lives. The role of student co-researchers is explained in more detail later in this chapter.

Scotland

The chosen school, Royal Mills, served slightly fewer than 600 students, ranging in age from 11 to 18, and employed approximately 60 full-time teachers. It was located in an economically-depressed area of Eastern Scotland: The number of students eligible for free school meals due to low income was more than double that of the national Scottish average of 15%; in 2010/2011, 14% of graduates from Royal Mills were going on to higher education, compared with the national average of 36% (Education Scotland, 2011). The school was ethnically homogenous, White Scottish. Royal Mills was seen as a leader for supporting students with complex learning and behavioral issues and, as such, attracted pupils with a wide range of needs from outside the catchment area. It was within this context, 5 years prior to the study, that restorative approaches (RA, the school's term for RJ) was formally brought into Royal Mills. I focused on first-year pupils, aged 12–13 years old, in the Winter of 2013.

Canada

The elementary school, Rocky Creek, in the western Canadian province of Alberta had just under 350 students, between the ages of 3 and 12. One third were new Canadians, English was a second language for approximately 80% of the families, and students came from almost 40 different countries. The neighborhood had 3.5 times as many low-income households as the city average and 3 times as many food hamper users. Similar to Royal Mills, Rocky Creek was seen as a leader in working with children with multiple and diverse needs. Within this context Rocky Creek implemented RJ 5 years prior to the study. I focused on the Grade 5 and 6 students, aged 10–12 years old, in the Spring of 2013.

Data Collection

The student experience was essential to this study. The student experience, however, cannot be fully understood without exploring the layers of meaning, the broader context, in which students are situated. Data that spoke to the student experience were gathered through student questionnaires, learning circles, and co-researcher activities. Data to understand the broad context and educator perspectives were gathered through document analysis, participant observation, interviews, educator questionnaires, and educator learning circles. Taken as a whole, the research attempted to illuminate the complex dynamics of the intersection between adult intentions and student perceptions.

Document Analysis

Throughout the study, I gathered public documents that related to RJ, as well as regional and national educational discourses. Documents were analyzed for patterns, both internally and in relation to each other. Studying public documents allows a comparison between what is officially stated as occurring or desirable, and what is actually happening.

Participant Observation

Before embarking on my study, I suggested to the management team in each school that I would participate in the life of their schools however they felt best. Thus, my participation looked different in each locale. I wanted to be part of school life, both in order to experience the school myself and to be able to, in a small way, directly thank the schools for their generosity in opening their doors to my study.

In Scotland, I spent 3 months in the region and three and a half consecutive weeks in Royal Mills. I was given free reign to wander, to sit in on lectures and classwork, and to speak to anyone. As Johnson, Avenarius, and

Weatherford (2006) point out, participant observation approaches vary between emphasizing observation or participation. My time as a participant observer in Royal Mills leaned more toward observation. I did occasionally work with pupils requiring extra assistance in the pupil support center and with pupils in the inclusion room, where pupils were placed who would otherwise be suspended or who were at risk of suspension. I observed innumerable interactions between pupils, between staff members, and between staff and pupils and was privy to many informal conversations in all parts of the school and with all members of the school community: from pupils smoking outside to custodial staff taking a break in the staff room; from teachers in the corridor to management staff before a meeting.

In Canada, I spent 2 months in the region and was present in Rocky Creek for 5 consecutive weeks. The longer time in the school, as well as other factors, led to my time in Rocky Creek being more participatory. Most days I worked directly with students: running reading groups, helping students set up displays in the gymnasium, assisting with special events such as a pancake breakfast, filling in for absent staff members, and providing extra assistance to individual students. Staff often asked me to sit in on the class-wide restorative circles they were running and I was usually asked for feedback, both within the circle and privately. My presence and the research activities I was conducting in Rocky Creek led to many conversations—informal and formal—and eventually resulted in several staff members requesting that I facilitate an all-staff circle focused on the issue of communication. The principal supported this request and I ran the circle on my last day in Rocky Creek. Again, the ability to be present in Rocky Creek was invaluable as I learned much about the school's priorities, values, and challenges from interactions and observations in the staff room, classrooms, playground, and office.

Interviews

I conducted interviews with members of the school management teams in each school and with significant individuals outside of the schools. In Scotland, I interviewed the headteacher, a male who had been at Royal Mills for almost 10 years, and one male depute headteacher who had served as depute at Royal Mills for 15 years—part of that as the person responsible for pupil support. I also met and interviewed: Anthony Finn, then chief executive of the General Teaching Council for Scotland; Drew Morrice, then national assistant secretary in the Educational Institute of Scotland (Scotland's largest educational union); the senior education manager for the local authority; the local authority's education officer responsible for

Royal Mills; and a principal for an elementary school using RJ within the same local authority.

In Canada, I interviewed the female principal who had been at Rocky Creek for approximately 5 years, and one female assistant principal who was new to the school. In addition, I interviewed two of the main RJ training facilitators in the area and was able to attend a 2-day board-wide training session put on by UNICEF on Rights Respecting Schools (RRS). RRS is an initiative that Rocky Creek had undertaken and had linked closely with their implementation of RJ.

Questionnaires

An educator questionnaire was developed to ascertain how RJ was understood and used by teachers, members of the management teams, and other staff. In Scotland, 29% of staff responded to the questionnaire; in Canada, the response rate was 49%.

A student questionnaire focused on student perceptions of school and direct and indirect indicators of RJ. In Scotland, there was concern among some of the members of the school management team, based on previous experiences, that the necessary parental consent forms would not be returned promptly or in sufficient numbers, and may not even be delivered to the parents by the pupils. Therefore, within the first week, an assembly was set up for all 90 first-year pupils so I could explain why I was in Royal Mills and how important it was for me to hear their thoughts. Beyond the attempt to improve the consent form return ratio, it was an opportunity to set the tone for my research with the young people. Both I and the depute headteacher emphasized that the young people were the experts of their pupil experience and had much to teach adults. Several pupils stopped me in the hallway in the next few days, wondering why I would travel from Canada to learn from them. The assembly was a success both in terms of planting the idea of the pupil as expert in the pupils' minds and in terms of the consent forms. Slightly more than 50% of the consent forms were returned, much higher than staff had predicted, and all of these pupils completed the questionnaire.

Similar to Scotland, there was concern amongst the Canadian staff that it would be difficult to convince students to bring back completed consent forms. Rather than hold a full assembly, I made presentations in the individual classes about what I wanted to learn from the students and why I considered it crucial that I hear from students directly. Since I had more opportunity to volunteer in classrooms and, thus, interact personally with students, I was also able to build more relationships before the consent forms were distributed. In all, out of 85 Grade 5 and 6 students, 38 returned parental consent forms and completed the questionnaire (45%). Of these 38, 12 were Grade 5 (32% of 38 Grade 5 students) and 26 were Grade 6 (55% of 47 Grade 6 students).

Learning Circles

Learning circles are focus groups conducted like restorative classroom circles, using similar guidelines. As with focus groups, learning circles elicit stories and in-depth explanations of people's thoughts and experiences (Kitzinger 1994; Wilkinson 1998). Learning circles, however, are meant to achieve more than just providing the researcher with desired data. Learning circles take the lead from Freire's cultural circles, in which participants are moved from objects to subjects in their learning. Subjects, according to Freire (2002), have "the capacity to adapt oneself to reality plus the critical capacity to make choices and transform [their] reality" (p. 4). Learning circles emphasize that participants are the ones with the knowledge and expertise and they are teaching each other and the researcher about their own reality. Viewing participants as subjects opens up the possibility that learning circles could be a stepping-stone beyond discussion into transformed choices and actions on the topics being discussed.

All learning circles were conducted with individuals who self-selected on the questionnaire or who later asked to be involved. With the educator learning circle, I wanted to learn how educators perceived RJ and its effect on their students and the school. What sorts of messages did they want to communicate to students through the use of RJ? In Scotland, 10 educators participated in learning circles. Three circles were held, one with two participants and two each with four participants, lasting between 35 and 45 minutes so as to fit within a free period. Of the 10 participants, one was male, three worked in the areas of guidance or pupil support and seven were employed as classroom teachers in a variety of subjects, with a few holding leadership positions within their subject area. Their experience in the school ranged from less than 1 year to almost 20 years. In Canada, 15 staff members, about one quarter of the staff, participated in circles. Four circles were held, ranging from between two and five participants each. The shortest circle lasted 45 minutes and the longest was one and a half hours. Of these 15 participants, one was male, and all but two were White; these demographics were representative of the larger Rocky Creek staff body. All participants worked primarily in the classroom, two as educational assistants and thirteen as classroom teachers. Together they represented the breadth of the school's programming; at least one teacher from each grade participated in the learning circles, as well as teachers from the early education program and the behavior learning assistance (BLA) program. Their experience in Rocky Creek ranged from less than one year to over 20 years.

For the student learning circles, 19 participants (8 male and 11 female) returned consent forms and participated in learning circles in Scotland; 20 (7 male and 13 female) did so in Canada. In Scotland, I ran four pupil learning circles, with four to six participants. In Canada, I had five circles, with two to five participants. The shortest was 18 minutes and the longest 42 minutes. Each student circle was focused on one of three themes: communication, rules, or community. These themes were selected from the literature to represent a range of aspects connected to RJ in schools.

Learning circles mirror the relational process inherent in restorative approaches and often have a ritualistic aspect to them. Each round was begun with a question or topic. One participant would offer to answer first and then, one by one, everyone around the circle would have a chance to answer. Following each initial round, the discussion on that particular question was opened up to flow more naturally. The facilitated rounds were done, in keeping with restorative values, to ensure that everyone's voice was valued and heard equally. A talking piece was used to focus the conversation and ensure that one person spoke at a time.

The learning circles provided an opportunity for educators and students to talk with their peers about their experiences at school. Learning circles acknowledge that the work of the circle is unique to its place and time, the people who are present, the dynamics between them, and how they contribute through their words and silences. The learning circles were introduced by me as opportunities not only for me to learn from the participants, but also for participants to learn from each other. Throughout the process, the conversations sometimes affirmed ideas that individuals put forward, and sometimes offered conflicting opinions; each statement reinforced how complex and layered schooling can be.

Student Co-Researchers

The concept of co-researchers was built on Grant's (1993) idea of shadowing, in which teachers were asked to follow a student in his/her own school for a whole day in order to gain an understanding of the student experience. By engaging students to be co-researchers, I *shadowed* the student from afar, as they recorded their experiences from their own perspective.

The idea of co-researchers highlighted two specific values often associated with RJ: the need to involve and give voice to those most affected; and the acknowledgement that process is as important—and sometimes more important—than end product (Cronin-Lampe & Cronin-Lampe, 2010; Hendry, 2009; Umbreit & Armour, 2010; Woolford, 2009). Engaging students as co-researchers embodied the first value as the student experience was prioritized; students were given a voice and asked to offer their expertise. Secondly, the focus shifted to the process, rather than the product. Although the results of the students' inquiries were one significant part of the study, results were intertwined with the process in which they were achieved.

Rather than use the vague term *co-researcher*, I talked about students as *detectives* or *reporters*. In Scotland, 11 pupils (2 male and 9 female) were co-researchers. In Canada, 19 (6 male and 13 female) were. Each participating student was given a notebook, chose a pseudonym, and was asked to record observations for 3 days. After the 3-day observation period, I met students individually so that they could give meaning to the notebooks.

In Scotland, they were asked to pay attention for 3 days to whatever theme (communication, rules, or community) was discussed in the circle. Without using names or identifying factors, they took note of everything they saw or heard that had to do with that theme. Taking note entailed whatever they were most comfortable with, including: writing detailed observations, drawing pictures, and repeating direct quotations. I emphasized to them that they were to record that which they felt was significant; I wanted to know what they personally thought. We also discussed how to keep the notebooks safe (treating them as personal diaries that would not be shared with others) and how to record observations so as to not disrupt the class or their own learning (using breaks and time between classes to jot down ideas). At the end of each of the 3 days, they returned the notebooks to me so that they would not be lost and then picked them up in the morning before school began. This also allowed me the opportunity to see how the notebooks were progressing.

The first day when I retrieved the notebooks I was impressed by the variety of ways in which the students had approached their task: Some had written pages of detailed notes, others had pictures and captions, some had a few point-form phrases, one had quotations from fellow students, and a few were blank. The second day, only a few of the students added anything to their initial notes. The third day, only one wrote additional observations. There was one that stayed blank throughout the whole process.

I was disappointed, wondering whether the task had been too onerous or too abstract, whether the students had simply gotten bored, or whether there had been anything of note for them to observe. I wondered whether this part of the research had failed, at least on two accounts—failed to teach me about the student experience and failed to give students the experience of inquiring into their own realities.

It was not until I met with each student individually, as they explained their notebooks to me, that the meaning of *taking note* became evident. Taking note was not confined to their notebooks. Some of the students with the least amount written down had the most to tell me about what they had seen, heard, observed, and thought. It seemed that the act of intentionally asking students to take note caused students to pay increased attention to classroom dynamics and interactions, regardless of whether the notebooks were used. If they had recorded observations in their notebooks, students began the interview by reading exactly what they had written or describing the pictures they had drawn. Then they spoke more naturally, elaborating on what they had seen: examples of behavior, generalizations about their classroom, and thoughts about why things were the way they were. I was thrilled with the depth and breadth of what they had to report.

Meaning—for me as the main researcher and for my student co-researchers—was created in two ways: through the student explaining the notebook and through the process of observing. The notebooks on their own meant very little to me as an outsider; each one needed to be given life through the voice of the student that had created it. The notebooks were used as a stepping-stone in the interviews into the students' actual observations and what he or she felt they meant. This echoes the findings of Ellis, Hetherington, Lovell, McConaghy, and Viczko (2013) who looked at the use of pre-interview drawing activities and found that participants who referred to these drawings during interviews had greater observations, analyses, or reflective insights.

Secondly, meaning was created through the very process of observing. Most of the students took my request that they take note of their school very seriously. Even though some of them felt unable to write down their observations, they all had ideas and thoughts they wanted to share verbally. The act of asking them to take note of their school heightened their awareness of their everyday experience.

My initial sense that the notebooks had failed raised questions as to how to approach the idea of taking note in a different way in Canada. Given that both the process of taking note and the process of explaining the notebooks to me elicited and validated the student perspective, I did not believe that the notebooks should be abandoned. I did, however, wish to make the experience more accessible to and satisfying for the student co-researchers.

I had hoped that by including the drawing of pictures under the rubric of note taking, the activity would be more inclusive of those students who, for whatever reason, did not have advanced writing skills or confidence. Indeed, one Scottish student who identified as having dyslexia chose to draw only pictures in his notebook. Yet, there were several individuals, regardless of writing ability, who found it difficult to take notes on what they were observing. One girl, Jemima,[2] expressed a common sentiment: "I couldn't put some stuff into words." On the other hand, other students thrived during the activity of taking notes and observing their classes, mentioning how fun they found it.

My intention was to ensure the activity was as open to interpretation as possible, to allow the students to decide what to include in their notebooks without my leading or intervention. The fact that several students seemed unsure about what to include, however, caused me to wonder if the task was too abstract for some. Thus, in Canada, I changed the activity slightly. In keeping with the idea of the student as expert, I brought the students together at the beginning of each observation day for a few minutes so that they could share different ideas for how to take note. I asked students to talk about how the previous day's observations had gone and to discuss any problems they had translating what they saw into their notebooks. Again, there was value in this strategy both as a product and a process. As product, the assumption was that students would be better equipped to record more of what they observed and share that with me. As process, the students were validated as having the answers within themselves. This practice also aligned with RJ's emphasis on collective problem solving.

Additionally, I altered the directions regarding the activity. In Scotland, I asked students to pay attention for 3 days to whatever theme had been discussed in their learning circle—communication, rules, or community. Therefore, the learning circle discussions potentially shaped what students thought of as appropriate for their notebooks. The learning circle discussions, while student focused, were still centred on questions that I, as an adult researcher, asked. In Canada, in an effort to lessen the effect that my own line of questioning might have had on the students' observations, as well as attempt to keep the activity fresh for the students, I asked all co-researchers, regardless of the learning circle in which they participated, to take note of all three themes: communication one day, rules the next, and community on the final day. This task was presented as their *mission of the day* during the short group morning meeting. Although I cannot attribute this directly to these changes, the majority of the notebooks in Canada contained significantly more observations for all 3 days than in Scotland.

What emerged from the students, in both Canada and Scotland, was a dialogue between the abstract and the concrete. Student co-researchers engaged in a three-stage dialogic (Bakhtin, 1992) in which student insights were formed and then informed by the thoughts of others and their own observations. This dialogic process facilitated both student learning and the expression of the student experience. The process began in the learning circle, moved to the observations, and continued with the student analysis of their experience.

The first stage occurred in the learning circles where, although concrete examples were given, the discussions often revolved around generalizations. Here are two examples: "People get along pretty good when they're not fighting. It's really peaceful and you just see friends being friends, and like, being funny. And you don't really see much big fights and people beating each other up here" (Canadian Learning Circle); The school is a community because "you've got a load of people that you ken [know] and even if you're not pals with them, they're still there for you when you need them" (Scottish Learning Circle). Through these generalizations about the student experience and life at school, students put forward an initial analysis, one that had not yet been tested by focused observation and further thought.

In the second stage, the co-researcher observations and interviews took those generalizations and gave them texture by offering specific examples that either strengthened or dismissed the initial generalized analysis. For example, detailed illustrations were provided of how students treated one another: "Somebody asked for a pencil, right, and she went, 'Nwa! You seen yourself, you're not gettin' my one!' And then she just starts being mean and cheeky and it's annoying…" (Georgia, Scotland). Other examples were given for how students worked to solve interpersonal issues: "We helped her with the problem. We walked her away, we calmed her down, we made her laugh, we played with her, we gave her cookies, and some of us gave her gum. We talked to her and we talked to the boy, too" (Kitty Pie, Canada).

The dialogic continued into the third stage as those concrete examples were then folded back into abstract generalizations and analysis during the final interview. I asked three questions at the end of each individual co-researcher interview: (a) "From what you observed, what would you like to see more of in your school?"; (b) "From what you observed, what would you like to see less of in your school?"; (c) "If there were a new student arriving tomorrow, what would you tell him or her about your school?" In answering these questions, students offered an analysis of what they had been observing over the three specific days combined with their general student experience in the school.

Lloyd-Smith and Tarr (2000) declared that, "The reality experienced by children and young people in educational settings cannot be fully comprehended by inference and assumption" (p. 61). Viewing students as experts of their own realities and providing opportunities for them to share that expertise and also to engage in an inquiry into these experiences, enriched both the body of knowledge in my study and, hopefully, the experience of the individuals involved.

By attending to the student experience in these two schools and situating that experience within the educators' understandings and the surrounding context, I began to decipher the purposes underpinning RJ in the Scottish and Canadian schools. The next chapter introduces the story of the Canadian school, Rocky Creek.

Notes

1. The names of the schools are pseudonyms.
2. All the names used are the pseudonyms that the students invented for themselves.

4

Rocky Creek

The Canadian School Story

In my study of two schools, the student experiences were primary, nestled at the center of the inquiry, yet engaged in a constant dialogic with other discourses that surrounded them. These discourses, evident in individual views and documents, both shaped and reflected how RJ was employed in schools in the different countries and formed the landscape by which to understand the student experience. It is this landscape that I describe in the following pages.

I have chosen to set the context of Rocky Creek public school, the Canadian school, by focusing on the province, Alberta, in which it is situated. In contrast to Scotland, education in Canada is a provincial responsibility. Given Canada's size and the differences that exist between provinces in terms of geography, economy, history, culture, politics, and sometimes, language, it seemed unwieldy and counterproductive to begin the discussion with Canada as a whole. As well, Scotland, although an autonomous nation, has a relationship with the United Kingdom that is in some ways analogous to Alberta's relationship to Canada: devolved responsibilities

Adult Intentions, Student Perceptions, pages 41–67
Copyright © 2019 by Information Age Publishing
41

alongside ones that remain the responsibility of the national governments of the United Kingdom and Canada.

Alberta

Provincial

Broad Discourses

The population of Alberta is just over four million (11% of Canada's population), making it the fourth most populated Canadian province (Statistics Canada, 2014a) and slightly less populated than Scotland (5.3 million). It is also the fourth largest Canadian province, more than 8 times the size of Scotland (Natural Resources Canada, 2005).

Although Alberta is not Canada's largest province, it commands disproportionate attention from the rest of Canada. Canadians outside of Alberta, of which I am one, are fascinated by the province. A land of prairies and oil, Alberta is often referred to as Canada's Texas, where the skies are big, the people are straight talkers, the money flows abundantly, and the politics are right wing. And yet, what fascinates us are the frequent contradictions—historically and currently—that poke holes in the convenient Texan stereotype. What becomes obvious, as one looks closer at Alberta, is that it is a land of independent thinkers, sometimes leaning right, sometimes leaning left, sometimes not leaning at all, that confounds any attempt by the rest of Canada to pigeonhole it.

Alberta is a relatively new province, having joined the Canadian confederation in 1905. Yet, the history of the region extends back thousands of years. The First Nations peoples who lived in the area "were as various and complex as the landscape itself, and are as various and complex today" (van Herk, 2001, p. 72). When White Europeans, Americans, and those from central Canada first ventured into the region, there were 10 tribes and four broad language groups firmly established (van Herk, 2001). Interactions between indigenous peoples and newcomers were, for the most part, mutually beneficial and respectful during the years of first contact, when relationships were essential, from the newcomer perspective, for survival and such activities as the fur trade (Saul, 2008). Once central Canada declared its ambition to create a nation that stretched from sea to sea, however, the First Nations peoples became seen as obstacles by White Canada. The disastrous results of this new engagement have been well documented. Between the inadvertent and intentional dissemination of communicable diseases, the near extinction of the buffalo population within two decades, the onslaught of missionaries and whisky traders, and settlers encroaching on traditional territory, indigenous people faced continuous threats to their very existence: "Facing famine and privation, they had no choice but to capitulate to the promises held out by the white man's treaties" (van Herk, 2001, p. 78). The differing understandings of what these treaties meant—the ceding of all land to the government or peace treaties that allowed newcomers access to the land—continue to resonate in aboriginal/non-aboriginal relationships today (Alberta Government, 2013; van Herk, 2001). The Indian Act of 1876 laid the foundation for Indian agents to rule over the lives of First Nations people in Alberta—as go-betweens, censors, bankers, moral and social arbiters—until 1969 (Alberta Government, 2013; van Herk, 2001). It was not until 1960 that First Nations peoples were granted the right to vote in federal elections without losing their treaty status; the Alberta franchise followed in 1964 (Alberta Government, 2013).

In 2006, the most recent statistics available, just over 80% of the population in Alberta identified as White, with approximately 14% identifying as a visible minority (Chinese and South Asian being the most common; Statistics Canada, 2009) and almost 6% identifying as aboriginal (Statistics Canada, 2008). These demographics are similar to the rest of Canada, with the exception of the aboriginal population, which is higher in Alberta than the national average, reported in 2006 to be 3.9% (Statistics Canada, 2013).

Today Alberta is home to more than 220,000 people descended from First Nations, Métis, and Inuit (FNMI) peoples, with the two largest groups being the Cree and the Blackfoot Confederacy (Alberta Government, 2013). Forty-three percent of Alberta's aboriginal peoples lived in the two biggest cities, Edmonton and Calgary, in 2011 (Alberta Government, 2013). Reserves today comprise 1% of Alberta's total area, with Métis settlements occupying less than 1% (van Herk, 2001). Alberta is also the only Canadian province to grant the Métis a land base, local autonomy, and self-sufficiency (Alberta Government, 2013). Since the 1970s, First Nation communities have had the power to make decisions on such issues as education, public health, band administration, and reserve roads (Alberta Government, 2013). The legacy of structural violence, however, continues to reverberate, and there are tremendous inequities on and between reserves, with some struggling to provide basic necessities to their members. Others, particularly those located near the tar/oil sands, run multimillion dollar businesses and use their economic power to bolster their social and political voice (Alberta Government, 2013; Helbig, 2014; van Herk, 2001). As one of the fastest growing segments of Alberta's population (Alberta Government, 2013; Alberta Government, 2014; van Herk, 2001), aboriginal people influence the past, present and future of the province.

Although foundational and essential, the aboriginal story is but one layer of Albertan culture. The other layers include—but are not limited to—cowboys, ranchers, feminists, oil executives, iconoclastic politicians, and the staunchly religious. With all of these layers and many contradictions, Albertans defy definition and description. Van Herk (2001), in writing a history of Alberta, selected the word *maverick* as the best description, defining it this way:

> Traditionally, a range calf without a brand and consequently without an owner. If cowboys couldn't poach them, they'd butcher them—fresh meat for the chuckwagon. Also a term applicable to Albertans, especially appropriate for a collective resistance to being caught, owned, herded, taxed, or identified. (p. 394)

She writes elsewhere that Alberta has "through time and experience become a sophisticated outlaw, a place where pedigree is unimportant and where migrants are encouraged to reinvent themselves, attracting a mélange of characters" (van Herk, 2001, p. 3). The acceptance of this mélange of characters—of all extremes, backgrounds, and interests—is part of what makes Alberta unique.

This uniqueness is particularly apparent in Albertan politics. Since the first election in 1905, Alberta has been primarily a one-party province, tending to punish and reward political parties in totality. As van Herk (2001) writes,

> Albertans have always hated government, its sticky fingers, its interfering ways. They hate politicians almost as much, although they practice a wild combination of adulation and revolt that swings politicians into power and then just as suddenly flings them out of power and onto the streets again. (p. 230)

The province started as a Liberal (Canada's center-left party) stronghold, with the party winning 23 out of 25 seats in 1905, and ruling for 16 years. The next political dynasty was the United Farmers of Alberta (UFA), working to promote the political position of farmers. The UFA, advocating for a new social order in which government favors were no longer distributed to the rich and well educated, ruled for 14 years (van Herk, 2001). Alberta experienced severe economic and social challenges in the 1930s; per capita income fell from $548 in 1929 to $212 in 1933 (Palmer & Palmer, 1990). In response to the economic hardships and scandals within the UFA, Albertans began to look for new answers, finding hope in one of Alberta's more colorful characters, evangelical radio preacher, William "Bible Bill" Aberhart (CBC, 2001; van Herk, 2001). Aberhart formed the Social Credit party, based on social and economic reforms, representing a populist protest against capitalism. Promising each citizen $25 a month in *social credit*, the party completely eradicated the UFA in the 1935 election. Initial social credit ideas mostly failed, however, due to a lack of ideological coherence and practical planning. Oil revenues soon eased the province's economic woes and the Social Credit party ruled the province for 36 years (CBC, 2001). Alberta of the 1970s, however, was secular and booming, a far cry from the Alberta that first elected Bible Bill; the Social Credit party was thrown aside in the 1971 election in favor of the new right-leaning Progressive Conservatives, who held power for 44 years. This party, too, has been led by memorable characters: Peter Lougheed, Ralph Klein, Ed Stelmach, and until 2014, Alberta's first female premier, Alison Redford. The reign, however, has been anything but monolithic, ranging from Lougheed's massive spending on industry and an expanded welfare state, to Klein's pursuit of government austerity through waves of privatization and outsourcing (Cosh, 2012). The party's rule has also weathered significant challenges from more socially conservative populist groups, such as the Reform party, which later became the Canadian Alliance (of which former Prime Minister Stephen Harper was elected leader), and the more recent Wildrose party. The year 2015 saw the end of the Progressive Conservative rule and a surprising election not of conservative populists but of social democrats, the New Democratic party, and the province's second female premier, Rachel Notley. Far from being a uniformly right-wing province, as it is often characterized by the rest of Canada, Alberta embraces a spectrum of policies and values, depending on the context and the draw of the leader. One need only look at Calgary's Mayor Naheed Nenshi, North America's first Muslim mayor, in power since 2010, and his broad appeal to those on both sides of the political spectrum to appreciate the complexity and contradictions present in Alberta's political scene.

This complexity extends to the role of women in Alberta. Within Alberta's male-dominated frontier society, Canada's first feminists emerged (van Herk, 2001). Alberta passed the suffrage bill in 1916, the third Canadian province to do so, giving women the right to vote in provincial elections (Parliament of Canada, 2014). Alberta was also the first province to set a minimum wage for women—$9 a week in 1917, raised to $14 in 1923 (van Herk, 2001). Louise McKinney was elected to the Alberta Legislature in 1917, becoming the first woman to sit in any legislative assembly in the British Empire (Famous Five Foundation, 2012; van Herk, 2001). McKinney, along with four other Alberta women who championed the rights of women and children—Emily Murphy, Nellie McClung, Henrietta Muir Edwards, and Irene Parlby— became known as the Famous Five. Together, they brought forward the Persons Case, a challenge to the interpretation of the British North America Act that only men could be considered *qualified persons* and thus appointed to the Canadian senate. In 1929, the Privy Council of England ruled that women were indeed persons and could become senators (Famous Five Foundation, 2012). Interestingly, no Albertan woman was appointed to the Senate until 1979, leading van Herk (2001) to suggest that Ottawa was rightfully afraid of the strength of Albertan women. The legacy of strong Albertan females continued with Alison Redford as the first female premier of Alberta; Danielle Smith as the head of the opposition, Wildrose party (until Smith's 2014 defection to the Progressive Conservative party); and current premier, Rachel Notley. The contradictions and complexity have continued, with some suggesting sexism as one reason that Redford stepped down as premier in 2014 (The Canadian Press, 2014). Van Herk (2001) warns against becoming complacent amidst the historical legacy of female equality: "... the hum of Alberta's boomeranging conservatism still pervades the province, and women here know that they better keep checking over their shoulders, twirling their lassos, and never take anything for granted" (p. 381).

The image of checking over one's shoulder could also be used to illustrate the uneasy relationship between Alberta and Canada's capital, Ottawa; a sense of western alienation that pervades today. Although Albertans had felt separate from central Canada since before confederation, this sense was most vivid during the 1980s when then Prime Minister Pierre Trudeau (father of Canada's current Prime Minister Justin Trudeau) unveiled the national energy program (NEP) as part of the federal budget. Seen as a battle over control of Alberta's natural resources and money, Premier Lougheed retaliated by cutting oil production, accompanied by the infamous quote by then Calgary mayor, Ralph Klein: "Let the eastern bastards freeze in the dark" (Finch, Varella, & Deephouse, 2012). Foreign companies began selling off energy assets and the Albertan economy crashed (CBC, 2015). Defenders of the NEP pointed to the influence of global markets and predicted an inevitable collapse in oil prices, regardless of domestic policy (CBC, 2015). Whether myth or reality, many Albertans were outraged at Ottawa and talk of separation exploded (van Herk, 2001). Although the outrage has long since been diluted, I found echoes of the NEP specifically and alienation in general surfacing in everyday conversation in Alberta.

Drawing on this complex history, van Herk (2001) portrays Albertans as enigmatic people who are full of contradictions and love breaking rules. I experienced the reality of this portrayal first hand while in Alberta. The quintessential example was found in Jordan (not his real name), a bus driver in the city in which I did my research. On my first day of conducting research in Rocky Creek public school, I mistakenly boarded a bus that finished its route well before the school; Jordan, the driver of that bus, offered to deliver me to that stop, anyway. Once everyone exited the bus at the official final stop, Jordan put on the *Out of Service* sign and drove me another 15 minutes to the school. We had a great chat about his job, my research, and Alberta in general. I had assumed that this would be an isolated incident; Jordan, however, upon seeing me waiting for a bus the next day, insisted that I board his bus. Jordan became my personal bus driver for the rest of my time in the city.

It was in those conversations, after everyone else exited the bus at the final official stop, that I was schooled on life in Alberta. According to Jordan, former Prime Minister Pierre Trudeau cheated Alberta with the NEP and made life even worse when Lougheed would not cooperate. On another day, Jordan delved into the topic of climate change as a hoax dreamed up by Al Gore and David Suzuki. According to Jordan, the hoax was created to make them a profit, giving an example of Gore's supposed 300-room house and private jet. A few days later, Jordan revealed decidedly liberal views on sexual politics and identity. Jordan epitomized Alberta for me, eluding all stereotypes. He did not respect bureaucracy (he decided to give me unofficial bus rides); he held very conservative beliefs (anti-Trudeau; climate change as hoax); and he held very liberal beliefs (sexual politics).

Educational Discourses

Responsibility for education in Canada rests almost entirely with provincial legislation. Thus, while there is a certain common expression of Canadian education (Tomkins, 1986), and the Canadian Council of Ministers of Education works to achieve a level of congruence across the provinces and territories, there exists a degree of differentiation (MacDonald, 2013). Educational discourses in Alberta—built on its history and context—are unique to the province.

Education in Alberta was shaped when it was still a territory and in negotiation to become a Canadian province. Schools were a particularly contentious issue in these negotiations as the territorial leadership at the time (the territory was eventually split into present-day Alberta and Saskatchewan) advocated for uniform, non-sectarian schools, fearing that different interests of the newcomers who spoke German, Ukrainian, Finnish, and French, among others, would splinter the West (van Herk, 2001). One-quarter of the territorial population in 1891 was French, however, and Prime Minister Laurier was under pressure from Quebec Catholic bishops to establish separate French-speaking Catholic schools. In the end, separate schools run by Catholic boards were established, with French as the language of instruction in French-speaking communities, and with teachers and curricula certified by the provincial government (van Herk, 2001). This same system exists today: Anglophone and Francophone publicly funded Catholic schools operate as part of the dual system of public education in Alberta (Alberta Catholic School Trustees' Association, 2010). In 2011, 69.1% of students in Alberta attended public non-denominational schools, 22.3% Catholic public schools, 1% Francophone schools, and 1.2% charter schools, all publicly funded. The remaining 6.4% of students attended private schools or received home education (Alberta Education, 2012b).

Educational choice has always been valued in Alberta. Von Heyking (2013) details how Alberta, unlike other provinces, has expanded rather than restricted opportunities for faith-based education within the public system. She claims that this acceptance was shaped by two Christian premiers—Aberhart (1935–1943) and Manning (1943–1968)—who gave school boards the responsibility to ensure public schools reflected and accommodated local religious views and diversity. Today there are publicly funded schools teaching Alberta's curricula but grounded, for example, in Christianity, Islam, or aboriginal spirituality (von Heyking, 2013).

Charter schools are another example of Alberta's emphasis on choice. According to Alberta Education (2012b), charter schools are "autonomous public schools" providing "education in ways that are measurably different or enhanced" (p. 4). Instead of school boards, charter schools are run by private organizations with particular educational agendas (Wagner, 1999). They cannot have a religious affiliation and must accept all students provided there is sufficient space and resources (Alberta Government, 2011). Alberta is the only province in Canada to integrate charter schools into the public system, introducing charter schools in 1994. Although criticized at the time by some as a radical step toward the privatization of education in Alberta, Wagner (1999) contends that the introduction of charter schools was merely an extension of the Progressive Conservative government's longstanding policy of promoting educational choice.

When Alberta first became a province, in 1905, it adopted the existing Ontario school curriculum. Although this was slightly revised in 1912, it did not embody a particular Alberta sensibility. As with other English-speaking parts of Canada, schools and their curricula reflected an Anglo-centric view and consisted mostly of British content (Tomkins, 1986; von Heyking, 2006). In a study of the evolution of the Alberta curricula, von Heyking (2006) demonstrates how the late 1930s curriculum documents represented the first evidence of a strong provincial consciousness. Politicians called for a curriculum appropriate for life in the West, free from Ontario prejudice. These calls coincided with education officials' interest in new approaches to education and, in 1942, resulted in a progressive curriculum that embodied a provincial identity (von Heyking, 2006). The progressive approach was unique within Canada, resulting in the production of made-in-Alberta textbooks. Texts emphasized such topics as cooperative organizations, the rise of alternative political parties such as the Progressive Conservatives and Social Credit, and the important contribution of Alberta's natural resources to the economy of the entire British Empire (von Heyking, 2006). The 1980s, with increased tension between Alberta and Ottawa—due in large part to the NEP—saw a renewed focus on curricula imbued with a strong sense of Alberta's identity and place within Canada. Political and economic grievances were highlighted within curricula, as were the values of freedom, individualism, persistence, and initiative, and their importance in the success of the province (von Heyking, 2006).

In many ways, curricula have continued to evolve to reflect current understandings of Albertan identity. Alberta Education (2012a) set as its goals for 2012–2015: success for every student, high quality education through collaboration and innovation, and success for FNMI students. The third goal is significant, given the history and legacy of education in relation to the indigenous people of Alberta. In 1894, the territorial government began forcing FNMI children to attend residential schools, often directed by missionaries of various Christian faiths, in an attempt to assimilate Alberta's aboriginal peoples (van Herk, 2001). Beyond the devastating loss of language, culture, and family ties, the schools often exposed children to communicable diseases such as tuberculosis, with many dying as a result (van Herk, 2001). There were 25 residential schools in Alberta, more than any other province (Truth and Reconciliation Commission of Canada, n.d.). The Truth and Reconciliation Commission estimates there are currently about 12,000 survivors of residential schools living in Alberta (Cotter, 2014). Although it is impossible to undo the poisonous effects of residential schools through policies alone, the Alberta Government Education websites and documents indicate a clear intention to engage with FNMI students and communities and prioritize their educational success. The development of culturally relevant learning resources and program supports for FNMI students, as well as increasing all Albertans' knowledge and understanding of FNMI cultures, worldviews, histories, treaties, and rights are highlighted within the documents (Alberta Education, 2013).

Based on province-wide consultations called the Inspiring Education dialogues, the Alberta Government began to implement a revised curriculum in 2018. Many of the designated changes match those of Scotland's national curriculum: student-focused, focus on competencies rather than content, and less prescriptive curriculum to enable teachers to meet unique student and community needs (Alberta Education, n.d.b). Yet, while in Alberta I heard no discussion about this proposed curriculum and its inspiring vision. I learned of the proposed changes online and through official documents. Instead, the dominant conversation among school staff and in the media focused on impending education budget cuts and a bleak vision of the future.

The budget, delivered in March 2013, the month before my study began, reduced operational funding for school boards by a total of $14.5 million for the 2013/2014 school year and cut some programs immediately, including a $41 million program which funded school authorities to develop and implement innovative educational projects (Alberta Teaching Association Staff, 2013). The threat of job losses and larger class sizes was already beginning to permeate and impact the atmosphere of schools in Alberta while I was there, even if that reality had yet to be realized.

Restorative Discourses

Canada has incorporated RJ into the formal justice system for over 40 years (Tomporowski, Buck, Bargen, & Binder, 2011). Worldwide, the first site of victim-offender facilitation is considered to be Elmira, Ontario, in 1974. Many RJ approaches in Canada are strongly tied to the indigenous people of Canada (Eagle, 2011; Elliott, 2011; Vaandering, 2009). Although some argue this indigenous connection is either dismissed without due respect (Eagle as cited in Enns & Myers, 2009; Vaandering, 2009) or artificially enhanced to lend credibility to restorative justice (Cunneen, 2012; Daly, 2002; London, 2011; Woolford, 2009), there is wide recognition that RJ in Canada has deep roots.

RJ has been applied in Canadian schools since the 1990s (Drewery & Winslade, 2003; Morrison, 2007b) and the popularity of the approach appears to be growing (Morrison, 2015; Tomporowski et al., 2011). In Alberta, it is difficult to find information on how and when RJ was first introduced to schools. There was no concerted effort to introduce RJ to schools across the province; most likely the introduction happened on an individual staff member or school basis, with much regional differentiation. The earliest mention of RJ in schools in Alberta was found on the Alberta Government's Education website: Between 2003 and 2008, two school boards discussed introducing RJ as part of their initiative for school improvement projects (the program which had its funding cut in 2013).

At the time of my study, besides these two school boards, there were very few references to RJ on the official provincial education website. RJ was identified as a best practice in a guide to effective collaboration between school administrators and police (Alberta Education—Cross-Ministry Services Branch, 2013); RJ was mentioned once in an almost 300-page document on character and citizenship education (Alberta Education, 2005a); and RJ received one mention each in a progress report on FNMI education (Alberta Education, 2008) and in a document on how to better serve the needs of aboriginal students (Alberta Education, 2005b). Clearly it was not through official education ministry channels that RJ was being accessed by schools in Alberta. Most schools were accessing training and resources from sources outside the government.

During my study, there were two RJ organizations, both located in Edmonton, working with schools province-wide: Alberta Conflict Transformation Society (ACTS), and the Society for Safe and Caring Schools and Communities (SACSC). ACTS provided most of the training for Alberta educators and students. In 2012, ACTS trained 450 people in Alberta, including educators, community members and police officers (ACTS, 2012). According to its website, ACTS took a broad view of RJ, focusing on relationships rather than behavior. In their school workshops, ACTS asked: "What is it we want students to learn through our discipline practices? How do we encourage students to do the right thing because it is the right thing to do? How do we encourage students to take responsibility and be accountable for their words and actions?" For reasons not publicly known, however, the board of directors for ACTS voted to dissolve the agency in June 2014. The individual trainers continue to work in the area.

The other organization influencing RJ in Alberta schools was SACSC. Building on earlier efforts by the Alberta Teacher's Association to develop safe and caring school initiatives, SACSC was incorporated as a nonprofit organization in 2004 (Alberta Education, n.d.a). SACSC provided free resources, workshops, and webinars on a wide range of topics related to safe and caring schools, including RJ. In one document, SACSC credited ACTS in the development of their RJ programming, suggesting a confluence of understanding of RJ between organizations (Pakan & SACSC, 2007).

Given the lack of attention in the ministry of education's websites and public documents, it was not surprising that there were few readily accessible documents on RJ to be found within the province. Even the websites of ACTS and SACSC had little in the way of documents. The only document I located during my study was a guide for teachers and parents published by SACSC in 2007, supported by a grant from the Alberta Solicitor General and Ministry for Public Safety. The message of this document—how to use formal restorative processes to improve student behavior—seemed inconsistent with ACTS' emphasis on a critical approach focused on relationships. Since there were so few Alberta documents focused on RJ, it was impossible to ascertain which of these messages was the predominant one being received by Alberta educators.

Regional

Broad Discourses

The neighborhood where my study was conducted is located in a growing urban center. As with many Alberta towns, it was established in the early 1800s on First Nations land, as a Hudson's Bay Company (HBC) fur trade post (van Herk, 2001). HBC, an entity established by the British monarchy, was given monopoly of almost a million and a half square miles of western and northern Canada, without regard to those already inhabiting the land, including this region (Manitoba Government, n.d.; Goldi Productions, 2007). The first languages in the area were French, Cree, Blackfoot, Gaelic, and very little English (van Herk, 2001); in 2011, about 75% of the region's citizens indicated that English was their mother tongue, 2% French, and just over 20% a non-official language, mostly Tagalog, Punjabi, and Chinese (Statistics Canada, 2011). English and French are Canada's two official languages. After a series of agricultural and energy booms and busts through the decades, the region, since the late 1990s, has seen a relatively consistent boom largely due to historically high oil prices.

In many ways, the region as a whole reflected the complexity of Alberta. The following vignettes of my personal experience from two consecutive days highlight the contradictory mix.

Day 1: While checking out the downtown YMCA, I asked an employee where I could find a business to print a 40-page document. The YMCA employee insisted he had time and would print it for me on their printer, no charge. Then I went to a café to work. The women's bathroom was covered in graffiti, 90% of which was both positive and intelligent. For example, there was a back and forth conversation between a 'conservative girl' and a 'leftie girl', each saying what they wished the other would know about them. Later, walking home on a main avenue, there was a protest outside of a tattoo and body-piercing shop. The workers were asking for it to be boycotted because of an unjust boss.

Day 2: I attended a performance of *Balletlujah*, a ballet based on the music and life of k.d. lang, an international music star who grew up in a prairie town in Eastern Alberta. The story followed a prairie girl who falls in love with another prairie girl. After a stint in Los Angeles and an affair, the protagonist comes back to Alberta and falls in love again. The prairie landscape was omnipresent: in the costumes, the background setting, and the music. Leonard Cohen's *Hallelujah* was the last song, with electric dancing symbolizing birth, life, and suicide. It left me weeping. This region is more than the stereotypes; yet, it is also absolutely those stereotypes. After the ballet, as I walked along the main avenue, the testosterone was palpable.

Every oil-money-bought truck, motorcycle, and sports car was revving; every screen in every bar was tuned in to either hockey or mixed martial arts; drunks were loudly pushing one another; vomit pooled in the street; and police tape marked off a gang-related shooting from the night before. Simultaneously, on the other side of the road, walked/lurched 50 people dressed as zombies. Ten minutes later, after smiling directly at me, a young woman passionately hugged a tree.

Educational Discourses

More than half of the students within the region attend public non-denominational schools; just over 20% attend public Catholic schools; and under 20% gave no response in the most recent census (Alberta City, 2012). As it is the school board affecting the most students, as well as the school board within which Rocky Creek public school belongs, this section attends to educational discourses as found within the public non-denominational system.

As in the rest of Alberta, the regional school board emphasizes choice as foundational to their approach to education (Alberta School Board, 2013b). Open boundaries allow parents and students to choose their preferred school. Students are guaranteed entry to their geographically designated school, but also have the option to attend any other school within the region, provided the school has room and the student meets entry requirements. As such, the region's schools offer numerous specialized programs ranging from Arabic, to dance, to Waldorf that attract students from across the area. Students choose between schools that offer regular programming, alternative programming with a focus on arts, athletics, language and culture, faith or teaching philosophy, or special education programming with specialized supports based on needs and abilities.

Since Rocky Creek public school offered two special education programs, I will briefly highlight one of those programs, the behavior learning assistance (BLA) program. BLA assists students whose "severe, chronic, extreme, and pervasive behaviors significantly interfere with learning at school" (Alberta School Board, n.d.a). Classes have a reduced number of students with close and constant adult supervision. All senior high schools provide this programming; 45 elementary and junior high schools also offer BLA programs. More will be said on this program in the section focusing on the school.

An annual education results report summary for 2012/2013 presents a mostly positive picture of the state of education in the region. Referencing the provincial accountability pillar, used by Alberta education to monitor school jurisdictions, the school district received a rating of *excellent* in the areas of safe and caring schools; student learning opportunities; and continuous improvement. A *good* rating was granted for student learning achievement; preparation for lifelong learning, world of work, and citizenship; and parental involvement (Alberta School Board, 2014). The summary reported that over 90% of teachers, parents, and students were satisfied with the overall quality of education.

One of the main regional goals for 2012/2013 was listed as a success for every student. According to the report, over 30% of students in the district self-identified as "outside of the traditional mainstream" which includes: FNMI, English language learners, refugee and newcomers, students in need of specialized supports and services, and sexual and gender minorities (Alberta School Board, 2014). Those outside the mainstream would also include, according to the report, the more than 30,000 children affected by poverty in the region. Rocky Creek reflected the diversity presented in the report.

As in the rest of the province, it was the budget that dominated educational discourse in the region. The province announced its budget cuts in March 2013, a month before I arrived at the school. The school board subsequently reported that it would need to drastically cut its budget, while at the same time welcoming more students. Conversations of which I was a part, in the school and throughout the district, ranged from anger to fear to acceptance. Some were angry that an oil rich province would not be able to properly fund its schools, others feared for their own jobs, some hated the uncertainty, and a few accepted the situation as the new reality and braced for larger class sizes. In the end, hundreds of full-time staff positions were cut, as were a variety of programs. Despite the official school board goals and accomplishments, the main discussion around education in the region centered not on vision, but on damage control.

Restorative Discourses

RJ was first introduced to the district as an alternative to suspension and expulsion. In 2002, the school board established a pilot project implementing the use of community/classroom conferences as an option in their school disciplinary procedures. Students were referred to conferences if there was a risk of expulsion or if their behavior was a chronic issue not successfully resolved by traditional means. There was no information available as to how long the pilot project lasted, nor how widespread it was within the region. An ACTS trainer, however, discussed the evolution of the project from a focus on lowering suspension rates through restorative conferences to a current focus on proactive measures to prevent the need for such conferences.

During the pilot project and after its completion, ACTS was contracted to facilitate community conferences. To gain an understanding of what messages educators in the region were receiving about RJ, I watched a 50-minute webinar offered by ACTS trainers on the SACSC Website (Hopgood & Missal, 2013). The main message focused on the importance of relationships. RJ, or RP (restorative practices) as it was called in the webinar, was framed as a developmental practice in which the philosophy needed to be embedded in everyday approaches. There was very little mention of utilizing RJ to change student behavior; rather, the focus was on building relationships and living out the philosophy in non-conflict situations. Adults, too, were encouraged to reflect on their relationships and were called to model all aspects of RJ. If this was the main training that educators in the region were receiving, they were being introduced to RJ as a proactive, all-encompassing philosophy that focused on building relationships and held adults to the same account as students.

Although the webinar presented a holistic understanding of RJ, it was still difficult to ascertain whether this understanding was widespread within the region. As was the case in the province as a whole, there was very little official attention paid to RJ within the board. Searching the school board's website for the word *restorative* turned up one result: the name of my own research project as having been approved. If RJ had been a priority of the board in the past (e.g., with the pilot project), during the time of my study, it evidently no longer was.

Rocky Creek Public School

General Discourses

Rocky Creek public school was built in the early 1970s. In 2012/2013, Rocky Creek served over 300 students, up almost 20% from 2008, and employed about 30 full-time (or equivalent) staff responsible for three separate programs: regular classes for Grades 1–6; half-day early education programming for students with special educational needs; and behavior learning assistance (BLA) programming for Grades 1–6. During the research period, out of the total student population, approximately 250 were in regular programming, 60 were in early education, and 25 were in BLA classes.

A profile found on the school board website provides a description of the student population as coming from diverse cultures and socioeconomic backgrounds. While some families are affluent, many struggle with low incomes. The profile identifies students as having almost 40 different home countries, with the predominant ethnic groups being Arabic, Somalian, and aboriginal. One third of students are new Canadians, many attending school for the first time. English is a second language for approximately 80% of the families.

Both the principal and the assistant principal, in their interviews, frequently referenced the backgrounds of students and families when explaining Rocky Creek's procedures, vision, and struggles. A significant number of students grew up in refugee camps and were fleeing various forms of social upheaval. Students at times arrived traumatized and trust needed to be built with both them and their families before learning could occur. Poverty was also an issue experienced by students at the school. Rocky Creek did its best to alleviate some of the effects of poverty by providing daily snacks to students and maintaining both a food and clothing bank.

Rocky Creek's multicultural nature was celebrated through events such as multicultural week, the inclusion of families and their traditions in school activities, and intentional class projects that highlighted cultural diversity. The principal praised the families of the students for their support and attitude toward education. She found that many placed hope in education to better the lives of their children, as opposed to experiences she had had with parents in other more typical inner-city schools where cyclical poverty had erased that hope. The principal discussed the ongoing transition of the surrounding neighborhood from a high-needs "rough, tough, rotten area" to a "nice, mixed little community" where, although dominated by public, often transient, housing, some ethnic groups were becoming more established.

There were also challenges brought about by the mix of cultures and newcomer status of many students. The assistant principal discussed the difficulty in translating societal expectations—particularly gender equality and how to handle conflicts—to families from cultures or social situations where violence was seen to be the norm and gender roles clearly defined. The principal mentioned this challenge as well, though placing more of the onus on staff to bridge the gap and be culturally sensitive. She gave an example of a previous practice, where recess supervisors would ask misbehaving students to stand against an outside wall, which "really upset parents because standing against the wall has certain connotations in a refugee camp or in war situations; it means you could, well, be shot quite literally."

Beyond these cultural disconnects, the large number of newcomer students was also identified as contributing to Rocky Creek's low academic performance. The 2012 provincial achievement tests saw only half of students in the school gain an acceptable rating compared to the provincial average of 79%. The principal explained the low achievement rates to parents this way: "We had 10 children come into our school, three of them are in

Grade 3 and two of them are in Grade 6 [the grades included in the provincial exams]. And guess what? They speak no English whatsoever and they will be writing the provincial achievement tests. What is going to happen to our mark?" The mix of cultures and backgrounds resulted in challenges both in terms of common everyday understandings and such public indicators of school success as test scores.

Yet many staff members I spoke with, including those in leadership, pointed out the often-overlooked indicators of school success. Part of the provincial accountability pillar is a student, teacher, and parent survey to assess if "students are safe at school, are learning the importance of caring for others, are learning respect for others, and are treated fairly at school" (Alberta Education, 2015, "How the Accountability Pillar Works" section, para. 3). In this measure, almost 80% of respondents from Rocky Creek agreed in 2012 that the school is safe and caring. Although still lower than the provincial 89% average, the gap is much diminished, as compared to academic measures. Anecdotally, the assistant principal reported that in 2013 she believed students increasingly felt safe in school and felt that adults were there to help them. The principal agreed that the ethos in Rocky Creek was continuing to improve. The effort that staff were making to connect with students, she believed, reverberated within the whole school community.

My own first impressions echoed this sense of Rocky Creek as safe and welcoming—for students, staff, and visitors. Inclusivity was evidenced in the patient manner in which many members of staff spoke with the students, in the programs and activities offered in school, in the way students were greeted by name in the front office, and in the impromptu circles that occurred in hallways and on the playground.

Seen as crucial to overall school culture was the leadership team, consisting of one female principal who had been at Rocky Creek for several years and one female assistant principal who had recently arrived. The principal acknowledged that her own brand of leadership was different from most. Her own educational philosophy was that "until you're fed, until you're accepted, until you're safe, you aren't going to learn very much" and she advocated putting student safety and inclusion at the heart of Rocky Creek, as necessary precursors to other directions the school might take. When she arrived at Rocky Creek, she did not push hard deadlines and directions; rather she wanted to work with staff to discover the school's next steps. The principal admitted that some staff members left Rocky Creek after her first year, not connecting with her style of leadership or the direction in which she was moving. She felt that she started to win over other members of staff once they realized that she was supporting them in the transition. The principal gave the example of bringing in various support staff—the aboriginal liaison, the school board social worker, and others—to meet monthly with teachers to conference on how to proceed with individual students. The fact that teachers were receiving such practical support gave the principal the traction she needed to continue implementing her ideas.

The principal's desire to support and work collaboratively with staff members continued during my study. She abhorred micromanaging but also wanted to ensure that staff members met fair deadlines. A difficult balance to achieve, staff members informally discussed how they sometimes felt imbued with too much freedom and sometimes with too little. With significant issues, however, the principal worked to elicit and consider the input of others. The upcoming budget cuts, for example, were a point of deliberation and the cause of much fear. In the monthly Rocky Creek newsletter, parents were asked to contact the leadership of the school with what they considered the most important student needs, so that those needs could be factored into budget decisions. Likewise, during a staff meeting that I attended, the principal put forward various budget scenarios. She requested input from staff as to which possibilities they preferred. Although the meeting was short and the discussion abbreviated, the act of requesting input invited further staff collaboration.

Collaborative, in fact, was a word often used to describe the staff at Rocky Creek. This collaborative spirit grew out of, the principal thought, a focus on how to best meet the needs of all students. Whereas staff previously felt responsible only for their immediate students, over the past few years, staff members had been working with the intention of connecting with all students within the school, regardless of which class they belonged to. One concrete manner in which this collaboration was facilitated was through the implementation of cross-Grade reading groups to improve literacy, where students were grouped according to reading ability regardless of age or grade. In a practical manner teachers needed to collaborate on how to create the groups, who would facilitate each group, and what report card marks would represent. Besides improved literacy, another result was, according to the principal, building "the notion that we're working together, we're doing this thing together. Everybody's kids belong to everybody." Another example of staff collaboration was the program called ROCKY.[1] Soon after the principal arrived, she asked staff what they really needed students to do for the wellbeing of all. Together staff created ROCKY: Remember to listen, Own your actions, Care for others, Keep your hands to yourself, and You can be a leader. ROCKY became the school rules and was posted liberally on the walls of the school; the acronym—and its focus on collective responsibility—were referred to frequently by students.

The practice of collaboration reflected a general sense of satisfaction among staff in Rocky Creek. In a survey conducted in 2012, almost 100% of staff felt that the school was a good place to work. Staff were described as having good relationships and being devoted to the students, evidenced by the running of clubs and after-school activities. Beyond the teaching staff, many others were applauded for their commitment and attitudes: front office staff, lunchtime supervisors, the school success coach, the family therapist and social workers, among others.

One staff issue that did emerge was a lack of adequate communication. In the 2012 survey, staff satisfaction with information on school happenings had dropped by close to 10% from the previous year. Staff circles to discuss issues and information had been used with some regularity when the principal first arrived. They had been discontinued, according to the principal, due to staff complaints that circles were "uncomfortable" and "not dignified." The principal admitted, however, that staff had started to ask for them again, to strengthen communication. In the staff learning circles that I ran, I also heard complaints about the quality of communication in the school. Some went as far as to call the staff *dysfunctional*. Many people said they longed for more discussion and would appreciate staff learning and discussion circles.

Part of the issue with communication seemed to be caused by the vast number of programs and groups operating within Rocky Creek. Despite the principal's insistence that the school operate as a cohesive whole, there were still many divisions. I do not believe that members of staff begrudged the presence of the various programs; they simply wished for better communication about and between these groups. Staff saw the programs as crucial for engaging the student population. Among the various partners offering services and programs in Rocky Creek were: child and family services, social work support, English language learning support, an aboriginal liaison, an art gallery, a peace center, UNICEF, before and after school care services, lunchtime supervisors, the school success coach, the family therapist, and a center for newcomers, among others.

One of Rocky Creek's main events, organized by staff, students, community members, and school partners, was a multicultural festival. The festival began about a decade ago when refugee families started to arrive at Rocky Creek in large numbers. According to one teacher, the families were often headed by single mothers dealing with trauma and culture shock. The school had a difficult time gaining the mothers' trust. At that time, this teacher told me, Rocky Creek also saw an increase in bullying, especially between various socioeconomic classes within African refugees and between different Arabic groups. Rocky Creek's culture at the time—built largely by the previous principal—was quite punitive and this did not improve matters. One teacher started a multicultural festival as a way to help mothers feel more connected to the school, reaching out to them through a focus on food and fashion. The event has grown ever since.

My first day in Rocky Creek coincided with a community multicultural evening event. The school was packed with students and family members, an incredible array of ethnicities and languages. Families all brought food to share and a line to sample the dishes snaked through the school. The evening's program consisted of a First Nations family drumming and dancing, a 7-year-old Punjabi girl dancing, and Arabic boys drumming and dancing. The whole week featured a variety of special guests and events. In later conversations, students often referred to these events as a highlight of their year and one of the things that made the school special; adults revealed behind-the-scenes issues and referred to it as a symbol of confusion, lack of communication, and stress. Regardless, for all, it represented a substantial bridge between the school and families.

Besides the celebration of cultures at Rocky Creek, inclusion was also addressed through other programs. Differing socioeconomic backgrounds, for example, were partly attended to through a program providing students with a daily nutritious snack. The program was funded by a nonprofit organization, and was a normal part of the day for all students, regardless of need. While I was in the school, the nonprofit arranged for a visit to inspect the facilities and present Rocky Creek to its board members. The event took an immense amount of organizing, as students in all rooms made and ate a pancake breakfast with the visitors. A number of media outlets also descended on Rocky Creek, holding a news conference and celebration in the library. One of the sponsors, in front of the television cameras, announced that they would be donating a 70-inch television and full sound system to Rocky Creek. The school also received a donated fridge and financial contributions. Not only was the snack program funding extended; it was also a successful fundraising day for Rocky Creek.

The other source of diversity addressed by Rocky Creek's programming was that of BLA. The BLA program was both a source of pride and despair. Rocky Creek had been chosen as a site for BLA programs, so students who met the criteria were bussed in from around the city. There were three classes: Grades 1/2, 3/4, and 5/6. The classes, with much fewer students than the regular classrooms, finished earlier and ran on a slightly different schedule than the rest of the school so as to allow for more supervision over lunches and breaks. Some students were integrated into mainstream classes part of the time; others stayed solely in the BLA rooms. They were both separate and integrated, attending some of the same assemblies and activities but seen by both themselves and other students as being a special group. The principal described the attitude within Rocky Creek to BLA classes as reflecting the phrase, "Everybody's in." She continued, discussing a student in a BLA class, "Yeah, I know, sometimes he kicks and screams and bites other people but it doesn't mean we can cast him into outer darkness. We have to get that kid back."

My initial BLA experience was with the Grade 5/6 class on my first day at Rocky Creek. All BLA rooms are equipped with time-out rooms, padded rooms where students go or are put when it is deemed that they need to calm down. The doors cannot be locked, so I would sometimes see a teacher sitting with his/her chair propped up against the door, keeping it closed. On the day I arrived, there was a child in the time-out room, thumping repeatedly against the walls. Apparently, he had torn up someone's book. He eventually came out and a mini restorative meeting was convened; he was asked who he thought he had affected and how he could make it better.

A few days later, I sat in on a circle in the Grade 1/2 BLA class, at the request of their teacher. They were having a restorative circle—which they did not often do—on issues that were happening on the school bus. The teacher wanted to deal with the fact that some of the boys were coming to class angry every day. Some students were filled with so much anger during the circle that they were shaking, punching their own heads, or using shoes to beat them. A teacher later told me this was extremely mild behavior; teachers get about three death threats a day from students. But the students did sit in the circle and eventually all spoke. After some talk, it came out that there were bullying issues on the bus. One boy decided to go with an adult to talk to an older boy, who had been instigating the bullying. The circle was framed as a way to figure things out together, not to get anyone into trouble. Interestingly, out of all the circles I witnessed, this one put the most onus on the students, even more so than those in the older *mainstream* grades: all the ideas came from the students, students were coached to speak to one another, and teachers kept going until they got to the root of the issue.

I also had positive experiences as I engaged with individuals from the 5/6 BLA class for the study. One girl and one boy from the class filled in the student questionnaire. Both were completely on task and they were the only two to spot (separately) an error I had made, referring to students as *pupils* in one of the questions. They also wrote the most in their detective notebooks and radiated when they had a chance to tell me what they saw. Their teacher used the notebooks as a teachable moment, too. The class had a circle where they discussed what the student detectives were observing.

My most memorable BLA experience came on the day that the snack program visitors were in the school. Every class was to prepare pancakes. It was an incredibly busy morning, so I helped out in the Grade 5/6 BLA class. A Grade 3/4 mainstream class joined them. The BLA students moved seamlessly into leadership roles. One boy, dressed in a suit, welcomed people into the class; two students gave up their chairs for younger kids; one girl ran around helping teachers; another boy told stories to entertain the younger kids; and one student helped me distribute food. All were pleased to be acting as hosts and role models.

From time-out rooms, with the doors held shut, to restorative circles that gave students ownership in their own issues, from self-abuse to vent a myriad of feelings, to playing leadership roles and taking care of younger kids, BLA students, with their range of emotions and needs, were an integral part of the Rocky Creek experience, and yet separate, physically and relationally.

One program implemented as part of a larger focus on building relationships across the potential divides—cultural, socioeconomic, behavioral, and learning—was UNICEF's Rights Respecting Schools (RRS), based on the United Nations convention on the Rights of the Child. Rocky Creek's staff handbook suggests that the RRS initiative fits perfectly with the school's vision, recognizing the rights and responsibilities of the diverse student population. The conduct philosophy section of the handbook states that Rocky Creek has a culture based on all individuals respecting one another, achieved through using the building blocks of RRS. According to UNICEF's own training materials, a RRS gives children meaningful opportunities to voice opinions, participate fully in all aspects of schooling, genuinely participate in decision-making that affects them, and helps to resolve obstacles to well-being.

Within Rocky Creek there was much visible evidence of the commitment to being a RRS. Each classroom had developed its own charter of rights and responsibilities based on the UN convention. I watched a kindergarten class create their charter. Although I was not privy to the lead-up activities and discussions that would have introduced the idea of rights, on the day that I was in the classroom, they created this charter: We have the right to be safe; We have the right to have friends; We have the right to talk; We have the right to play; and We have the right to an education. The hallways were filled with posters featuring student versions of what it meant to have both rights and responsibilities. As even greater evidence of the RRS focus, the older students that I worked with consistently referred to conduct in their classrooms not in terms of behavior, but in terms of rights and responsibilities.

Many in Rocky Creek felt that there were strong connections between RRS and RJ. One of the educators, Barbara,[2] voiced the feeling of many: "I see a pretty natural fit between respecting rights and wanting to repair harm that you've done to someone." Although RJ was introduced to Rocky Creek a few years prior to the introduction of RRS, there was a sense that one could not work without the other. The assistant principal named RRS the "precursor" to RJ, setting the tone and developing necessary characteristics in children to be able to then restore broken relationships through RJ. The principal described the interaction between the two approaches this way:

> Rights Respecting Schools talks big-time about how students need to be involved in meaningful decisions. They need to be part of making the policies, their dignity needs to be respected at all times, you need to extend that same courtesy to parents. You know, they have a right to be safe and they have a right to be honoured in their own home and culture. And I think that restorative practices really look at treating people that way. They are about healing, about ensuring that everyone is included in the larger society.

This is the context within which RJ was implemented.

Restorative Discourses

Prior to implementing RJ, Rocky Creek relied on a standard discipline model. For any misbehavior, a student would receive a timeout and the teacher, principal, and parents needed to fill in forms detailing the student's behavior. Upon her arrival, the principal recalled finding three binders full of these forms. The principal's initial goal was to move away from the form-filled binders and the discipline model they represented.

Knowing she wanted the school to move in a different direction, but not entirely sure what that might mean, the principal booked the entire Rocky Creek staff into a professional development session with Barbara Coloroso, an American author and speaker on parenting, school discipline, and RJ. After that experience, she sent staff members, in groups, to whatever professional development sessions they thought would help them discern how to move forward with a different discipline model, and had them present their findings to the whole staff. In the end, "the staff latched on to the notion of restorative practices as something that was small enough that we could take a piece of it and use it. Which was specifically the restorative justice circles."

The principal described the first efforts to implement RJ in the school as "rocky." Teachers were asked to conduct weekly circles with their classes; many did not follow through. By the third year, however, the principal believed that most staff members had come on board. As RJ became more integrated into Rocky Creek's philosophy, the leadership team also reached out to families, holding presentations on RJ to inform parents of the move away from the punitive model. The principal found that parents were quite supportive of this new direction.

It was also at this point that RRS was introduced to the Rocky Creek. The principal thought that if the staff had not already embraced RJ, RRS would never have been accepted. The shift that RJ caused in thinking—particularly involving students in decisions that affected them—facilitated discussion about children's rights and children's voice. Both RJ and RRS, according to the principal have the same message: "This is the students' process, not just ours. You are not God sitting on a hill dispensing the commandments, you know? You're down there and everybody's working together. And you need to model what you expect to be done." The assistant principal also saw the two working together, but viewed RRS as the proactive part and RJ as the reactive piece. RRS was a "stepping stone" into RJ. During my study, 5 years into RJ implementation, Rocky Creek was committed to both initiatives, RJ and RRS, with many seeing the two as intertwined.

In considering the importance of RJ for students, the principal discussed RJ in regards to the culture it produced—both in Rocky Creek and in the larger society. She felt that RJ ensured that everyone was included and respected, and that relationships were healed. The assistant principal, too, focused on the big picture, how RJ could lead to better citizenship and to being a "good person." She also identified the many skills and attitudes that she saw RJ instilling in students: self-confidence, inner sense of calm, respect for others, willingness to take responsibility, and skills to deal with conflict. One of the main benefits, as the assistant principal voiced it, was that RJ provided students with "that understanding that they can fix it. They're not dead in the water. They can fix it."

RJ in Rocky Creek was mainly actualized through circles. I was able to view a variety of circles for different ages and different purposes. I sat in on a circle with a kindergarten class. They reviewed how to be in circle: look at and listen to the person talking, pass the talking piece, and do not talk while someone else is talking. Then the teacher introduced the topic of being a leader at school. The teacher asked students to think of a time when they had been leaders. She gave them time to think about their answer and then went sequentially around the circle. They listened attentively. If a child could not think of a time he/she had been a leader, the teacher gave an example of when she had seen that child as a leader. The teacher reminded one girl of how she had been scared to go on the playground because an older boy was being mean to her. They had a restorative meeting and the girl spoke directly to him about how he was making her feel. He had denied any culpability to the teacher but when he spoke to the girl in person, he was honest and apologized. The girl beamed at the memory.

The Grade 5/6 class ran circles on Thursday afternoons. The students were able to get their desks into circle in a matter of minutes. They explained to me how and why they do circles. The students told me it was to solve issues or simply to share thoughts. They need to listen to each other, not talk when others are talking, and not put anyone down. The week I joined the circle they wanted to discuss playing soccer at recess. The circle discussion was not sequential, but rather jumped wherever there was a hand up. It took awhile for the issues to emerge: The main issue was how boys acted toward the girls who were playing and how some girls did not seem to take the game seriously. The students were open about the issues but still shied away from letting the conversation get too personal. The teacher was very competent at encouraging students to talk; she also, however, shaped the conversation through her questions. Later she said she would prefer students to run the circle, but did not yet feel they had the maturity. Within the circle she asked if I had any thoughts. I noted that I had seen some students smirking during the circle and I wondered if there were dynamics that still needed to be discussed. The students got a bit more specific about some of the issues and suggested a few solutions. I remarked on how brave it was for them to talk honestly and I asked if they had been able to do that at the start of the year. They reacted quite strongly and said, "No, not at all." Only now do they know each other and feel safe enough to speak honestly.

Circles seemed to be a natural part of Rocky Creek life and the students relished them—from the young ones who shared stories of their lives to the older ones who had confidence that issues would be dealt with. In the learning circles for my study, students told me they appreciated circles, but also voiced their frustration at the tendency for some students to make false statements or false commitments in circle. Teachers, too, had mixed feelings, being particularly frustrated that the same issues kept coming up in circles.

The expectation from the leadership team was that staff also use RJ among themselves to address any potential conflicts. As the principal stated, "If we're doing it with kids, why wouldn't we do it with ourselves?" Although staff restorative circles had been run when RJ was first introduced to Rocky Creek, staff circles did not appear to have been used with regularity within the last few years. Several staff members intimated that they would appreciate more opportunities to practice the restorative work they were requiring of their students.

Within the staff learning circles that I ran for my study, some participants requested that I conduct a whole staff circle. One of the participants talked to the principal about it, who agreed, and it was planned as a special staff meeting for my last week in the school. Although it was an idea that originated with staff participants, it quickly came to be seen as a top-down initiative, due to how it was communicated by the principal. It was presented to staff as a mandatory meeting, making initial acceptance of the circle difficult.

On the day of the circle, all the tables were cleared out of the staff room and we set chairs into a large circle. On each chair, I placed a piece of paper divided into four. As they came in, people were instructed to answer four designated questions with words or pictures. They were told that they could choose later how much they wished to share. The questions were: "What do I like about working with students?"; "What do I appreciate about working at Rocky Creek?"; "Who is the teacher/educational assistant/principal I strive to be?"; and "What support do I need to better be that person at Rocky Creek?"

I reviewed the circle guidelines (which I had posted on the wall) and introduced the circle as their own circle, requested by staff, that they could use however they needed. The first round went quickly, with almost everyone focusing on the first two questions. Only positive thoughts were shared. Since staff members, in asking for this circle, were hoping to open communication and build bridges, this feel-good round seemed necessary. In the second round, I asked for people to share based on the last two questions. Here, more issues arose and there were a number of tears. Some people spoke of their own insecurities, others were very specific about what was not working in their current situations, and one talked about the lack of respect she saw in how adults spoke to one another. Overall, the circle experience seemed to be positive for most. It occurred on my final day in the school so I cannot comment on whether there were any follow-up actions or whether it succeeded in opening communication. As a participant researcher, however, it felt like a tangible way to give something to a community that had opened their doors to me for almost 6 weeks; something that was very much in line with Rocky Creek's stated desire to use RJ as a way to build health and wellness in both staff and students.

In the province, the region, and Rocky Creek, I was impressed by the embracing of complexity at each level and around each issue. Although not formed by a systematic coherent vision, this is not a province that attends to the status quo. Building on the strengths and challenges of the past and present, relying on a maverick spirit to see them through, the people and documents reflect a context that is both highly individualistic and highly community-oriented. RJ reflects the same reality. This reality will be explored in greater depth in the next chapter.

Notes

1. This is not the actual acronym used by the school but is representative of their program.
2. All names used are pseudonyms.

5

Rocky Creek Public School

Educator Intentions

It is time to listen directly to the staff and students of Rocky Creek, the individuals implementing and experiencing RJ within its context. We continue moving from the outer rings of the story, drilling down into the center of the experience—the students. I have chosen to introduce the understandings of the educators first, before the students, in order to attend to the purposes, goals, and intentions underlying the use of RJ in their school. The students, in the next chapter, then have the final word. They will tell us how well adult intentions match with the actual student experience.

Educator Intentions

In listening to the educators in the learning circles and examining the educator questionnaire, the purposes underpinning the use of RJ in Rocky Creek start to emerge. As could be expected, intentions are not homogenous: It is clear that there is a mixing of transformative and affirmative discourses within the school. What is interesting, however, in this mixing, is what rises to the top—social engagement and transformative RJ.

───

RJ Hopes: "I want them to learn how to do it so that people will listen to them."

Rocky Creek educators articulated four main understandings of RJ: a chance for students to take responsibility for actions, a collaborative way to solve problems, an approach that gives voice to all involved, and a way to make things right.

The most common reason mentioned for using RJ was to help students take responsibility for their actions. For many, taking responsibility simply made common sense. Barbara[1] explained: "Yep, you made a mistake; we all do. Let's fix it. Let's take responsibility for it, and let's take responsibility for fixing it." In order for students to take responsibility, educators felt they first needed to develop an awareness of others. This awareness was crucial since, as Aaron suggested:

> Sometimes [students] don't know that what they're doing is wrong or how it affects other people because they're just thinking about themselves. Well, I was mad because you didn't want to play with me, so I did that. But then having people explain, oh, when you do that it makes me scared and I don't want to play with you or be around you.

By understanding how their actions impacted those around them, educators hoped that students would take responsibility for those actions.

After taking responsibility, educators hoped that students would then engage in collaborative problem solving. As a first step, educators hoped RJ would help students "develop skills and vocabulary to talk about problems" (Mai). Those social and communication skills, although essential for school, were also thought to be beneficial for students in the long term. Kimi offered this wish:

> It's just a really powerful skill for them to have to solve their own problems. And that's what it teaches, in the end, when they go off into the world on their own, they're going to approach conflict and problem solving in that way, if they've been here long enough to gain that skill.

The third understanding of RJ was that of an approach that gave voice to all participants. Participants appreciated RJ's ability to empower students to express opinions that would otherwise be unheard and to allow students to feel fairly treated. Although the understanding of RJ as an empowerment tool did not surface often in the learning circles, the few educators who raised this as a goal were adamant. Mai hoped that participating in circles would impact students positively: "Making them feel like, 'No, I'm capable, I can solve my problems, I've got some skills.' Empowerment." Beth more explicitly made this hope part of her practice:

> I'm thinking that they'll be able to stand up for themselves. Because there's a lot of kids that can't voice their concerns. I have a lot of quiet kids that are too scared to rock the boat, kind of thing. So hopefully I'm also teaching them how to stand up respectfully for yourself, not just mouth off at somebody and go "Shut up!" at everybody. I want them to learn how to do it so that people will listen to them.

Although not mentioned often, those who did mention the hope that RJ would give voice to students were firm in their belief.

Finally, a few educators saw RJ as a way to "make things right." Making things right was interpreted in two ways: restoring the situation to the way it was before the conflict, or making the environment better than it was before the incident. Incorporating aspects of the other three goals—taking responsibility, collaborative problem solving, and giving voice—making things right was seen as an all-encompassing goal. Kirsten discussed kindergarten girls who she saw as working to make things right: "And the language that they use and the caring that they show towards other people and, even at such a young age, their willingness to admit their mistakes and their efforts to make it better, and to make the school better, it's just, it's really great to see." Making things right expanded aspects of the other goals to a holistic hope that RJ could restore or create better school environments.

The hopes educators had for what RJ could do—assist in taking responsibility, teach how to problem solve collaboratively, facilitate empowerment, and make things right—mostly focused on students. The hopes, however, did not attend only to changing the behavior of students, an affirmative RJ focus. They also expressed the desire of the Rocky Creek educators to help students develop empathy, cultivate social skills, and find their voice.

RJ Concerns: "I sort of feel it's being done in a half-assed way."

Educators also identified areas of concern with RJ. Those that supported RJ felt that RJ sometimes got lost amidst a slew of other priorities and felt it needed to be implemented more consistently across Rocky Creek. Others took issue with the process itself, asserting that: RJ did not work if students did not take responsibility, circles in isolation were ineffective at changing behavior, and that some students manipulated the restorative process.

Understanding what the Rocky Creek educators point to as issues helps to reveal how they viewed RJ and its purposes.

Most of the educators who participated in the learning circles felt that RJ was valuable for Rocky Creek. Some, however, named concerns about both the process and philosophy of RJ. Lisa was particularly unconvinced by the process:

> A circle isn't restoring. That's part of the restoration piece. But what is actually happening that's restorative? And part of restorative justice—I wouldn't say it needs to be public but it needs to be made...people need to know. Like, if so-and-so is cleaning the graffiti off the school because they graffiti-ed it, we all need to know that it's so-and-so doing it so we feel like it's been restored. So if I feel like somebody's gotten away with something and isn't having to make good, then I'm not—like, not me, but the person who's been wronged—is not having their faith restored. So it isn't restorative justice, right? So it's being done, but sometimes I sort of feel it's being done in a half-assed way. Like, kind of lip service. We're going to have circles. Good idea—I think we should totally have circles. And what else? Like, a circle isn't enough.

For this educator, RJ needed to include visible restitution for the process to be considered restorative. Kate was equally skeptical. Although Kate attempted to implement the processes in her classroom, she found RJ ineffective with her students. As a result, Kate questioned her own understanding of RJ:

> But when it comes to things that have happened in the classroom that need to be resolved...At the time, it gets resolved with the language, but then I don't see an effect. Because I'm missing something that makes it so that they're not going to do it again. Because the next day, it's the same thing; the next week, it's the same thing. I don't see an effect to it.

Neither of these educators saw their understanding of RJ—an approach that results in behavioral change and visible amend-making—reflected in Rocky Creek's implementation.

A final concern voiced about RJ was its susceptibility to manipulation by students. Kirsten, Brenda, Aaron, and Sonya all provided examples of occasions when they felt students "wasted time" intentionally by insisting on circles. Aaron's example was typical of the others: A certain group of students "were a little bit of manipulators and they knew, oh, if they called for a circle they could take the time out of class. And some of those circles were, what, over an hour, hour and a half with nothing accomplished." These educators spoke of how they dealt with this concern—by structuring circles, limiting circle time, or agreeing to circles until students exhausted their interest. All felt that the manipulation needed to be dealt with; and once addressed, circles could be used to greater effect.

Identified here are the concerns the educators associated with RJ as practiced in Rocky Creek. Underlying these concerns were various discourses about how educators viewed RJ. The concerns that RJ was ineffective if people did not take responsibility, did not offer visible restitution, or did not change their behavior, suggest an affirmative understanding of RJ as an approach limited to addressing individual incidents or behaviors. Although such goals are not inherently negative and the frustration is understandable, the focus here remains on seeking compliance rather than transforming structures or relationships. The educators concerned with RJ's susceptibility to manipulation raise questions of who needs to control the process; in this case, these educators were clear that adults are in control. Their concern, however, was related to ensuring a more meaningful circle process for students, speaking to the mix of affirmation and transformation present in Rocky Creek.

RJ and Other Initiatives: "It's really hard to problem solve when students don't know who you are."

Educators consistently mentioned that RJ could not work in isolation in the school. In order to create an environment conducive for RJ, staff discussed the importance of building respectful relationships. Educators were clear that RJ would not be effective if groundwork was not laid first.

Building mutually respectful relationships—between adults and students, among students, and among adults—emerged as both a necessary precursor to RJ and a product of RJ. Referring to relationships as a product of RJ, 91% of respondents to the educator questionnaire indicated that they use RJ to build relationships in their classroom. Within the learning circles, however, the majority of discussion focused on relationships as a precursor to RJ. In reference to adult relationships, Leona and Tanya pointed out that restorative processes used with staff only worked if a sufficient level of trust existed. Relationships were deemed essential to using RJ with students because, as Kirsten expressed it, "It's really hard to problem solve when [students] don't know who you are." Many educators spoke of having strong relationships with students, with some referring to them being similar to parent-child relationships. Eve described her relationship with students: "I always tell them at this school, I'm like your mother. Because if you've done wrong, you know that I'm going to come to you and we're going to deal with it. But if somebody's hurting you, know that I'm going to look into it, too." Relationships needed to be in place first, before RJ could assist in maintaining or repairing them.

When discussing relationships between teachers and students, most educators focused on the idea of respect. Interestingly, although mutual respect did emerge occasionally, most discussed teachers needing to show students respect. Mai felt that showing students respect was "the big piece" for building relationships. Although respect could be defined in a variety of ways, educators in the learning circles often described it as students feeling heard or being given a voice. Leona felt that:

> Voice is really important. But I think our kids, when I talk with kids, I feel like they're being heard....And they have that little, little power. Like, it gives them that voice, so I think it reduces a lot of anxiety for kids. And they know darn well that yes, they do have a voice in this building.

In the written portion of the educator questionnaire, the idea of respect for students also surfaced. Here respondents appreciated how RJ validated and honored student feelings, treated students with dignity and respect, and allowed students to maintain pride. Again, there appears to be a virtuous loop in that respectful relationships both are increased through RJ and ensure that RJ is implemented successfully.

In order to create an environment in which students felt respected and relationships among students were strong, educators had a variety of techniques. Some focused on building a sense of community through weekly circles or other activities. Aisha provided this example:

> We try to have a lot of positive circles where the kids have to say something nice about somebody in the circle, in the class. Something that somebody's done good for them, that's been nice for them. Whether Johnny helped him pick up the toys or something like that. And that reall...the kids really enjoy that. Because it makes everybody feel good to hear something good about them.

RRS was also mentioned as a crucial way to create a respectful ethos; restorative circles were only possible within a rights-respecting environment.

Difficult to pinpoint exactly what was considered *restorative* by the Rocky Creek educators and what was seen to be preparation, it was clear that educators did not feel that RJ was a stand-alone option. Although educators believed RJ helped maintain respectful relationships, allow students to be heard, and build a sense of community, educators did not feel that RJ could accomplish this in isolation. A chicken and egg question, the school environment needed to be conducive for RJ, and RJ needed to maintain and strengthen that environment. This holistic view of RJ, as part of the broad ethos, speaks to a transformative understanding of RJ at Rocky Creek.

RJ's Impact on Rocky Creek: "And they may have a dispute but then they'll talk about it and I don't have to intervene."

RJ was seen to be very different and more effective than previous approaches. Seventy-four percent of respondents to the educator questionnaire felt that RJ had impacted Rocky Creek significantly. In general, educators identified changes to Rocky Creek's culture as a whole, in classrooms, and on the playground. Educators found the impact easiest to see in students exposed to RJ for several years, contrasted with new students. Students were described as listening to each other, being willing to talk things out, helping with group decisions, learning skills for the future, and being empowered.

Educators who had been at Rocky Creek for more than 5 years discussed the stark contrast between the previous approach and RJ. Barbara and Mai described the previous atmosphere in which broken rules resulted in set sanctions that got progressively more severe with repeated offences. When the current principal arrived and staff embarked on a series of professional development workshops to determine a new way forward in terms of discipline approaches, Mai reported that staff looked for approaches that better fit Rocky Creek's "value system." Once RJ was decided upon as the way forward, Mai recalled a comprehensive shift: "First year, or 2 years, there was almost 100% staff trying to do the same thing and so we had all the skills being built everywhere consistently, vocabulary. And so I saw that transfer into every aspect of the school—office, playground, classrooms."

When discussing the impact of RJ, some educators focused on the overall atmosphere of Rocky Creek. Leona and Mai spoke of a sense of caring being present in the classroom and on the playground. Aaron explained the impact by contrasting playground behavior before and after RJ's implementation:

> There's less problems outside at recess than before we had circles. Because I remember when I was outside on supervision we'd be breaking up fights almost every recess before, and I'd have some big problems. Since we started the circles I think the frequency of those major eruptions is far less. I can go outside on supervision and watch kids playing together. And they may have a dispute but then they'll talk about it and I don't have to intervene. So, in the last 2 years I think I've intervened in just a handful of, you know, physical altercations, fights. Whereas before, it was pretty regular.

As is evident from these comments, the impact that RJ had on Rocky Creek—the creation of a more peaceful environment—was due to the change in student behavior and attitudes.

Educators in the learning circles reflected on how RJ's impact on students depended upon long-term contact. A few educators provided examples of how new students behaved differently than existing students, citing this difference as evidence that RJ was changing student attitudes. Sonya shared this story:

> You can tell the ones that just came in this year and have no idea. Like, [a student] came in and when she has a problem, she's just up in tears: "No, I don't want to deal with it, no, I don't want to talk to anybody!" And she's really isolated. But the other girls, when they have a problem, they'll approach one another.

Long-term exposure to RJ impacted students and such exposure was seen to affect the culture as a whole.

Beyond a sense that RJ was generally improving student behavior and attitudes, educators shared examples of specific impact. Kimi found that RJ helped students articulate their thoughts and feelings. Aisha, Beth, and Sonya all gave examples of how RJ had improved group decision-making skills. A significant impact identified by some educators was the willingness of students to talk out problems rather than resort to other methods. The willingness to talk referred not only to students talking to adults or those in authority positions, but also to one another.

Students talking directly to one another emerged as a main indicator of RJ's success, in the eyes of educators. Most educators encouraged students to talk directly rather than use the teacher as an intermediary, seeing minimal teacher involvement as a sign of success. Kimi shared this moment:

> When they come to me tattling, saying, oh, so-and-so said I wasn't going to be able to go on the field trip and that hurt my feelings. And I said, "Okay, are you done talking to that person already or did you need to discuss that more with them?" "I need to discuss it more with them." And then I hear them go over to that person and say, "That was not kind words when you said that I couldn't come on the field trip, I already got my paper signed." And explaining the details. And the other person is like, "Oh, okay, I didn't know." And so in having that conversation, they work it out themselves. And I don't have to go over there and say, "Don't do that" or "Those aren't kind words" or whatever. They know it all themselves.

Educators delighted in the stories of students either working out issues on their own or helping others to work through conflicts.

Educators believed that RJ had impacted Rocky Creek. Due, in part, to RJ, Rocky Creek was seen to be warm, caring, and supportive. Students—especially those who had attended the school for all grades—were seen to be willing to talk out problems, both with teachers and with each other; had good social and communication skills; and acted as peer mentors and peer supporters. Although the focus was primarily on the impact RJ had on student behavior and attitudes, educators were not fixated on improving student behavior for the sake of calm and order. Most educators felt RJ's most significant impact was on empowering students in their interactions with their peers—whether working out issues, or mentoring and supporting one another. The focus on empowerment was a clear indicator of transformative RJ.

RJ and Staff: "The kids do a better job of it than we do."

A main topic of conversation in the learning circles was the extent to which staff members were practicing what they were teaching. Learning circle participants continually moved the focus away from whether students were acting restoratively to whether adults were acting restoratively. Beth voiced a common sentiment: "The kids do a better job of it than we do."

As evidence of Rocky Creek staff embodying RJ principles and practices, examples were shared: There had been staff circles to deal with concerns in the past, one educator invited others to her classroom to view circles in process, and some staff members approached one another when in conflict. Corroborating these examples, 30% of questionnaire respondents said that RJ was used to address issues among adults *often* or *always*. That said, another 30% of respondents indicated that RJ was used among adults *never* or *hardly ever*. Sonya admitted her response to the survey question: "The kids do it, yeah, we do it with the kids. But when it comes to the staff? I was like, no, no. I'm being totally honest here." There were numerous examples provided in learning circles as evidence of RJ not being present in Rocky Creek staff culture: Staff members talked behind each other's backs, one educator yelled at another in front of students, disrespectful comments were made by staff about staff members and students, and the use of circles for discussion or dealing with issues among adults was rare. Hypocrisy, in terms of how RJ was taught to students and how it was enacted by and among staff members, was openly discussed in the learning circles.

Cohesion between words and actions was deemed important by staff for two reasons: for the sake of the students; and for the sake of the adults. Cohesion was seen to affect students because, as Eleanore expressed it, "if it becomes a part of us, it will become a part of the kids." There was discussion about being "role models of the school" (Beth) and that working on RJ among adults was the best way to "engage our kids and have our kids reap the most benefit out of it" (Eleanore). On the flip side, the issue was raised of what happened when students saw the opposite:

> The kids see it and they see, like, well, they do it. You know, [a teacher] is mean to [another teacher] and she's allowed to do it. And she doesn't get in trouble for it. So why do I have to be nice? And kids will say that. (Sonya)

Beyond being good for the students to see, RJ was also discussed as being an inherent good for adults. Several participants gave examples of festering conflicts that they thought would be helped by restorative processes. Tanya provided a typical example: "I hear comments in this school that are quite embarrassing—not from the kids. The kids are kids. Adults. Who have been harmed by other adults in the school. Do we need a circle? Yes." Mai, to the agreement of her fellow circle participants, felt it was "issues of trust and fear, risk" that really kept adults from fully engaging restoratively with one another at Rocky Creek. Those issues, others agreed (Eleanore, Kirsten, Beth), were both hindering the use of RJ and exacerbated by not using RJ. Mai summed it up this way: "If you've got people, there's going to be conflict. But there's, I mean, it's a big trust issue. That's where I'd like to see us grow more, as a staff."

The consensus seemed to be that adults were falling short of practicing the RJ they were teaching at Rocky Creek. Yet, the educators engaged in honest discussion about their own practices and attitudes; they did not see RJ as focused only on students. This sense of mutual involvement is again an indicator of transformative RJ.

Overall, affirmative RJ did exist in the school—in the desire of educators to change student behavior and control the way students engaged with circles, and the consequences that arose from circles. Yet, overwhelmingly, educator intentions focused not on changing student behavior but on empowering students. As educators took a comprehensive approach, transformative RJ seemed to dominate Rocky Creek. Layering the student experience into this context allows for these discourses to become more evident, to see if adult intentions were actually student perceptions.

Note

1. Names here are all pseudonyms given to the learning circle participants.

6

Rocky Creek Public School

Student Perceptions

Although staff spoke freely about RJ and its impact on Rocky Creek, students themselves were almost completely unaware of the term, RJ. This lack of awareness meant that I needed to reach beyond RJ to the students' general experience of schooling. Setting aside the idea of transformative and affirmative RJ, I listened deeply to their portrayal of their broad Rocky Creek experience, in the questionnaire, learning circles, and co-researcher interviews. The majority of student comments and observations revolved around the primacy and quality of relationships at Rocky Creek—student–student and adult–student.

Rocky Creek Context:
"Our school is a rights respecting school and other schools aren't."

For the most part, students referred to Rocky Creek in positive terms, focusing on the relationships that made the school feel like a family. Students discussed the RRS program, the BLA program, and the multicultural nature

Adult Intentions, Student Perceptions, pages 81–95
Copyright © 2019 by Information Age Publishing
All rights of reproduction in any form reserved.

of Rocky Creek. Overwhelmingly, these aspects were spoken about with pride. Connected to some of these unique features of the school, however, were also issues of racism, sexism, and aggressive behavior.

Several students mentioned how the overall school and each individual classroom felt "like a family" (Corcork). This familial feeling was evidenced for students in the ethos of welcoming new students, and in the various events and programs that Rocky Creek ran to support students and their families. Students repeatedly discussed the importance of ensuring that new students felt welcomed at Rocky Creek and held themselves responsible for this welcome. Co-researcher Kiwi explained what happened when someone new arrived: "We would just catch them. Like, we would say hi already and we would have a big conversation with the new kid. And they would feel comfortable, like, they would feel like they were part of the big family already." Although students felt responsible on an individual level to be welcoming to others, they also spoke of Rocky Creek's role in supporting students. Several mentioned appreciation for the snack program where "kids that don't get to eat breakfast at home, they can eat breakfast at school" (Code7). Students found it natural for Rocky Creek to meet a wide variety of student needs. Lily discussed her needs being met through the clubs offered by the school; Kitty Pie talked about individual staff members being supportive of her needs. In her co-researcher interview, Kitty Pie had this to say in praise of one staff member:

> He brings us together so that we can feel, so we feel we belong together, that the school is a Rights Respecting School and that we feel like we have friends and that we don't feel like trash. He brings us together, he makes us communicate, he puts us on teams, he also gets new students, and he plays with us, talks to us.

Overall students described Rocky Creek as a supportive and nurturing school.

The idea of a supportive school related, for many students, to Rocky Creek's multicultural nature. Most students talked about the variety of cultures in the school as an asset: "And it's just cool to have fun with your friends and know lots of people you don't know, have new friends from other countries and other languages, learn other stuff about other countries and stuff like that" (Soccer); "A good community has lots of different cultures in it and our school has lots of different cultures" (Kiwi). Indeed, Rocky Creek did have a whole variety of cultures and languages. My participants identified their own languages: English, Arabic, Somali, French, Spanish, Turkish, Punjabi, Hindi, Urdu, Persian, and Ukrainian. Sam, Soccer, Sunflower, Corcork, and Bob all mentioned specific multicultural events held by Rocky Creek as proof that students' cultures and languages were valued and respected.

Layered into this background of respect, was Rocky Creek's designation as a RRS. This designation was mentioned with pride by most of the students. As Bob said, "Our school is a rights respecting school and other schools aren't." Most mentions, however, were simply a mention of the term—Rights Respecting School—with little clarification or elaboration as to what that actually meant. A few, such as Soccer elaborated when I asked explicitly what being a RRS meant: "We have rules and the rules are just the rights of the child. And we respect each other. And we don't make fun of other people and their cultures, language..." One student, Justice, felt Rocky Creek did not deserve the RRS title, and shared this opinion: "I've never thought it was a rights respecting school. I just have to go along with it.... 'Cause kids never respect one another. Teachers respect each other, but kids don't." Although Justice's view was in the minority about RRS, similar concerns did emerge about Rocky Creek in general.

Students voiced concerns about racism, sexism, and the presence of harmful behavior. Many of these concerns were attributed to Rocky Creek's unique nature; others stood in contrast to what students expected from Rocky Creek. Some students thought that racism, for instance, was prevalent due to the multicultural nature of the school. Corcork talked about occasional issues arising between cultures during soccer games: "There is some discrimination, like, you're not allowed to play 'cause you're from a different country and all that. But most of the time, it's like, all good." Kitty Pie felt racism was actually more widespread, citing this scenario as a typical example in her co-researcher interview:

> Yeah, in our class, we see [racism] a lot, we see that a lot. When [the teacher] is here, we don't, like, say it aloud, we would, like, whisper it or people send notes to each other saying, like, ewww, go back to your country, ewww, I don't like your hair color, ewww, your breath smells like this, ewww, your skin color's ugly.

Kitty Pie continued, explaining that racism was never addressed by teachers due to widespread secrecy among students:

> Because if you tell what other people do, the class will, like, gang up on you and start yelling at you and saying, "Why do you have to be such a snitch? Why are you such a tattletale?" No one gets it why you would do that.

She felt that racism would remain an issue since it was so hidden.

Gender discrimination was mentioned by several students—both boys and girls—as an issue at Rocky Creek. Most examples involved the playing of soccer. Kitty Pie provided a typical example, "Soccer's a big problem, 'cause if the girls want to play soccer, the boys say, no, they're not worthy, they're not good soccer players and that they suck at passing, they suck at scoring." In contrast to the issue of racism, however, suggestions of sexism were dealt with openly by students and teachers. Several students mentioned having circle discussions about how boys could treat girls more fairly. Corcork shared the class' recent decision about soccer behavior in her co-researcher interview: "We'll at least have to pass to the girls so we're not excluding the girls in any way possible." There was optimism from both males and females that gender issues were being dealt with effectively.

The other issue that students discussed as part of Rocky Creek's context was aggressive behavior exhibited by some students, particularly members of the BLA classes. The members of those classes who acted as co-researchers provided innumerable examples of such behavior. One BLA co-researcher shared the events that took place within 5 minutes in her classroom: "Kid moaning. Kid said no. Kid said that did not like one another. Kid angry, defiant, not being kind. Kid is being disrespectful. Kid not listening to teacher. Kid saying shut up. Kid threw chair across the room and said F You. Kid talking out. Body contact."

According to the other BLA co-researcher, such behavior was "completely normal" in BLA classes. The behavior was accepted by most students as simply a necessary part of Rocky Creek; although some, as Justice observed, found Rocky Creek "kind of scary" due to the behavior of BLA students. The BLA students themselves felt uncomfortable in BLA classrooms. One BLA co-researcher shared her own plan to escape BLA classrooms: "There's a thing, it's called integration and BLA kids use it to get into a formal, a normal, class. And, well, it's kind of really hard to get into. But once you finally learn how to get into it, then you just know how to get in." Although deemed necessary, no one had much positive to say about the BLA program or its students.

Overall, the Rocky Creek context described by students was one in which they felt cared for and supported. Rocky Creek had several unique aspects—RRS, multicultural student body, BLA program—that both created an ethos of respect and provided a diverse student population that tested that ethos.

The Daily Student Experience:
"People get along pretty good when they're not fighting."

When speaking generally, students described an atmosphere in which students, for the most part, supported one another. Support was not universal, of course, and students also shared numerous instances of harmful behavior—gossiping, excluding, fighting, bullying, and more—between students.

There was no topic more discussed in learning circles and co-researcher reports than student relationships. All participants had something positive to say about student relationships, with some students speaking of them in glowing terms. Bob represented the positive views: "It's a terrific school to be in 'cause a lot of people get along." Most, such as Liby, were more measured in their responses:

> People get along pretty good when they're not fighting. It's really peaceful and you just see friends being friends, and like, being funny. And you don't really see much big fights and people beating each other up here. So, I would say, sometimes it's okay, I guess.

Liby's measured view was reflected in the student questionnaires. In response to the statement "most students in our school respect one another," 52% of students *agreed* or *strongly agreed*, 21% *disagreed* or *strongly disagreed*, and 26% neither *agreed* nor *disagreed*; when asked if students felt like they belonged, 50% *agreed* or *strongly agreed* and 47% neither *agreed* nor *disagreed*. The large portion of respondents that chose the neutral response for both questions suggests the complexity of student relationships; they encompass a gamut of both positive and negative emotions, thoughts, and behaviors.

On the positive side of student relationships, participants felt that students demonstrated support for one another in a variety of ways. Students were quick to help those who were struggling. RaRa shared this example in the co-researcher interview:

> I liked how people, if somebody was having trouble with something, maybe, like, say, if you were having trouble in math, like, if you had partners, they would come and help you even if they're not your partner. You're allowed to go around helping.

As already mentioned, befriending new students was something most participants felt responsible for. One of the co-researchers, Tay-Tay, shared the experience from a different perspective: "I think that you should be able to feel included because I was a new kid this year—me and [student]— and we felt really included at the beginning." As further evidence of this inclusive atmosphere, students shared examples of peer encouragement, standing up for others, and helping peers solve their own problems. Inclusion and support were described as being encouraged both by other students and by teachers.

Although students spoke in general of a supportive, inclusive atmosphere, they were also quick to point out negative behaviors. Joe Bob characterized the way students communicated with one another as "really mean." Sunflower revealed in her co-researcher interview that despite insistence otherwise, not all new students were welcomed like family: "Cause some kids, like, sometimes, they go and pick on new kids for some reason. And they'll say, 'Oh, you don't belong here, you're new.'" The co-researcher reports were full of examples of students being rude to one another. Most participants felt that the older students—of which they were all apart—were less respectful than the younger ones. Shadow007 was at a loss for words, saying "People who are in Grade 6, just some of the boys, they just . . . I can't even explain how bad they are."

Other students were able to provide specific references to what they believed constituted bad behavior. The main complaints revolved around gossiping, telling lies, physical fighting, and bullying. Gossiping was mostly an issue raised by the female participants. Kiwi, Tay-Tay, and Lily all shared personal examples of being victims of gossiping; most were examples that occurred during the 3-day co-researcher observation period. The telling of lies, sometimes connected to gossiping, was of interest to both genders. Students felt that others told lies to stay out of trouble and to make themselves look better: "They did communicate to the teachers when they got in trouble. But like they wouldn't tell the whole truth sometimes. It's like they didn't want to get in trouble" (Corcork). The telling of lies annoyed student participants, but they felt that the truth usually emerged, either by the lying student's own volition in circle discussions or through witnesses. Shadow007, however, during his co-researcher interview, spoke of the relationship toll taken when he had been a witness. Students he called out for lying refused to continue the friendship. Though, he claimed, "I don't really care if they're not my friends. 'Cause they're liars, anyway." Although such behavior was thought to be widespread, it was also universally denounced.

Fighting—both physical fights and "talking fights" (Sophia)—was prevalent. Most of the co-researcher reports focused on examples of students fighting. Students related the incidents with great detail and often, significant emotion, even if they themselves were not involved. Their reports frequently indicated how the incident was or was not dealt with. Co-researcher Kitty Pie shared this example which covers all of the above:

> Yeah, last week, it was a huge problem 'cause a boy in our class got punched by another boy in the other class and he had a black eye and a bloody nose. So, he wasn't here. And a girl, too, she got, she was being, she felt like she didn't belong to the school because someone was being racist to her. She

felt, she felt really, she felt bad for her own color because she told [teacher] that she didn't want to be that color anymore, she felt like being a different color. And the other boy that was, like, yelling at her and stuff started laughing and calling her names in Arabic and swearing at her, making fun of her parents, making fun of her. But then we helped her with the problem. We walked her away, we calmed her down, we made her laugh, we played with her, we gave her cookies, and some of us gave her gum. We talked to her and we talked to the boy, too.

Although fights were a common aspect of student relationships, so was the solving of them. As raw as the details and emotions surrounding fights sometimes appeared in the retelling, students felt confident that they would not be left to fester for long.

Students, however, were not as confident that bullying could be addressed effectively. Most felt that bullying was too widespread, especially for a school that was supposed to be a "no bullying school and a Rights Respecting School" (Soccer). Faith expressed this wish, "What I would change is most of the bullying, because it happens a lot. And it bothers me, seeing other kids being bullied. And they don't, the bullies don't realize how much it hurts." Although participants discussed how Rocky Creek used similar approaches to address bullying as to address fighting—teacher intervention, circles, peer intervention—bullies were often seen to be immune to most approaches. As Corcork described it, "Circles do help most of the time, but for some of the kids they don't help 'cause they'll just keep on bullying other kids and we'll just keep on having circles every day." Bullying was grudgingly accepted by most students as an unfortunate fact of the student experience.

Student relationships were complex. Students felt both supported by their peers and undermined by them. The drama of relationships surfaced daily and dominated the thoughts and reflections of student participants. Although many of their examples were of negative behavior, most students gave measured assessments of student relationships.

The Role of the Adults of Rocky Creek:
"Students can talk to teachers and teachers listen to them"

When discussing student–teacher communication, student participants often focused on the student side of the equation. Students felt that most students were respectful of teachers; the exceptions, they felt, were often disrespectful for no reason. Joe Bob explained that "most students listen but sometimes students think the teachers are just being mean to them when they're just trying to help. So they get mad at that teacher." The student participants almost always viewed the student as being in the wrong. They expressed sympathy for adults in the school.

Students felt almost unanimously supported by the Rocky Creek adults. Overall, students had more faith in the adults in the school than in each other. Only 52% of student questionnaire respondents felt that students respected each other as compared to 87% that felt respected by adults. Soccer thought that relationships with adults were as important as those with other students: "Everyone in the school has a friend and, like, there is no one in the school that doesn't have anyone to talk to. There's teachers, there's staff, there's lots of people to talk to." All student participants had something positive to say about the Rocky Creek teachers, who they described as: "caring," "nice," and "funny." Many students expressed appreciation that "students can talk to teachers and teachers listen to them" (Bobby); or, as Sam put it: "When we have a problem we can tell the teachers what's going on and we can be open with them." Seventy-four percent of student questionnaire respondents found it easy to talk to adults in the school. Notably, there were only two instances recorded by the co-researchers, over 3 days, of adult behavior that students found unsupportive—one of a teacher "by accident" (Shadow007) getting the wrong student in trouble and one of adults ignoring bullying on the playground. Overall, students had confidence in the Rocky Creek adults.

Many students also felt as though they had a say in decisions adults were making about Rocky Creek: Sixty-six percent of respondents agreed that students help make classroom decisions and half of respondents felt they could make changes in the school if something was unfair. Liby was unequivocal in her belief that student voice was considered by adults:

> And, most decisions made in our school... it's not that the teachers, or the principal, is being unfair and saying, no, I want this, or no, I want... The principal's fair because she goes around to the students to see what the students think of it. And if they don't like it, she wouldn't do it. If they did like it, she would do it.

One of the responsibilities that students attributed to adults was that of enforcing school rules. Most students equated rules with the ROCKY program (Remember to listen, Own your actions, Care for others, Keep your hands to yourself, You can be a leader) and thus felt that rules were logical and not arbitrary. RaRa believed, like most students, that "the only reason that there are rules are so we're safe in school." Students felt that adult enforcement of the rules also made sense. Bob believed that "the teachers like the rules because they want students to be safe and come to school in a safe environment." Connected to the enforcement of rules were actions adults took if students broke rules. There were a variety of measures that adults were known to take to deal with students who broke rules or in other ways made the school unsafe. Although there was some mention of exclusionary practices ["They get sent to another class or she asks them to move their desk back from around people. And, like, yeah, if they're really bad, then they get sent to the office" (Bob)], most teachers seemed to employ discussion or a circle approach. Soccer gave this example of a mixed approach: "If anyone bullies, they will get detention or something 'cause bullying isn't something from our school 'cause our school is a rights respecting school. Well, we have circles about it and then we solve it." Again, for many participants, the way that teachers handled negative behavior and rule breaking seemed to make sense.

For students, relationships with adults may have been secondary to those with other students, but they were still significant. Adults played consistent and coherent roles for students—adults were supportive, listened to students, kept Rocky Creek safe, and engaged in sensible measures when rule breaking needed to be dealt with. Students had faith that adults had their best interest at heart and would work collaboratively with students to solve issues.

How Issues Are Solved:
"It's like you don't have to leave the classroom, really, to solve a problem."

Building on the previous theme, students were entirely confident that issues would be solved, often with help from Rocky Creek staff. Discussion revealed that teachers could be counted on to help solve issues, usually through the arrangement of a circle. Students were seen as equal partners in the solutions.

Students were confident in the ability of adults to help them work through problems. Seventy-nine percent of questionnaire respondents agreed that the school would help them sort out conflicts. As Corcork said, "When we try to solve a problem all the teachers help the students solve the problem so that we can minimize it so it's not as big a problem so we can all get together again." Although in the questionnaire, students felt that they would be listened to more readily if they were the one hurt (84%) rather than the person deemed to have been misbehaving (73%), learning circle and co-researcher participants provided examples in which stories from either "side" of the conflict were heard equally. RaRa provided a typical scenario in her co-researcher report:

> Like, when [teachers] see kids fighting they come in, like, a little place and talk to them. And they talk to them about their feelings and they get one story at a time from each person. And the stories are both heard and eventually it gets resolved and they become friends again.

Beyond bringing students together to talk, adults assisted students through other measures to solve issues. At times, students looked to adults to be arbitrators of disputes ["Teacher called them back in and told him not to talk about people's weight 'cause it's rude. And they both said sorry to each other and they started working again" (Code7)]; other times students would seek help directly from teachers ["Sometimes it's just too bad, they need to talk to a teacher about it" (Sophia)]; and some students took advice from teachers to heart ["But the teacher tells us, like, if you rage or if you get angry, take 10 breaths, take 10 steps away and just, like, be calm. Try to be calm" (Monkey)]. The action most often cited as being taken by teachers, however, was arranging a circle discussion.

Most students expressed appreciation for circles, viewing them as necessary components of the classroom community. Seventy-nine percent of questionnaire respondents were confident that issues that affected the whole class would be dealt with as a collective. In practice, circles were the way in which such issues were approached. Circles were seen as a safe place to share emotions and thoughts. Sunflower stated that "in circles, I like how all the kids can be really honest and they can actually share their true feelings" because, as RaRa articulated it, "whatever goes on in the circle, stays in the circle." Circles were viewed as a place where the truth emerged, where everyone was able to share his/her side of the story and as a way to minimize problems. Co-researcher Liby believed that if some students "don't have a circle it gets bigger and bigger and bigger and they just go to the point where they want to, like, beat each other up." Circles were also practical, seen as a process in which actual solutions were decided upon. Code7 shared an example from the co-researcher period of a complicated, multi-person, multi-grade dispute that resulted in a large circle that ran for an hour and a half. Although it might take time, students trusted that, for the most part, solutions to problems could be found in circle. In circle, those solutions might be provided by adults or by other students. Sophia praised the process, stating that "it's like you don't have to leave the classroom, really, to solve a problem. Like you can discuss it with your whole class. And your classmates might have solutions for the problem." Although circles were overwhelmingly relied upon to solve problems, students did share a few examples in which circles did not work. In these cases, individual students were seen to prevent the circle from working, either refusing to listen to the other person or not being honest in circle. Kitty Pie also pondered whether the solutions suggested in circle might really only work for young students, and not for the more complex problems of Grade 5 and 6 students.

Outside of circle discussions, participants relayed stories of student intervention in conflicts. A few students referred to an official peer mediation program in which students were given training and badges and "you go around and you try to fix the problem and you try to help" (Liby). Most of the examples, however, were of students voluntarily intervening in conflicts simply because they wanted to "calm them down and, um, try to stop their fighting" (Sophia).

Participants also shared some examples of students working out their own issues. Cupcake, for instance, wrote in her co-researcher notebook about two students who argued over a toy, figuring out an acceptable solution on their own. One way for students to solve their own problems was to take time away from the person they were in conflict with. As Bob explained it, "Well, they don't always become friends but they eventually become nice to each other and just don't fight anymore." However, examples of students working out their own conflicts—even deciding to walk away—were rare. Joe Bob felt that she had "seen it once. Once or twice." The questionnaire responses back up the sense that student-solved issues were rare: compared to 79% of respondents who believed the school would help them sort out conflicts, only 34% had confidence that students could do it themselves. Co-researcher Liby felt it was difficult for students to solve their own problems "because you can't just, like, fight and be screaming at each other and then be, like, [*whispers*] 'sorry.'" Although that seemed to be a reasonable explanation of the difficulty of student-led interventions, Tay-Tay did not believe it an adequate excuse. In her co-researcher interview, she explained her reason for not approaching teachers with her problems: "We've got to learn how to solve things. We're going into Grade 7 soon."

Students had the utmost confidence that problems would be solved at Rocky Creek. Although most of their faith lay in adults to facilitate appropriate processes, some students were able and willing to intervene in conflicts themselves. Regardless of whether the process was teacher- or student-led, students were involved in the process and the outcome.

Explicit and Implicit Lessons:
"In a democracy, you put your hand up and the majority rules."

Students identified two lessons that they were taking from their time at Rocky Creek: learning how to solve problems, and how to responsibly make choices. These lessons were sometimes taught to students explicitly; most of the time, the lessons were absorbed from modeling and seeing them in practice.

As noted, students had continuous opportunities to see problem-solving in action. A few students felt that explicit teaching of problem-solving skills and approaches was necessary because some students only realized how to solve problems when shown in circle (Liby). During the co-researcher interview, Liby also shared a personal example of how she learned to be a problem solver. She was prone to conflicts when she was younger and her teacher decided to make her a peer mediator. Liby felt taking on this role impacted her life significantly "because it makes you do a good deed—you see the difference between being bad and being good—and you see how much you become a better person if you do those kinds of things." Students internalized messages about problem solving from their teachers, either from their words or actions. Sam shared something he had learned:

> If you have a problem, like, two students, then a lot of times you go to the teacher and talk it out. But sometimes, like, our teacher says it's better if you go talk to the person. 'Cause that's the person you're having the problem with so you should sort it out with them.

Interestingly, during one of the learning circle conversations, the lessons they had internalized about talking through disagreements were put into practice. Two students—Sunflower and RaRa—spoke about their frustration with a reading activity. The other students—Bob, Corcork, and Sam—disagreed with their assessment. In the middle of the learning circle the five students facilitated their own discussion about the topic, expressing their thoughts without dismissing the opinions of their peers. The spontaneous conversation was a clear indication that problem-solving and communication skills were not only discussed at Rocky Creek, they were practiced as well.

Another lesson being taught to the students at Rocky Creek was how to make choices. Students felt that adults were open to having student input in many choices. Kiwi gave this example: "If we have something to do, like a subject or something. Or if there's, let's say, math or gym and she asks us, oh, what do you want to do, math or gym? In a democracy, you put your hand up and the majority rules." One practical venue for having student voice heard, students thought, was through the student council. Students had learned that their voice made a difference. Although students felt they had a say in many school choices, they were still eager for more opportunities to be heard. Some students, such as Faith, also acknowledged that although students wanted more choice, "sometimes they don't make good decisions." A lesson articulated by some students was that with choice comes responsibility. Soccer related an instance where this lesson was clear:

> We made a decision that we can play on the far field 'cause there's lots of soccer fields. So they said, would you guys like to play there and open the field? But you have to respect each other, play with each other. And we made a decision that we will.

For these students, making choices was something desirable, but also laden with responsibility.

Students seemed to have adopted many lessons from Rocky Creek— how to solve problems, make choices, and be responsible. The lessons were mostly implicit, though backed up by explicit teachings. Students discussed these lessons as works in progress. As Corcork said, in reference to some students still feeling excluded: "We've been working on it a lot and we've come very far with it." Students felt comfortable with the lessons they were learning and saw them as ongoing.

Overall Assessment:
"People actually get along sometimes. And if anyone fights they would actually be solving it."

Consistent with the examples provided of a school ethos in which problems were unfailingly dealt with, students reported that, overall, their Rocky Creek experience was positive. And, consistent with the mixed assessment of relationships, the areas of improvement identified by students all focused on student–student relationships and student–adult relationships.

Most students appreciated Rocky Creek and compared it favorably to other schools. Bobby exclaimed, "I love this school because it has nice teachers and it's cooler than all other schools." In the individual co-researcher interviews, students were asked to offer an analysis of Rocky Creek. They were asked to consider their observations and answer the question, "Of what you observed, what would you like less of?" Without exception, every response centered on relationship issues. Students responded that they would like less fighting, rude behavior, and gossiping. Shadow007 voiced his desires this way: "I would want, um, none of them to be nasty and stuff like that. Like, you know how normal people, they don't keep secrets and stuff like that." In a similar vein, when asked the question—"Of what you observed, what would you like more of?"—students also focused mainly on relationships. Within student–teacher relationships, students wished for better listening and more respect toward teachers. Within peer relationships, students wanted to see more students getting along, helping one another, and solving problems together. It is notable that students identified all of these aspects as being present in Rocky Creek; they simply wished they were more widespread. One different response came from a BLA co-researcher who wanted the BLA's early dismissal changed so that BLA students went "home when the normal kids do." This response also expresses a relational desire, to fit in with peers.

Throughout the learning circles and co-researcher reports, students occasionally offered suggestions for how to move the classroom environment closer to their ideal. A few students suggested there be more rules or more discipline. Shadow007 liked the idea of electing a student president who "checks if there are any fights and he tries to think of a rule that stops that." Others like co-researcher Sophia felt teachers "could, like, encourage them a lot. And reward them for everything they accomplish." In line with Sophia's suggestion, a few participants felt that control for a better classroom environment rested in the teacher's hands: One student suggested teachers give more timeouts to calm the classroom environment; another thought teachers should entrust students with more choices so as to encourage better behavior. Most students, however, felt that responsibility for the ideal classroom environment lies within the power of students. Faith recommended that students talk about what they want their classroom to be like and "set it as our goal before the end of the year." Liby agreed, stating:

> We have to learn how to do the things that you're supposed to do more. Like, we have to learn how to respect each other more and more and we have to learn how to talk things out more and more. And we have to learn how to do—basically, the rules of the school, like, kind words, show pride,...we have to learn that.

Since the breakdown in the classroom environment was seen to be the responsibility of students, participants felt students needed to be the ones to improve it.

As a final question in the individual co-researcher interviews, students were asked to imagine a new student arriving the following day and to explain Rocky Creek to that student. In answering this question, students considered what they had been observing over the three specific observation days combined with their general Rocky Creek experience. Although students took into consideration some of the negative aspects about student relationships, their final analysis painted a positive, realistic picture of Rocky Creek. Cupcake succinctly summed it up: "It's fun and we learn lots and sometimes there's fighting." Code7 was more verbose:

I'd say it's actually a pretty nice school. People actually get along sometimes. And if anyone fights they would actually be solving it. So you wouldn't have to worry about after school, what would happen to you if you got in a fight. And we eat lots of good stuff. And we get lots of community-like stuff so parents can come in for, like, events. Lots of amazing events.

Although students recognized the reality that human relationships are complex [or, as Faith put it: "Every day is a different day...you'll either get along really nicely with people or you won't get along with anyone"], the confidence they had in their own, their peers', and Rocky Creek's ability to deal with issues as they arose, made for a positive overall assessment.

Conclusion

Viewed together, the educator and student themes reveal how RJ in Rocky Creek was understood by educators and experienced by students. Relationships played central roles in both educator and student comments.

Educators, for the most part, understood RJ as a relational approach in which students—and, potentially, adults—are provided with skills and processes that improve both their current and future ways of relating with one another. Students described a complex reality in which relationships—with adults and with peers—are continually navigated. In relating their general Rocky Creek experience, students pointed to RJ as an approach that transforms those relationships into associations of trust, in which people work together to deal with issues and learn from one another. Although there were instances in which that trust was broken, those instances were the exception. Transformation and social engagement was how RJ was understood by educators; transformation and social engagement was how RJ was experienced by students.

7

Royal Mills High School

The Scottish School Story

This chapter and the next now turn to focus on the Scottish school, Royal Mills High School. I begin, as with Rocky Creek, by looking at the national, regional, and school discourses—the landscape—within which the students experienced RJ.

National

Broad Discourses

Scotland is a semi-autonomous country; part of the United Kingdom but with its own parliament and government. Scotland covers nearly one third of the total land area of the United Kingdom, but contains just 12% of its population (5.3 million; Scottish Government, 2013a; United Kingdom Office for National Statistics, 2013). Based on Scotland's 2011 Census, 4% of Scotland's population identified as part of a minority ethnic group with most (2.7%) identifying as Asian, Asian Scottish, or Asian British (National Records of Scotland, 2013). Despite historically being Western Europe's

Adult Intentions, Student Perceptions, pages 97–124
Copyright © 2019 by Information Age Publishing
All rights of reproduction in any form reserved.

poorest nation (Herman, 2001), Scotland is no longer regarded as such, mostly due to the North Sea oil and gas reserves. Some estimates even place an independent Scotland as the sixth richest country in the world, 10 places above the United Kingdom as a whole (BBC News Scotland, 2011). Still, in 2012/2013, 16% of individuals in Scotland were living in relative poverty (Communities Analytical Services, 2014b).

In 1999, an act of the United Kingdom Parliament created the first Scottish Parliament since 1707, bestowing responsibility on Scotland for a range of issues known as devolved matters: education, civil and criminal justice, agriculture, environment, health, housing, local government, planning, police and fire services, social work, sports and the arts, and transportation (Scottish Parliament, 2012a). The U.K. Parliament remains responsible for the United Kingdom and international issues such as foreign affairs, defence, immigration, and social security. The Scottish government was also formed in 1999 and, since 2007, has been led by the Scottish National Party (SNP). The 2011 elections handed the SNP the first majority government in modern Scotland, with the SNP holding almost double the seats of the next largest party, the Scottish Labour Party. The SNP is "a social democratic political party committed to Scottish independence" (SNP, n.d.a., "About Us" section, para. 1). Following the 2011 win, then First Minister Alex Salmond, announced that a national referendum on independence would be held within 5 years. For the SNP the devolution of power enacted in 1999 was only the first step to make Scotland into a "more ambitious and dynamic" independent country (SNP, n.d.b., "The New Scotland," para. 2). The independence referendum was scheduled for September 2014 and dominated most conversations—political and otherwise—while I was in Scotland. Symbolic of its prominent presence in the minds of many Scots, the SNP website featured a countdown to the referendum in days, hours, minutes, and seconds.

It was not only the Scots who were interested in the referendum; the world watched with rapt attention as the day of the vote approached (BBC News Scotland, 2014a). Although Scottish citizens eventually decided to remain part of the United Kingdom with 55% of the vote (BBC News Scotland, 2014b), the referendum had a huge impact in Scotland. In Scotland, the mere existence of the referendum spurred discussions and thought on what made Scotland unique and what the future of Scotland could entail. I witnessed these conversations taking place in Holyrood (the Scottish Parliament), in the media, on the street, in schools, and around the dinner table. It was an exceptional time to be present in Scotland, as its citizens debated the particulars of independence and imagined the ideal version of their country. Much was made of the growing chasm between the political direction being taken by the Conservative Party in Westminster (United Kingdom) and the more social democratic agenda being heralded by the SNP. As Richards (2013) wrote in the *Guardian,* prior to the vote, even if the independence vote were to fail, the political and cultural separation between the two countries had already been solidified. Many Scots saw their vision of Scotland as a "better and fairer nation" (Yes Scotland, n.d., "What Independent Scotland Can Mean") running antithetical to the stated political priorities in England. Indeed, in recognition of this divide, Westminster granted additional devolved powers to Holyrood once Scotland voted "no" (Black, 2014). Talk of separation, however, has not disappeared. After Brexit, when the United Kingdom as a whole voted to leave the European Union but the majority of Scots did not, Scottish independence was once again on the table (Bourgon, 2017).

As a way to differentiate themselves from England, conversations and public documents often referred to what were seen as Scottish values. As an example, the mace, originally a practical weapon intended to protect the king but now used in parliament to symbolize the authority of the sovereign, repeatedly arose in conversation. Engraved on the head of the Scottish mace in 1999 were the words: Wisdom, Justice, Compassion, and Integrity. These values seemed to represent Scotland to many of the people with whom I spoke. In one interview, the senior education manager in the local authority where I conducted my research described the mace values as "a set of aspirations in the context of a Scottish culture which is in transition." I attended a lecture by Sir Harry Burns, then the chief medical officer for Scotland, who, at the end of a complex presentation on national health and wellbeing, suggested that the most important catalyst for societal change was one of the mace values: compassion. He concluded, "Scotland has a tradition of this. We need to reignite that" (2013).

My visit to the parliament to attend *question time* confirmed the central place of these values, at least as aspirations. The chamber itself was designed to "reflect the Parliament's commitment to openness" (Scottish Parliament, 2012b). Members of the Scottish Parliament (MSPs) sit in a semi-circle, clustered according to their respective party affiliation. Although I cannot claim my experience to be representative, discussion was, for the most part, civil. The Minister for the Environment and Climate Change discussed a report revealing that Scotland had missed their first emissions reduction target and was on the road to miss the second. As the minister was asked questions by opposition members, he frequently agreed with the person and often asked to meet later to collaborate on any suggestions. Everyone was in agreement that climate change was an important issue; the disagreement centered on how to go about addressing it. A later debate on the civil justice system was more combative, but only marginally. MSPs continually juggled Scottish needs with English demands/interests, in some ways portrayed as the common foe around which to unite disparate ideologies.

Modern Scotland today is built firmly upon and around its history, both recent and distant. Scotland of the 17th century was a nation shaped by an unforgiving Calvinist religious faith with frequent trials for witchcraft and blasphemy (Herman, 2001). Although there are traces of this history in modern Scotland, much more evident is the Scotland that came into being by the end of the 18th century, that of the Scottish enlightenment. The Scottish Enlightenment seems to still strongly influence society today. Ironically, Herman (2001) asserts that this Scotland of innovation and change was made possible by the Act of the Union in 1707, joining Scotland and England into Great Britain. The very union that is today hotly debated provided Scots, Herman suggests, with peace and order within a strong administrative state that also largely ignored them. This union, he argues, allowed for rapid social and economic change. Considered by many to be the first modern nation and culture, Scotland has made crucial contributions to science, philosophy, literature, education, medicine, economics, and politics (Herman, 2001). One of the great insights of the Scottish enlightenment was intellectual liberation that encouraged people to "free themselves from myths and to see the world as it really is" (Herman, 2001, p. 428). This ability to see the world as it really is, what we might today term *critical thinking*, was evident in many of my interactions with Scottish individuals and within organizations.

Scotland in the 20th century was marred by poverty, unemployment, poor health, class conflict, political tribalism, and religious sectarianism (BBC History, 2014). The Scottish economy was built mostly on heavy industry, bringing periods of great prosperity as well as scarcity. When Margaret Thatcher came to power, these traditional industries—with coal mines being hit the hardest—no longer received government support and the power of the unions began to be eroded. In the first 2 years of the Thatcher administration, one fifth of Scotland's workforce became unemployed (BBC History, 2014). Scottish society was turned upside down. I happened to be visiting London the weekend Margaret Thatcher passed away in April 2013. The English press carried accolades and tributes; in Glasgow, 300 people gathered to celebrate her death (Daily Record, 2013).

Although obviously still a sore spot for some Scots, Scotland has, in large part though not entirely, moved beyond these ills. "Confidence in both the economy and Scottish society at large increased through the 1990s and culminated in the re-opening of the Scottish Parliament" (BBC History, 2014, "20th Century Scotland—An Introduction," para. 6). This confidence and guarded hope is represented beautifully in the poem written by the Scots Makar, Edwin Morgan, for the opening of the Scottish Parliament Building in Holyrood in 2004. "Open the Doors" reads, in part:

> What do the people want of the place? They want it to be filled with thinking persons as open and adventurous as its architecture. A nest of fearies is what they do not want. A symposium of procrastinators is what they do not want. A phalanx of forelock-tuggers is what they do not want. And perhaps above all the droopy mantra of "it wizny me" is what they do not want. Dear friends, dear lawgivers, dear parliamentarians, you are picking up a thread of pride and self-esteem that has been almost but not quite, oh no not quite, not ever broken or forgotten. (Morgan, 2004)

The past—both positive and negative—shapes Scotland of today.

Educational Discourses

Education has long been seen as integral to forming the Scottish character and culture; a national education system was set up in 1696, well before that of other countries. The Scottish Parliament of the day passed an act establishing a school in every parish in Scotland, the intention being to equip all children of both genders with the skill to read the Bible (Herman, 2001). Scotland became Europe's first modern literate society; some estimate that male literacy stood at 75% in 1750, compared with 53% in England (Herman, 2001). In the 18th century, this high literacy rate meant that most people were exposed to books on a variety of subjects and ideas. The appreciation for literature continues: One of the main institutions of Scottish life is Burns Night, the annual celebration of the national bard, Robert Burns.

Education in Scotland today remains within a national system, distinct from the systems of England and Wales, delivered through 32 regional councils, called local authorities. The delivery of curriculum is the responsibility of these local authorities and local schools, under the guidance of the Scottish government and a public body called Education Scotland, established in 2011 by the Scottish government. This national system is often contrasted to that of England and Wales where there are a number of means of providing education, including a strong tradition of independent schools not funded by the state (D. Morrice, personal communication, March 26, 2013). In 2013, there were about 2600 state-funded schools in Scotland, including 370 state-funded faith schools—366 Catholic, one Jewish and three Episcopalian (Scottish Government, 2013c). Statistics from 2012 show that the teaching profession is not fully representative of the demographics of the Scottish population: There is an overall gender imbalance among teachers (77% women to 23% men) which is reversed with secondary school headteachers (33% are female); ethnic minorities are also underrepresented (2% of teachers compared to 5.5% of pupils) (Scottish National Statistics, 2012).

My research period in Scotland coincided with renewed discussion about the direction of education. In an interview, Anthony Finn, the then chief executive officer for the General Teaching Council for Scotland (GTCS), the independent professional body that promotes and regulates the teaching profession in Scotland, characterized 2013 as a moment of "systemic coherence" in which both policies and people—teachers, unions, government—had aligned. The main symbol of this alignment was the national curriculum framework, Curriculum for Excellence (CfE), which began to be implemented in 2010.

CfE aimed to achieve a "transformation in education" (Scottish Government, n.d., "Curriculum for Excellence," para. 1). The reform emerged out of a 2002 national debate on education which highlighted a variety of needs including: more active, challenging, and enjoyable learning; less crowding in the curriculum; and more choices to meet the individual needs of young people (Kidner, 2010). CfE was a broad curriculum framework for pupils between the ages of three and 18. It aimed to develop *four capacities*: successful learners, confident individuals, effective contributors, and responsible citizens. CfE was referred to as a lifelong learning strategy or a broad framework since the government stated it did not seek to "micromanage what goes on in individual schools" but wanted schools to take responsibility for how CfE was interpreted and implemented (Scottish Government, n.d., "Curriculum").

The management board, the body responsible for overseeing how CfE was implemented, consisted of seventeen different organizations, including: the Scottish Government, various unions, GTCS, and associations such as School Leaders Scotland and the National Parent Forum Scotland. The inclusion of this vast array of organizations resulted in widespread official support for CfE.

The systemic coherence as articulated by Finn and embodied in CfE had two main threads: the professional autonomy of teachers and pupil-centered education. On the first point, significantly different from the approach used previously in Scotland, CfE explicitly moved away from prescriptive implementation and allowed teachers more professional autonomy. As Donaldson (2010), in a frequently referenced review of teacher education in Scotland, wrote, CfE "sees schools and teachers as co-creators of the curriculum" (p. 4). This same point, however, received the most criticism from teachers who sometimes critiqued CfE as overly vague. One study found that although teachers welcomed the principles of CfE and voiced appreciation for more autonomy, they had difficulty implementing it; teachers also identified tensions between the big ideas articulated in CfE and the continued emphasis on accountability, attainment, and inspections (Priestley & Minty, 2013). Informal conversations with teachers confirmed some of this critical sentiment. One secondary teacher told me that CfE effectively dumbed down the curriculum, providing breadth but not depth, and did little but put new packaging on old ideas. Teachers, he said, have always worked to assist pupils in becoming successful learners, confident individuals, effective contributors, and responsible citizens; they simply did not refer to them as the four capacities.

Complementing CfE's focus on professional autonomy were a number of other policies and documents. The 2010 Donaldson Report on teacher education recognized teaching as complex and challenging and called for the strengthening of both the quality of teaching and the quality of leadership. In addition, new professional standards from GTCS were announced while I was in Scotland, and came into effect in August 2013, highlighting teachers' professionalism and the need for them to take ownership of their own learning (GTCS, 2013).

The other thread comprising systemic coherence had to do with making education more pupil-centered. Again, in the interview with Anthony Finn, he suggested that a cultural shift was occurring: The school system no longer pivoted around teacher needs but around pupil needs. Central to this shift was Getting It Right for Every Child (GIRFEC), an approach that focused on the well-being of children and young people and was threaded into all policy, practice, strategy, and legislation affecting youth and their families. GIRFEC encouraged individuals and agencies to work together to meet the needs of children and took a whole child approach, putting the child at the center of all decisions that affected them (Scottish Government, n.d., "What is GIRFEC?"). Aligning with GIRFEC, the Additional Support for Learning Act, introduced in 2004 and amended in 2009, provided "additional support where needed to enable any child or young person to benefit from education" (Education Scotland, n.d.b, About Additional Support Needs section, para. 1). In 2012, 17.6% of all pupils were identified as requiring additional support (Scottish Government, 2013b). Thus, the two concepts combining to create Anthony Finn's "systemic coherence" are greater professional autonomy for teachers and pupil-centered education. It is within this context that RJ should be understood.

Restorative Discourses

Scotland introduced a national RJ pilot project in schools in 2004 (Hendry, 2009; McCluskey et al., 2008b). Scottish practitioners drew on the experience of other countries to glean information, apply previously developed ideas, and build their own model specific to Scotland (Hendry, 2009). Although formally introduced in 2004, some principles and practices of RJ had been previously evident in Scottish schools. A tradition of involving pupils and families in decision-making through inter-professional meetings provided a context where the principles were in place to embrace RJ (McCluskey et al., 2008b).

Finn, who worked as a head teacher before moving into his role at GTCS, recalled RJ being discussed and used 20 years prior, albeit without the restorative title. One impetus for RJ, according to Finn, was a high rate of exclusions.[1] The goal was not simply to bring the rate down, but for schools to substantially address the needs of pupils that were leading to exclusions and to help them feel included in the school community.

Not every inclination in Scottish schools, however, was a natural fit with RJ. In their interviews, both the senior education manager for the local authority in which Royal Mills was located and one of the region's education officers recalled the challenging educational environment into which RJ was introduced. Corporal punishment had only been banned in the late 1990s and most teachers, according to my interviewees, were filling the vacuum with what are termed *punishment exercises*, the writing of lines. It was into this environment that the newly devolved government stepped. The education minister at the time, Peter Peacock, campaigned to bring RJ into the education sector. In the words of the senior education manager, Peacock was "opening up the idea that there might be more in the toolbox than simply punishment exercises, which were being deployed pretty heavily" (Senior Education Manager, personal communication, April 15, 2013).

The connection between RJ, discipline, and exclusion rates was clearly evident in the initial presentation and framing of the concept. In 2003, the Scottish Executive (called the Scottish government after 2007) formally introduced the idea of RJ in a document on school exclusion (Kane et al., 2007). In this document RJ was suggested as a way to re-integrate pupils after exclusions and encourage positive school atmospheres (Scottish Executive, 2003). There was a sense in the late 1990s—confirmed by the Discipline Task Group convened in 2000—that discipline was seen as a growing issue in schools (Scottish Executive, 2001). In 2004, as part of their *Better Behaviour, Better Learning* initiative, funding was provided by the Scottish Executive for a 2-year pilot project on RJ in 18 schools (including 10 secondary schools) in three local authorities. This funding was later extended by a further 2 years (Kane et al., 2007). The aim of the pilot project was to learn more about the impact of RJ on school culture, to improve schools, and to identify a distinctively Scottish approach that both complemented existing practice and offered more (Kane et al., 2007; McCluskey et al., 2013). At the launch of the pilot project, an evaluation team consisting of researchers from the University of Edinburgh and the University of Glasgow was created. The 2-year evaluation (Kane et al., 2007) and its follow up (Lloyd & McCluskey, 2009) comprise the largest evaluation of RJ undertaken in the United Kingdom to date (McCluskey et al., 2013). Active involvement of the schools and local authorities in the evaluation allowed "different definitions and criteria for success to be developed, acknowledged, and applied" (McCluskey et al., 2013, p. 145) so that schools were judged according to their own aims.

Although there were diverse approaches across these schools, initial development in secondary schools was strongly linked to dealing with discipline, which is consistent with the impetus of using RJ to lower exclusion rates (Kane et al., 2007). This initial focus, however, morphed throughout the pilot project. At the start, many school managers envisioned RJ mainly taking the form of isolated formal conferences to deal with serious issues; in reality, this use was limited and RJ became seen as "a broad framework of values, strategies, practices, and skills" (Kane et al., 2007, p. 97). For all schools, the development of a comprehensive restorative ethos was the touchstone of success. A restorative ethos was defined in the report as including: an understanding of the importance of preventing harm to others and of resolving harm and conflict in helpful, supportive ways; respect between staff and pupils and among pupils; a feeling among pupils and staff that they are included and treated equitably; a sense that school processes are carried out with fairness and justice; and that staff and pupils report feeling safe and happy.

The follow-up report in 2009 found schools continued to develop RJ successfully in a way that suited their own local needs and circumstances and RJ was identified as becoming *embedded* in school culture (Lloyd & McCluskey, 2009). Acknowledging the difficulty in studying such factors, the report points out that among schools that felt they had been most successful at embedding RJ, it was also more difficult to "isolate it as a distinctive practice and as the identifying characteristic of success in developing a positive ethos" (Lloyd & McCluskey, 2009, p. 4). Despite the move to a broad restorative ethos, the report also found that schools were divided as to whether RJ was the main response to disciplinary issues or worked alongside other more punitive responses. This outcome highlights some of the inherent tensions between values that underpin RJ and those that underpin more common approaches based on behavioral theories (Hendry, 2009; McCluskey et al., 2008a; Morrison, 2007a; Reimer, 2009).

In terms of what constitutes a distinctively Scottish approach to RJ, Kane et al. (2007) stress several aspects. They found that RJ in these Scottish schools derived more from humanistic/person-centered psychology, social models, and sociological perspectives on education—all which underpin other social and educational interventions with children in Scotland—than from the theoretical underpinnings of RJ in the criminal justice field. As opposed to the approach taken in many countries, Scotland utilized few external facilitators and instead focused on developing school staff and pupils in line with individual contexts and complexities. The Scottish model attends to these complexities by being "broadly focused, encompassing prevention, response and intervention, and sometimes, reparation" (Kane et al., 2007, p. 98).

While being broadly focused in practice, there continued, at least officially, to be a tendency to link RJ with behavior and disciplinary matters, rather than ethos. Toward the end of the first evaluation, in response to a 2006 national discipline survey, the Scottish Executive, teaching unions, GTCS, and others put forward a joint plan on how to respond to discipline issues, or indiscipline as it is termed in Scotland. In the plan, there was an expectation that every local authority and headteacher use a mix of approaches, including RJ (Kane et al., 2007). At the same time, the Scottish Executive established a Positive Behaviour Team to support local authorities in embedding such approaches in schools.

Linking RJ to behavior and exclusion was confirmed in my interview with Drew Morrice, then assistant secretary for Employment Relations for the Educational Institute of Scotland (EIS), the largest teaching union in Scotland and the oldest teaching union in the world. EIS was supportive of initiatives such as RJ, provided that teachers maintained the freedom to use their professional judgment in dealing with behavior issues. Morrice's one caution was when RJ was "used almost politically" to reduce exclusion rates. As he put it: "If you reduce the exclusion rates, does that mean you're finding more effective solutions? Or are you just internalizing difficulties? And are schools becoming more difficult to work in? A lot of our evidence is that teachers are being expected to put up with more indiscipline" (Morrice, D., personal communication, March 26, 2013).

In this instance, Morrice was suggesting that RJ might lead to more discipline issues, by keeping disruptive children in school. Morrice shared an internal report that showed that the exclusion rate had indeed gone down in recent years, from 60.4 pupils per 1,000 in 2005/2006 to 40.0 in

2010/2011 with RJ—along with a list of other strategies and changes such as CfE—deemed responsible for the reduction. Over half of the local authorities that responded to a call from EIS listed RJ as one of the approaches they have used to reduce exclusion rates.

In other instances, the link between RJ and discipline is framed as a response, one undertaken to reduce the need for exclusion. A 2012 national survey on behavior suggested positive overall changes to discipline issues. Within secondary schools, the survey showed that 99% of headteachers, 88% of teachers, and 61% of support staff felt that all or most pupils were generally well behaved (Black, Chamberlain, Murray, Sewel, & Skelton, 2012). In the report, 88% of secondary schools listed using RJ to encourage positive behavior, up from 75% in 2009. Among the large number of other approaches used, the most commonly listed was the promotion of positive behavior through whole school ethos and values. Although situated around behavior and discipline issues, this framing paints too simple a picture of how RJ is intended. The narrow emphasis on RJ as a way to improve behavior seemed to expand each year. The 2012 report concluded that "staff were far more inclined to refer to 'relationships,' rather than 'behaviour management' or 'indiscipline' when talking about the ways in which they deal with negative behaviour" (Black et al., 2012, p. iv). Even the mandate of the Positive Behaviour Team, despite its rather narrow title, supported local authorities to "promote positive relationships, social and emotional wellbeing, and positive behaviour" (Education Scotland, n.d.a, "About Positive Relationships and Behaviour"). In recognition of this mandate, in 2013, after I left Scotland, the team underwent a dramatic name change to the Rights, Support, and Wellbeing Team.

The messages surrounding RJ in a national context appear mixed, focusing either on positive behavior or on developing good relationships and a positive ethos.

Regional

Broad Discourses

The region where my study was conducted had a population of over 300,000 and was a blend of urban, suburban, fishing, and rural communities (Kane et al., 2007). The area had a long industrial and agricultural history. The motto of one of the burghs within the region refers to coal mining and sailing, an indication of the two interdependent industries which, at the time, brought with them development and prosperity. For centuries, the sea provided a living for many people in the towns and the area could boast of one of the largest fishing fleets in Scotland. Coal mining replaced fishing as the key socioeconomic activity in the area from at least the 17th century up until the 1980s. Beyond the production in the mines, coal also drove many other industries, particularly shipping. By the early 1900s more coal was being shipped through the region's ports than in any other port in Scotland. Housing was often provided by coal and railway companies, making the region an attractive place for prospective workers. Through most of the 19th and early 20th centuries, unemployment was not an issue. Images and personal recollections displayed at the local history museum reveal bustling, prosperous towns full of optimism, modern conveniences, and even the latest international styles thanks to the many foreign ships in the ports.

A series of historical events resulted in a gradual downturn in the region's economy. A general strike by miners in the 1920s to address poor working conditions and low pay rallied the community around the workers; it did not, however, improve relations with the mine owners. After World War II, the use of the docks declined, with their final dismantling and demolition in the 1970s. This overlapped with a fatal coal mine fire and the closing of it and several other coal mines. In the words of another visitor to the local history museum, the town had once been prosperous: "But, the strike, then the fire, then Thatcher, killed it all."

Today the region's economy and socioeconomic indicators are mixed, with some areas of significant economic deprivation and other areas organized around new ventures. Between 2002 and 2008, in the region overall, poverty rates were slightly higher than the Scottish average (Scottish Government, 2010). However, in the town in which Royal Mills High School was located, the situation was substantially worse. School staff often referred to children in the area as being *third-generation unemployed*, meaning their parents had never known sustainable employment and their grandparents had likely been the ones to lose their jobs in the mines and docks. In fact, a school document from the 1990s indicated that well over three quarters of the pupils in the catchment area fit this category. Most of the housing in the area were either owned by the council, a form of subsidized housing, or were council flats bought by private citizens, a controversial plan implemented during Thatcher's rule. Driving back to the school from the local history museum, I was struck by the stark contrast between the booming company town displayed in the museum and the impoverished town of the present.

Educational Discourses

The local authority is well aware of how the region's history and current situation impact pupils and their educational experience. In an interview with the senior education manager in the local authority, I was told that there was a "strong political commitment in [the region] to trying to break the cycle of disadvantage" that was seen to affect the 20% of pupils who were the least successful in school. Although this manager associated the cycle of disadvantage with families that had been involved with mining and heavy industry, he was quick to point out that contrary to the usual framing of the issue as an economic one, it was in fact a cultural, psychological, and social phenomenon. Thus, the local authority saw the greatest hope for breaking the cycle of disadvantage within the context of education, rather than primarily in economic solutions. Specifically, the senior education manager mentioned quality engagement and school relationships as key to breaking the cycle.

As in the rest of Scotland, the history of education in the region is multifaceted, revealing values and principles that both align with and contradict the discourses of engagement and relationships. On the one hand, a long religious tradition of seeing punishment as the route to redemption led to the leather strap being designed in the late 1800s by a saddler in a nearby region and manufactured for over 100 years. Teachers apparently liked the design of this particular strap because it was easier to wield and had no sharp edges to cause serious damage. After a booming market in the 70s, corporal punishment was banned in state schools in 1987 and in fee-paying schools in 1998. The straps are still being made today, though as commemorative items. On the other hand, the region was an early adapter in prioritizing the needs of pupils; it was one of the first to set up pupil support centers in schools, where learning and behavioural support were undertaken as an integrated endeavor. Thus, there is a history of innovation and attention to pupils that is tempered by a culture that sought order and obedience in schools through the use of force.

That tension between pupil needs and school order was present in other less extreme ways, as well. The local education officer told me that much of the 1980s and '90s were characterized by behavioral psychological approaches to managing discipline and behavior issues within schools. Educational psychologists, of which the educational officer was one for 20 years, have played a key role in Scottish schools since the '70s, influencing the various approaches implemented by schools. The reliance on behavioral approaches is not surprising as it mirrors the general popularity at the time of behaviorism (Graham, 2010). Although feedback from teachers to these approaches was positive, the education officer eventually realized that behavioral approaches were "making teachers very, very good at controlling and managing children, but weren't making children very good at controlling and managing themselves."

The local senior education manager suggested to me that there had been a recent move from the concept of behavior management to discussions about relationships and how to nurture students. This shift is reflected most visibly in a name change for the region's school improvement strategy. Previously entitled the Behaviour and Discipline Strategy, it was renamed the Strategy for Relationships and Behaviour in 2012. The name change, according to a preamble in a report on the strategy, reflected an evolving understanding of how relationships shape behavior within organizations, and a shift to helping youth develop the capacity to manage their own behavior.

From most accounts, this approach appears to be working. The Strategy for Relationships and Behaviour reported that recent surveys and inspections all indicated that both the quality of relationships in local schools and the overall behavior of pupils are good and improving. In a regional pupil survey conducted in 2012, 81% of pupils felt that their school helped them feel safe and cared for; 81% felt their school helped everyone to feel included; and 77% agreed that their school helped them understand how to make friends and build relationships (Pupil Survey, 2012). Interestingly, 68% (and, broken down further, only 42% of secondary students) felt their school helped pupils behave well. The staff survey on relationships and behavior in regional schools showed an increase in staff who identified having access to effective strategies for dealing with challenging behavior, from 68% in 2005 to 88% in 2012. Despite these strategies, however, 79% of teachers felt that managing challenging behavior seriously detracted from their teaching time and duties. An analysis in the report suggested that the response to this statement was an indicator of the importance of "good order" to effective learning and teaching (Education and Learning Directorate, 2012). This stress on *good order*, as well as the fact that most staff survey questions focused on behavior and not relationships, suggest that the practice and even priorities lag behind name changes and aspirations. Even when relationships were emphasized, they were sometimes framed as a vehicle for good behavior.

In the survey, teachers were asked about the extent to which various initiatives were helpful in addressing relationship and behavioral issues. Both primary teachers (89%) and secondary teachers (69%) rated RJ as the most effective. Within this context, with a historical focus on order and a more intentional move toward relationships, we can begin to understand the various purposes behind the introduction of RJ in the region.

Restorative Discourses

This region was amongst those chosen to be part of the national restorative pilot project in 2004. A handful of schools within the region—both primary and secondary—were selected to participate. According to the local education officer, there was a confluence of interests as the local authority was questioning its approach to behavior at the same time that the government launched the initiative into restorative practices, as it was called then. The conversations taking place within the region at that time, around relationships and engagement, shaped the restorative pilot project in a number of ways unique to this local authority.

For one, rather than utilizing the national government's preferred term, *restorative practices*, the local authority made an intentional choice, after the first year of the project, to use the term, *restorative approaches* (RA). As the local education officer explained, "What we came to realize, collectively, as an education community... was that, actually, the practice bit of it was quite secondary to the values bit of it. It was actually what you thought and what you believed that made the difference." Using the term RA signaled recognition by the local authority that the concept was broader than simply learning steps and technique. In acknowledgement of this intentional choice of words, I use the term RA when referring to the approach in the region.

This particular local authority was, in its implementation of RA, unique amongst regions in other ways: Schools were encouraged to develop their own approaches and to visit, share, and learn from each other; schools were supported in the development of individual action plans; many schools focused on low-level interventions (informal restorative conversations in the classroom and corridor) to create positive change as opposed to more formal processes; and, schools built on existing educational initiatives that were seen as supportive of RA (Kane et al., 2007). Prior to introducing RA into a school, the local authority attempted to gauge values, understandings, and practices as expressed by school staff. The rationale for this approach was to delay the introduction of RA into schools where RA would most likely not be sustained or would only be implemented in a narrow form. It then allowed the local authority to identify how to support schools preparing to adopt RA.

There have since been a number of changes in terms of RA in the region—steps forward and steps backward. For one, during the time of the project, there was money available for speakers, trainers, site visits, and dedicated staff to promote and develop RA; austerity, precipitated by the 2008/2009 global recession, caused a significant reduction of resources, and schools were asked to network and train internally and at low to no-cost. Nonetheless, as evidenced in a primary school I visited, some schools continued to embrace RA wholeheartedly. The education officer estimated that although almost every school in the region would claim to be restorative, about 25% would "pass a fairly high threshold and the rest would be spread out along the continuum." The challenge, as articulated by the education officer, was to move away from simply using restorative language to actually enacting the principles and values. This challenge was being made greater by a lack of funding and other resources.

In examining various RA documents in the region, I discovered a more nuanced picture of RA than in the national documents. Values were frequently discussed, including, notably, asking what values were currently being taught and enacted through behavior management policies. RA was framed as a value-laden approach; not simply a technique. Although there was still a primary focus on pupils in terms of changing behavior and building relationship skills, these documents all emphasized the importance of adults being cognizant of the values, skills, and attitudes they wished to foster in students. There were calls for teachers not only to teach such approaches, but to model them, as well. While the national documents split the focus evenly between building relationships and managing behavior, seemingly unsure of which was the center of RA, the regional documents merged the two, much of the time, seamlessly. By emphasizing both the underlying values of RA and the responsibility of adults to model these values, the focus was on the quality of relationships and how such relationships changed how schools responded to behavior issues.

Royal Mills High School

General Discourses

Royal Mills High School was built in the 1960s to serve over 1,000 pupils. By the late 1980s, the number of registered pupils dropped by a few hundred; the Scottish government website showed just over 500 pupils registered in 2012 (Education Scotland, 2012). Royal Mills was a public, non-denominational, 6-year comprehensive school. Essentially all of the pupils in Royal Mills were White Scottish. This differed from the national Scottish demographics, in which 5.5% of pupils indicated being from a minority ethnic group (Scottish National Statistics, 2012). As one teacher explained, immigrants are not drawn to places where there are no opportunities for employment. The percentage of pupils entitled to free school meals (an indicator of low income) in 2012/2013 was more than double the national average (Education Scotland, 2013). Several staff members, including those who had attended the school when they themselves were pupils, told me that Royal Mills had had a greater socioeconomic mix in the past; in the last decade, middle-class families had started sending their children to schools seen as more upper class. The depute headteacher confirmed this evolution, adding that once Royal Mills became known for supporting pupils with high needs—and thus attracted students with such needs—even more middle-class families withdrew. At the time of my study, with falling numbers and aging infrastructure, Royal Mills was in administrative limbo.

Staff frequently referred to a disconnection between the culture outside the school walls, the broader community, and that within their walls. According to the depute headteacher, "...out there it's dog-eat-dog, and they hit each other and fight with each other and so on and so forth. It's reasonably violent, which we don't get in the school. It bubbles over sometimes but we don't pick up much of it." Several members of the senior management team called the school an "oasis of calm" within a chaotic, violent environment in which the pupils spent the rest of their time. The depute headteacher lamented the fact that within public perception, the school was seen to be as unruly as the surrounding neighborhood: "There is a perception out there that young people about [Royal Mills] run amok and are loud and cause bother and are riotous and there's no teaching takes place. And when you're in here, it's relatively calm."

Part of this perception seemed based not on Royal Mills' current situation, but its recent past. The headteacher, who joined Royal Mills in 2005, recalled entering into a very aggressive environment. He illustrated this environment by describing his first day on the job: He walked in the front door of Royal Mills to find two prefects, the pupil leaders of the school, physically fighting and the two depute headteachers holding them back. For his first 2 years at Royal Mills, there was not a week that went by without the police being called in to deal with an incident. Conflictual relationships, according to the headteacher, extended to parents and staff, as well. Parents did not trust the school and brought their issues to local counselors rather than speak directly with the school personnel, teaching unions were involved with pupil discipline issues, and relationships between many members within the Royal Mills community were tenuous.

As a first step, with the intention of sending a message to the community and staff that the leadership of Royal Mills was serious about bringing order to a chaotic environment, senior management began excluding pupils at a much higher rate than previously:

Indeed, at one point [our exclusion rates] were the highest in Scotland. And I make no apologies for that. Other than I don't believe in exclusion. I generally don't believe in exclusion. It doesn't work. But in order to support the staff where they were, and how they felt—because they felt quite low, in terms of their morale. They needed to be supported. (Headteacher)

From 2006 until the time I spent in Royal Mills, there were significant changes. A 2008 school inspection identified the following key strengths in the school: pupils' increasing academic achievement, high quality support for vulnerable pupils, well-considered curricular innovation, improving pupil behavior and attendance, and staff involvement in school initiatives. The noted improvements were mostly attributed to the leadership of the headteacher. The inspection highlighted how the school, although still struggling to help pupils attain appropriate national levels in reading, writing, and mathematics, was becoming increasingly successful at helping pupils achieve academically. Pupils were also beginning to have higher expectations of themselves.

The improvements were noted by more than official inspectors: The headteacher talked about a recent visit from a retired colleague who commented on how much less violent Royal Mills had become; a 2012 report on the school improvement plan, evaluating progress since 2007, mentioned how parents regularly commented on the productive, supportive, and inclusive atmosphere they experienced when entering Royal Mills; and a 2010 teacher survey cited one teacher's observation that Royal Mills was starting to feel more cohesive. The Royal Mills of 2013 was remarkably transformed from the Royal Mills of 2006.

Indeed, my first day in Royal Mills left me with similarly positive impressions. From the moment I walked in, I found staff and students to be friendly and open. There was little evidence of the chaotic and violent school of the past. As I waited in the reception area to meet the depute headteacher, I examined a shiny mock-up of a new school, that some students would be attending. A first-year pupil approached and asked me what I was looking at. I replied, "I think it's your new school." I pointed out how nice the stained glass was, and he sighed and said, "Yeah, but I want to stay here. I like *this* school."

Of course, first impressions are only that. My entire experience, my data, and other documents, revealed a much more complex situation. The 2010 teacher survey showed, among other indicators, that while over 50% of teaching staff agreed that staff and pupils respected each other, no one strongly agreed, 30% disagreed, and just under 10% strongly disagreed. Reflecting this, in conversation, teachers continually referred to Royal Mills as a *challenging* school. Challenging was defined sometimes as aggression and disrespect on the part of the pupils; other times it was defined as refreshing honesty. Three teachers, in informal conversation, told me early on, "There's no culture like this school's. In most schools, classrooms are silent, teachers are addressed as Miss or Sir. Not here. We have kids who want to have a voice."

In observing a drama lesson a week into my time at Royal Mills, I witnessed an example of both the challenging realities and the pupils' desire to have a voice. The pupils sat in a circle, preparing for their next acting assignment which involved portrayals of the police; they were sharing personal examples of interactions with police officers. All but two or three of the 15 pupils had had formal meetings with police. These were first year pupils, most of them 12 or 13 years old. They went around the circle telling their stories: One girl had smashed someone's window because she was bored, another had been extremely drunk, and a boy had been in a violent altercation. As the teacher told me later, "The thing is, they're absolutely honest. They're not devious."

The culture at Royal Mills was shaped by both the pupils' realities and by the school's response to those realities. The depute headteacher stated emphatically, "We never give up on young people, no matter what they've done, no matter how difficult it is, we'll always keep trying and trying and trying." This insistence on working with all pupils garnered both praise and criticism from staff. Many staff pointed out to me that Royal Mills was inclusive. Several followed that statement with the refrain: "Sometimes too much so." All staff agreed that it added to the challenge, whether they found the inclusivity positive or negative.

Royal Mills attempted to address some of the wide variety of challenges faced by and from their pupils by establishing links with external organizations. These included colleges, social workers, businesses, and local elected members, among other agencies and individuals. One of those relationships brought about *School of Football*, which many (particularly male) pupils raved about. Pupils chosen to be part of School of Football followed an altered timetable which used football[2] to motivate students and included a period of football activity every day. Three male pupils, part of School of Football, were selected, they told me, not because of their football skills, but because their teachers reported that they had both positive and negative traits and recommended that they needed this program. The pupils agreed on all points.

The Pupil Support department, an internal mechanism, was widely cited by both staff and pupils as key to Royal Mills' success in dealing with its vast challenges. Pupil Support represented an integration of three areas formerly seen as separate entities: behavior support, guidance, and learning support services. Pupil Support staff worked with pupils who found it difficult to cope with aspects of school life due to social, emotional, or behavioral issues; they also worked with teaching staff to promote positive behavior and good relationships. According to one school document, approximately one quarter of pupils had access to Pupil Support. Some pupils had regularly scheduled periods in the Pupil Support Center; others were sent there by teachers when they were having difficulties. I spent an hour in the center on my first day, speaking with pupils and staff. When I walked into the center, one member of staff was with a male pupil who had an interview the following week at the local college. The teacher was attempting to prepare the pupil for all possibilities, including discussing the bus timetable and other logistics. He later explained how such logistics are sometimes the biggest hurdles: Some pupils and their families never leave town so any sort of arrangements can flummox and sabotage the best-laid plans. Pupil Support staff were lauded in several reports for being skillful, sensitive, and rigorous in meeting pupils' emotional, physical, and social needs. The depute headteacher called Pupil Support "a victim of their own success, because they are constantly really, really busy. I feel that the young people trust them enough to go in there and deal with [any problem]."

For those pupils who required more intensive support, a new initiative, the Inclusion Room, existed. The Inclusion Room was an in-school room for pupils who were being excluded or were at risk of exclusion from regular classes. Activities in the room were meant to introduce students to a range of learning techniques and coping strategies. The Inclusion Room staff member was not a certified teacher, but a community educator employed by a company contracted to work in the school. She ran a number of groups (anger management, girls group, first year group) on specific issues with pupils. The staff member described her room as a safe place for pupils to be honest about their thoughts and feelings. Amongst the broader staff, reviews were mixed. Some staff appreciated the work being done in the Inclusion Room; others were unsure what the room was accomplishing. Testifying to the confusion about the Inclusion Room felt by some in the school community, I overheard the headteacher, while escorting a pupil to the room, respond to the pupil, "No, it's called the *inclusion* not the *exclusion* room."

Similar to Rocky Creek, another initiative undertaken by Royal Mills was Unicef's Rights Respecting Schools (RRS). Royal Mills had achieved Level 1 status as a RRS as recognition that it is a school that "not only teaches about children's rights but also models rights and respect in all its relationships:

between teachers/adults and pupils, between adults and between pupils" (UNICEF, n.d.). Achieving this status was a joint effort between staff and pupils, especially the Pupil Union, as part of a RRS committee. Being identified as deserving of this status seemed to validate how far Royal Mills had evolved as a school, in both the students' and teachers' eyes. Royal Mills was working toward Level 2 status while I was visiting, the highest level available through UNICEF, which is a recognition that the values and principles of the Convention on the Rights of the Child are fully embedded in the school ethos. In light of the endeavor to achieve this level, Royal Mills had recently compiled a report, shared with me, in which each department identified how RRS values and principles were evidenced. Interestingly, RA was often mentioned as an indication of rights respecting ethos.

Royal Mills was guided by a leadership team consisting of one headteacher, two depute headteachers, and a business manager. Their leadership was uniformly praised, in official reports and by all the staff members with whom I spoke. The team was described as being collegial, consulting staff on important issues. The 2008 school inspection suggested that the headteacher was one of the main reasons for the school's revival. According to this report, the headteacher and his vision had won the respect of pupils, parents, and staff. The headteacher attempted to visit each classroom every day, creating a sense of familiarity and connection. Although I did not have experience in any other secondary school in Scotland, I was assured by staff members that the team's collegial, open-door approach was not typical of Scottish management teams.

During interviews, the two members of the management team with whom I had the most contact—the headteacher and the depute headteacher responsible for pupil support—both highlighted collaboration and inclusivity, in the pursuit of meeting pupils' needs, as part of their broader visions. The depute headteacher described his philosophy of education as wanting to "make a difference in the life chances and life expectancy for young people, and make Scotland a better place. It seems pretty grand, but that's what it's all about." The headteacher expressed similar ideas, wanting to make a difference in pupils' lives, and challenged himself to do so through continual reflection and revision. Throughout my time in the school, I was impressed by how the headteacher and depute headteacher interacted with the pupils: They knew each pupil's name as we walked about the school and often used a personal question, joke, or anecdote to relate to that pupil.

The management team is, of course, one significant component of a school; another significant factor is the teaching staff. Royal Mills had a staff of about 60 teachers. Two of the words used most frequently to describe the staff—by staff members themselves—were *supportive* and *reflective*. Several staff members lauded the level of support they received from colleagues and described such support as crucial to surviving the school environment. The statistics showed a slightly less consistent sense of support: The 2010 teacher survey indicated that three quarters of staff agreed that they, the staff, communicated effectively with each other. This number dropped to about two thirds in a more recent survey asking if an ethos of mutual support and collaboration existed across staff. The headteacher, while describing the staff as collegial and forward-thinking, admitted that there were members of staff who were dubious about the direction Royal Mills was taking, thus detracting from staff cohesiveness.

As in most schools, the Royal Mills' staff room was a microcosm of staff dynamics. I witnessed honest grappling with issues as teachers struggled to do their best as individuals and in support of one another, embodying the reflective nature and critical thinking that I had come to identify with Scottish culture. The staff room was a large, open room with couches, a kitchen, and a whole variety of posters and information. The teachers I spoke with felt that the staff room dynamics were representative of close and collegial relationships between staff. As an example of this, every day the pupil-run café set big kettles of tea and coffee, and snacks, in the staff room for break/tea time, and staff members joined one another for food and conversation. The staff contributed money each month to support the pupil-run café and most members participated. When I remarked on this wonderful practice, I was rather pointedly told by one of the teachers, "we are a cooperative staff."

In the staff room, I also witnessed teachers putting up barriers against one another—whether due to insecurities, ideologies, fatigue, or other reasons. On my first day at Royal Mills, I remarkably found the staff room split between men and women: Men sat on the couches; women sat at the table. Only once in over three weeks did I witness mingling: One man sat at a table with his female colleagues once. As an outsider, I often felt awkward at lunch and the conversation was forced. One day, however, when only females were in the staff room (the men had a tradition of eating in the pupil-run café on that particular day of the week), the talk focused on specific pupils and the teachers' struggles with them. A few teachers wondered if they had done the right thing as they relayed various examples. The conversation felt extremely supportive and reflective, providing a window for me into the type of encouragement that teachers provided one another. Yet, the next day, one of those same teachers confided that she found the staff room demoralizing. She said when she arrived it took 6 weeks before anyone spoke to her.

Staff relationships—whether those that supported or those that iso-lated—were featured in the daily experience of staff at Royal Mills. Rela-tionships were also a feature of the staff's experience with pupils. Build-ing healthy relationships was seen, by many, as key to creating an effective learning environment. This was especially true in interviews with the senior management team. The depute headteacher identified the building of re-lationships as the most important aspect of education. The headteacher concurred, praising the strong relationships between staff and pupils and referring to the school as one big family. As he said, "For some of the young-sters in this area, school is the most stable part of their lives. And it's very important to them that they have relationships with the teachers and the teachers here know that." The depute headteacher also suggested that a focus on relationships simply made sense: "If you shout at a young person here, they will shout back at you twice as hard and you will lose, so there's no point." Building relationships with pupils was seen as both morally and practically sound.

The depute headteacher admitted, however, that a focus on relation-ships was not universal; some staff members still relied heavily on disciplin-ary measures such as detentions. The 2010 teacher survey corroborated this focus, revealing staff members who were unsatisfied with the relational approach being taken by Royal Mills, with almost half of the staff indicating a desire for more emphasis on behavior. Several written comments on the survey referred to pupils being given "far too many chances."

Official documents, too, did not reflect a universal relational focus. The Royal Mills' code of behavior, for example, distributed to pupils in a brochure, did not refer once to relationships, except in terms of being po-lite to others and not challenging the authority of teachers. Among other points, the brochure stated that the pupil commitment to Royal Mills was to follow the school rules and follow the teacher's instructions in class. The clear message was that good pupils are orderly and behave.

What I saw at Royal Mills reflected a tension between building mutu-ally supportive relationships and maintaining order through behavior man-agement. I witnessed numerous examples of strong relationships between pupils and staff, particularly with pupils who were less engaged in school. Within the Inclusion Room, for instance, relationships were being built and maintained that kept pupils returning day after day. Yet these same pupils were required to carry yellow behavior slips every day. On it, each period, the class teacher would record comments about the pupil's behavior and sign the slip; the pupil was required to then ensure that his/her parents/carers signed the slip in the evening and would return the slip to the school the next morning. I wondered how it felt for the pupil to carry this slip around and be constantly evaluated on his/her behavior. I also wondered if the slip had the desired long-term effect of changing behavior and ultimately engaging the pupil.

According to the custodial staff I spoke with, more practices such as behavioral slips were needed to ensure control and discipline. They felt that there had been a steady increase in indiscipline at Royal Mills since RA had been introduced. They blamed the increase on *soft* practices—such as RA—being implemented in the school. Although some teachers might have agreed with the assessment of the custodial staff, the leadership of Royal Mills was interested in moving the school decidedly toward the soft approaches and away from a focus on only behavior. Currently, however, it was teetering between the two approaches.

Restorative Discourses

Although the region was selected to be part of the restorative pilot project in 2004, Royal Mills was not one of the pilot schools. The school did benefit, however, from the regional focus on RA, learning through the experiences of the schools involved. Once the pilot project finished in 2008, the local authority was determined to expand the use of RA in the region. Royal Mills was deemed "ready" by the local authority and key staff members were invited for a 2-day course offered by an external facilitator.

Building on the initial training, school staff worked to integrate RA organically, rather than embark on a structured implementation plan. As the depute headteacher told me, "We've kind of almost fallen into it by being part way along the road and then identifying, here, we do some of that, and then kind of building that." The depute headteacher, in analyzing figures from different departments at the time, found that some departments had low exclusion rates and high levels of pupil engagement, where other departments were unable to engage the same pupils. He discovered that "some members of staff were actually very good at getting sworn at because of their interactions with young people." In response, Royal Mills chose to introduce RA in 2008 as a way to improve interpersonal interactions.

After engaging an international facilitator to train all staff in the use of restorative language to encourage positive interactions, a group of 15 teachers committed to using restorative language in their classrooms. The teachers documented their experiences and met regularly to discuss successes and challenges. The teachers reported significant improvements in their interactions with pupils, particularly those pupils deemed most challenging. Building on their success, the senior management team dedicated all of Royal Mills' in-service days in 2008 to training staff in RA. One third of the staff were trained as restorative facilitators that year by regional educational psychologists.

The first year also saw intentional efforts to educate pupils and parents about RA. The school produced a parent leaflet, assemblies for pupils, and offered a half-day of training for S1 pupils focused on RA and emotional intelligence. Both the headteacher and the depute headteacher felt pupils were open to RA, especially because many had been exposed to similar approaches in their primary schools. The headteacher admitted, "Actually, they were better prepared for it than we were, in many respects." Some parents were unsure of the value of the approach, seeing punishment as essential. The depute headteacher, however, thought that those families who participated in restorative meetings soon recognized the benefits.

In that first year, there were over 100 requests by staff members for restorative meetings. The school continued to exclude pupils, though exclusions went down considerably, as did referrals to the office. Importantly, some staff members felt that the need for exclusions and referrals—disruptive behavior—had also decreased. There were, however, issues they needed to figure out: Some staff felt the timing for restorative meetings was not right; some pupils felt that teachers were using restorative meetings to punish them. A steering committee used what they were learning in that first year to continually revise the school's approach.

In the following year, the number of staff asking for restorative meetings dropped considerably. Two explanations emerged: (a) Staff felt able to deal with issues themselves in a restorative manner rather than ask someone else to facilitate, or (b) Staff simply did not believe RA was the right approach. The senior management team had no illusions that the staff were unanimously supportive of RA, but they did believe the majority were. The support, however, needed continual encouragement. As the depute headteacher said: "It's a constant drip feed that you need to keep going and going and going."

The constant drip feed was necessary as it was not an easy transition from the previous discipline approach to RA. According to both the headteacher and the depute headteacher, an attitude had existed among staff that discipline problems were the domain of senior management. The depute headteacher thought that "the staff found [RA] quite hard at the start because, you know, they were having to give a bit of themselves." The management team, however, wanted teachers to be able to deal with behavior issues on their own, within the classroom. RA was seen as a way to fully empower and support staff to do so. Staff, they felt, needed to view discipline issues as part of the process of teaching and learning. Prior to RA, the depute headteacher would be requested by teachers to enter into their classroom and ask pupils to remove their jackets or to put their phones away. As staff grew more confident and relationships with their pupils improved, such requests diminished.

The headteacher felt RA assisted everyone within the school to work together. The ultimate goal of RA, he said, was a "more ordered society in the school." Elaborating, that ordered society would include: greater respect, less violence, more engaged pupils, and a safe environment where learning for life was promoted. The depute headteacher was equally as ambitious in his view. He hoped that RA would provide pupils with the "best learning experiences, to build their confidence, build their resilience, to give them hope that there's things better than they're suffering outside." They felt that most pupils responded well to RA and preferred being actively involved in creating a solution rather than passively receiving punishment. The depute headteacher noted a greater degree of trust and honesty from pupils: "Pupils are much more likely to admit to doing something wrong because they know that they're not going to get a row or shouted at, and they know they're going to get an opportunity to sort it out."

Although there was a concerted effort in 2008 and the subsequent years to ensure RA was the dominant approach at Royal Mills, it was unclear how dominant it was in 2013. The depute headteacher summed up the 2013 state of RA in Royal Mills: "There is a fine line between it being embedded and it being lost." RA, he said, was not as visible as a few years ago. Gone were the explanatory pamphlets, the pupil assemblies, and the training sessions. RA had either simply become part of who they were at Royal Mills and no longer needed explicit explanation; or staff had forgotten RA and were ceasing to implement it. There was evidence that pointed to both scenarios.

In the embedded scenario, there had been a cultural shift, moving away from facilitated restorative meetings for isolated incidents back to the origins of RA in Royal Mills: restorative interactions. The depute headteacher defined this as "restorative, interactive classrooms involving the young people and their learning; making the learning interesting, interactive, making communication purposeful and positive." The cultural shift had been initiated and modeled from the top down, with the senior management team applying the same restorative expectations to themselves as to staff and pupils. The depute headteacher felt that the longer pupils were in the school, the more embedded RA was in their own interactions, that is, S4 pupils were more restorative than S1 pupils. RA also fit well with other initiatives within the school, suggesting that RA was integrated into the greater aims of the school. The headteacher described RA as a *catalyst* bringing together a diversity of approaches: capacity building amongst staff, inclusion, reduced exclusions, improved learning experiences for pupils, nurturing environments, and RRS. During my period at Royal Mills, I observed several incidents attesting to the embedded nature of RA, such as impromptu restorative meetings in the hallways and staff members actively engaging pupils in finding solutions to issues.

In the lost scenario, one survey suggested inconsistency in the use of RA across Royal Mills. The depute headteacher agreed with the survey results, identifying a minority of staff as desiring more punishment. Interestingly, he thought the least restorative staff were the most recent graduates from teacher education programs. The headteacher, too, felt that RA was "part of our menu of approaches that we can use to work with and manage pupil and, indeed, staff behavior. It's part of a menu; it's not the only thing that's in there." Realistic, for certain; but *part of a menu* could also lead to the identified inconsistencies and the potential for RA to be lost. In informal conversations, several teachers admitted either misgivings about RA or lack of awareness. On my first day at Royal Mills, I met one of the staff members who had been trained as a restorative facilitator. She had recently returned to Royal Mills after teaching at another school. The other school, she said, had, unfortunately, gone "the other way." I said, a bit naively, "Oh, more punitive?" She responded, shocked, "No, totally restorative, nothing punitive at all!" This was one example of the tensions circulating in the school. Was the school fully restorative, focused more on punishment, or a mixture?

A key metaphor used to describe RA in the school was that of a journey. The depute headteacher said, "We'll just keep going and going. I don't think anyone ever gets there, but you can keep going." The headteacher hoped to find out "what could we be doing next. Where now? You know, because we don't want to be complacent about it. What other things could we be doing that could make an even bigger difference?" The school wanted to know how embedded RA was and then decide how best to move forward on their RA journey.

In the nation, the region, and Royal Mills itself, I found people willing to "see the world as it really is" (Herman, 2001, p. 428), engaging with complexity, contradictions, and self-critique. The individuals I spoke with and the documents I studied were, in many ways, just as the drama teacher described his students: refreshingly honest. There were minimal attempts to present a false image of the state of RA or to provide simplistic answers to questions posed. In this honesty, then, nationally, regionally, and in Royal Mills, tensions emerged between a historical focus on behaviorism and punishment and more recent aspirations of engagement and relationships.

The reality was *both/and.* The educator intentions, one part of this reality, will be explored in the next chapter.

———

Notes

1. Called *suspensions* in North America
2. Soccer in North America

8

Royal Mills High School

Educator Intentions

It is now time to listen carefully to the staff of Royal Mills, the individuals implementing RA. The pupils, in the next chapter, again have the final word, showing how adult intentions do or do not match with the actual pupil experience.

Educator Intentions

Listening to the educators—through the questionnaire, in the learning circles, and in informal discussion—the purposes underpinning the use of RA in Royal Mills start to surface. As in Rocky Creek, the presence of both transformative and affirmative discourses within Royal Mills are revealed; in contrast to Rocky Creek, discourses of affirmation emerge as dominant.

RA Hopes: "They're obviously not learning that from their home."

The group that responded to the educator questionnaire actively used RA in the school. Ninety-six percent of respondents indicated that they

Adult Intentions, Student Perceptions, pages 125–133
Copyright © 2019 by Information Age Publishing
All rights of reproduction in any form reserved.

used RA at least occasionally. In their use, educators hoped that RA would model or teach pupils a different way to: behave, deal with their emotions, handle conflicts and issues, and take responsibility for their own actions.

There was an oft-repeated sense that RA was a vastly different approach from what pupils experienced outside Royal Mills and that, therefore, teaching them this alternative was both ambitious and necessary. Some educators saw the school's influence and the impact of RA as limited, as it was difficult to "break the trend" (Margaret) of the surrounding environment. As proof of this limited influence, Margaret commented on how pupils behave after brief school holidays: "There is a wildness about them where they've had no routine, no boundaries and almost we have to start with some of them again. Because we can't, sadly, change the society that they live in." On the other hand, the difficult environment in which pupils lived was also seen as reason to persist in the use of RA. Pupils were thought to have few stable relationships in their lives and educators who used RA to build relationships with them sometimes took on the role of surrogate parents. Several participants alluded to the responsibility that comes with this role, with pupils sharing difficult aspects of their lives with adults. Sophie framed it this way:

> It's probably a very alien thing for someone—for an adult—to turn around and speak to them and show that they care. But they need to learn that that's an important thing in life. They're obviously not learning that from their home; so that's showing them, this is how you can deal with a situation or a conflict. And hopefully they'll go out into the real world and remember that.

Margaret concurred with the idea that RA taught their specific cohort of pupils crucial skills:

> They're very good at anger but they're not very good at expressing where that anger comes from. So maybe it's a way of helping them not get so angry or when they do get angry, of being able to deal with that. So that they can actually, therefore, modify their behavior . . . But maybe, try to get into their heads a little bit and make them emotionally intelligent about how they, about how other people feel. I think maybe that's . . . and improve behavior.

The hope seemed to be that RA would offer pupils an alternative approach through which they could learn new skills for the present and new habits for the future.

That alternative approach, it was expected, would also bring order to a chaotic classroom. It was rare to hear an educator refer to him- or herself as desiring more authority in the classroom. Yet discussions in the learning circles, while utilizing progressive language, pointed to an inherent belief that the teacher has final authority, particularly when keeping order within the classroom. As Margaret stated, she uses RA "very much as a tool to make the pupils understand that if they've done something where I've had to put them out of class, how it makes me feel about them and their behavior." The focus here was not on discovering the roots of the behavior or on recognition of mutual accountability, but on *making* the pupil understand the *teacher's* perspective. Interestingly, Sophie offered this observation about the purposes of RA in the classroom: "So restorative isn't just about, I suppose, order and control; it's also about teaching them, isn't it?" Although in this discussion Sophie expanded her understanding of RA to include a role for educating pupils, the comment revealed her primary understanding of RA as being about the order and control of pupils. Her comment, though more explicit than others, nonetheless showed how RA was used as a behavior management tool in Royal Mills.

In both the learning circles and the questionnaire, it is apparent that educators hoped that RA would offer improvements in pupil behavior, pupil relationships, and in pupil responses to incidents of conflict and harm. Due to the pupils' apparent *deficits*—familial or personal—educators felt that teaching social skills was crucial for the pupils' well-being. To this end, many felt the staff members of Royal Mills formed a surrogate family for the pupils, instructing them in how to survive and thrive in the world. This obvious care for pupils and focus on relationships facilitated social connection and was evidence of transformative RA. The deficit lens used by some adults to view the pupils and their families, and the focus on using RA to manage behavior and bring order to the classroom, however, meant that adults were sometimes more focused on controlling pupils than engaging them, using RA in affirmative ways.

RA Concerns: "If there is no consequence and no punishment, right, therefore society will run in chaos."

The two main concerns identified by some educators in the learning circles were that RA was too lenient and that RA was ineffective. A minority of participants voiced the first criticism, that RA was too lenient. Some educators, such as Margaret, claimed the critique as their own: "Sometimes, restorative has become a way to avoid dealing with serious consequences. And I still believe that they should go hand in hand." Most educators who raised this point, however, attributed the feeling to pupils ("I know some of the pupils who are maybe, like, have never been in trouble, for instance, maybe feel sometimes that restorative is a softly, softly approach with the ones that misbehave" [Jean]) or to other staff members or to both. Sophie wondered about the difference between an approach that is lenient and one that is restorative:

> There's a fine line, I think, sometimes between the two. Sometimes a lot of children see that. And staff will complain that we're crossing over into that leniency, as opposed to just restorative. There's no discipline as such. Rather than understanding that the discipline procedures have changed; they just don't think they're there at all.

Connected to the leniency critique, the other criticism, also voiced by a minority, was that RA was not effective, either with certain pupils or in general. As Margaret said, "To me, it's a combination of punishment and restorative. You can't abrogate all responsibility by saying having a wee chat with some of the pupils will work because with some of them, it doesn't." Some educators felt that RA was too lenient for a vocal minority of "hard-core" pupils who had become "so well-versed in restorative" as to use it to their advantage (Jack). The suggestion by those who felt RA could be too lenient or ineffective was that RA must be backed up by consequences, punishments, or, at least, the threat of those measures.

Among the learning circle participants, there were a variety of beliefs about punishment. A few dismissed punishment outright, such as Giselle: "It doesn't come together, the punishing side and the discussion side. They don't go well together, that's my experience." Most rejected the use of punishment exercises, the writing of lines. Teachers recognized, however, that there were other forms of punitive action available to them and a few participants called for greater use of those measures. Margaret justified her response by referring to general society: "What stops people breaking the law? The fear of getting into trouble. There has to be some element in society to stop people disrupting and disregarding the laws and rules of society. If there is no consequence and no punishment, right, therefore society will run in chaos." Educators concerned that RA could not deliver in the management of individual pupil behavior reinforced their authority through punitive measures.

A final concern of some educators was specific to how RA was handled in Royal Mills, not a critique of RA itself. A few educators took issue with the lack of communication that they felt accompanied RA. Again, most participants, such as Jack, who voiced this concern, raised it on behalf of pupils:

> I think also, maybe I'm sort of second-guessing here, that pupils will have a gripe about what they see as persistent, repeat offenders, ones that repeatedly disrupt learning. And as far as they're concerned, nothing, nothing has

happened to the pupils. But what they don't see are all the levels of intervention that are going on with people.

This educator and others who voiced similar apprehensions supported RA
in general, but voiced concerns about how RA had been implemented in
Royal Mills. They believed that better communication would improve the
use and perception of RA.

The first two concerns suggest that at least a minority of educators believed RA should have a role in controlling pupil behavior and, if it does
not, then it is ineffective. These concerns, along with the continued reliance on punitive measures, reveal an affirmative understanding of RA. The
third concern, that there be better communication, spoke to a desire to
more fully engage pupils and staff in the use of RA at Royal Mills—a move
toward a transformative understanding.

RA as a Relational Approach: *"I think of us as a team."*

Although there was a view of RA as a behavior management tool in
Royal Mills, RA was also used to increase empathy and connection to others and to build relationships. Importantly, the focus here was not only on
pupils, but also on adults and the mutuality of their interactions—mutual
respect, mutual challenge, and mutual expectations.

Beyond a focus on changing or improving behavior, educators utilized
RA to create understanding into how one person's actions impacted upon
another's life. Giselle described her usual approach to classroom issues: "So
usually I speak to them outside the class and I discuss basically, you know,
why there's a problem and then what their perception of it is, and what my
perception of it is, and what effect it can have on the others in the class."
Similarly, Mairi used RA to encourage pupils to empathize with others' feelings, "And I kind of put him in the position, 'How would you like someone
saying those things to you?' 'Oh, I wouldn't like it.' So when he came back
in, I got no more of it, no more of the nastiness." Although still engaged in
shaping pupil behavior, the focus in the above examples was on an outcome
of empathy and connection rather than order and control.

It was also acknowledged among educators that pupils were not the
only ones who benefited from learning to see the world through others'
eyes; adults required that same lesson. Jean revealed a lesson she learned
through a restorative meeting:

> Kids can kick off at you but when you then hear about the fact that in the
> morning, such and such had happened and, you know, then you realize al-

most that it wasn't aimed at you, it was just they needed to vent some form of anger or something like that. And then being able to sit down with that kid, talk it out, and then that has a huge impact on your relationship from then on because, you know, it's been dealt with and it's been sorted. Whereas previously, the old way, where you'd try and discipline them and they'd rebel against it, they never got the respect back for you and you never really got the respect back for them. So, it's almost, getting that relationship thing again, building relationships and trying to get everybody settled.

This excerpt speaks to the teacher's recognition that interactions in school need to be based on mutual respect and mutual understanding, and that RA can assist in building this mutuality. Giselle described the mutuality of education this way: "I think we're all there together for their learning. I think of us as a team." The team that Giselle refers to consisted of multiple members—pupils, family members, teaching and other staff, and the management team.

The majority of participants acknowledged the importance of relationships, but had varying descriptions of what healthy relationships in a school looked like. In the educator questionnaire, respondents identified the building of relationships as the number one way in which they used RA. They elaborated on their use of RA: to build respectful, positive, trusting relationships; to deepen existing relationships; to give a new start to broken relationships; and to focus on rights and responsibilities within relationship.

In the learning circles, most staff felt very positive about relationships they had formed with pupils. Adults recognized how vital those relationships could be to pupils who may otherwise have had few stable relationships. Many staff members discussed having daily conversations with pupils, from checking in about the weekend to life-changing issues such as pregnancies. They declared that pupils were very open with the staff about their lives and that this built empathy in staff for the pupils. Staff recognized the mutual benefit of such relationships: "When you have a good relationship with the pupils you look forward to your work, to coming into work everyday" (Margaret); "And there is a level of respect on the whole between the staff and the children in this school. There are a lot of very positive relationships and some very, very difficult individuals. And yet they're achieving, at their own level, eventually, within the school system; which they might not have given different circumstances and not the use of restorative" (Charlotte). Although the mutuality of relationships was emphasized in many comments, there were also comments revealing how relationships could be used in the employ of affirmative RA. Ella, for example, in praising fellow teachers, showed the dual purpose of building relationships:

You can see it in staff because they have a lot more time for the young people and it's not just about teaching the subject, it's about building a relationship with that young person. And I think that's really important, a really
important part to restorative approaches especially. Without that—because
I think once you do that, once you have that relationship with young people,
that young person will have a lot of respect for you and will probably work
better within the class. Because at the end of the day, they don't want to let
you down, or that staff member.

In this instance, RA built relationships with the outcome being that pupils
were more compliant.

It is clear that transformative RA existed in Royal Mills. Educators
viewed RA as building empathy, creating connections, emphasizing mutual
respect and mutual trust, and building relationships. Yet, those ideas of
transformation were sometimes intertwined with affirmation.

RA's Impact: *"I think it's made a huge impact
on the way kids behave and the way we behave towards them."*

Most respondents to the educator questionnaire (84%) either agreed
or strongly agreed that RA had impacted Royal Mills significantly. Learning
circle participants described the impact on pupils in multiple ways: Pupils
exhibited "more of a willingness to cooperate and to work together" (Donalda); were able to see the other person's point of view (Jack); and had
come to "rely on" RA (Ella). The focus for most participants was on how
RA affected pupil relationships. Donalda echoed the sentiment of several
educators: "I do think it has an impact on how the pupils behave with each
other and their ability to restore relationships." By repeatedly using RA,
some educators noted that pupils were beginning to take their own initiative to repair harm. Ella gave this example:

I built a really good relationship with one of the young people. And yesterday
they were just really out of character, I didn't know what was going on, I tried
to speak to them and just very, let's say, cheeky behavior back and attitude and
I was, like, okay. But then they came in today and they did apologize—about 5
minutes after they left, they came back and apologized—but today they came
in with a big note and it actually says, "I didn't mean to take it out on you, I
should know better, blah, blah, blah." But they've obviously went away and
thought about it and reflected back on it and came in on a new day.

Although still mostly focused on changing pupil behavior, the responses
showed an interest in empowering pupils, not controlling them.

In the learning circles, educators did not see RA as having a big impact on their own staff culture. Several educators referred to RA as a "natural way to think" (Donalda; Heather) and "just the way we are" (Heather). RA was described as simply giving a name and focus to common ways of being. Jean summed it up for many: "I was here when restorative approaches came in and although maybe we never used that term previously, we had really done it." Most educators who participated in learning circles did not see RA as a paradigm shift either for themselves personally or for the staff in general. Corroborating this natural acceptance of RA, 92% of respondents to the educator questionnaire either *agreed* or *strongly agreed* that RA fit well with the school's values.

In the educator questionnaire, there was a real divide as to whether RA were ever used to address issues among adults: one quarter of respondents said *often* or *always*; one quarter said *never* or *hardly ever*. Sixty-two percent of questionnaire respondents believed that RA helped to empower adults to deal with their own conflicts; 21% *disagreed* or *strongly disagreed*. References to using RA to deal with adult conflicts were also rare in the learning circles. When mentioned, it was predominantly in reference to the senior management team's "open door policy" (Charlotte), not to teachers approaching one another directly. In contrast to the Canadian educator learning circles, there was no discussion of how RA might be better practiced by staff members.

Although not seeing a change in staff culture, learning circle participants described the impact RA had on how some staff members related with pupils. Jean admitted that she goes "in much more sensitively to issues now" after participating in "eye-opening" restorative meetings. Sophie appreciated how "it's easier, as well, as a teacher. The last thing you want to be doing is getting yourself upset and stressed at pupils. I've got two options here, they're both going to work, but it's easier to do restorative." Key to making situations *easier* was the idea that RA is "just discussion rather than shouting" (Heather). This switch in communication styles was seen to provide a "better rapport" between teachers and pupils (Heather) and to allow an opportunity to substantially transform a situation. As Jack said, speaking to pupils rather than shouting at them "wrongfoots [pupils]. And then you get to the real root why they're behaving like that, you know. The tears come and they open up." Jean continued, focusing on the mutual impact of RA, "Rather than, you know, 'you did this,' 'you did that,' actually listening to their side of the story. I think it's made a huge impact on the way kids behave and the way we behave towards them." Learning circle participants elaborated on this mutual impact, describing how RA was impacting the school ethos ("I think, generally, the whole school is calmer"

[Mairi]; "There's more of a kind of culture of that's the way things are dealt with" [Charlotte]. The idea of RA being a *calm* approach came up repeatedly in the educator questionnaires, with respondents referring to RA as a non-confrontational, constructive approach that reduces both shouting and anger. As Charlotte stated in a learning circle, RA made Royal Mills "very different and it is a nicer place to work."

A few participants suggested that RA was increasingly embedded in the school culture. Evidence of infusion of RA was provided through examples such as the reduction of shouting in the school (Sophie) and the development of the school's welcoming environment (Ella). Margaret gave this example:

> It's so embedded now, you know, we take the pupils out [of the classroom] and we say, "Well, where do we go from here? Do you want to stand here? Do you want to let me know how we're not going to do this again?" Because it's now embedded in what we do, I think sometimes we don't even realize we're doing it.

Others were less convinced that RA had become the underlying approach. Charlotte feared that the lack of explicit discussion about RA indicated not that RA was embedded but that it might be getting lost: "There's a feeling that a lot of people are using restorative more automatically now, but also it hasn't been re-visited for a while. Maybe people are forgetting, so I'm not really sure."

Whether RA was embedded or not was debatable in the educators' eyes; also debatable was which form of RA—if any—was taking root at Royal Mills. As described by educators, there were indications that both transformative RA and affirmative RA sat side by side in the school context. The next chapter builds on how pupils experienced this dual understanding of RA.

9

Royal Mills High School

Pupil Perceptions

Pupil Perceptions

As in the Canadian school, pupils at Royal Mills were almost completely unaware of the concept of RA. This again required that I listen deeply to their portrayal of their broad schooling experience in order to see how RA was influencing that experience. As in Rocky Creek, the majority of pupil comments and observations revolved around pupil–pupil and adult–pupil relationships on display in Royal Mills.

The Context of Royal Mills: "You've got a load of people that you ken and even if you're not pals with them, they're still there for you when you need them."

In the educator circles, educators stressed the discrepancy between the perceived shortcomings of the pupils' environment outside of school and the calming refuge adults saw themselves offering within Royal Mills; in contrast, only a handful of pupils made any reference to this divide. Sheldon raised the reputation of the surrounding neighborhood, acknowledging

Adult Intentions, Student Perceptions, pages 135–148
Copyright © 2019 by Information Age Publishing

that "I know, like, everyone says it's not good." Two other pupils attributed some of their aggressive tendencies to experiences they had suffered within their families. Georgia, in her co-researcher individual interview, told a heart-wrenching story of witnessing abuse as a young child and ended the conversation by saying, "I will just automatically lash out at somebody if they actually, like, shout at me. Or they punch me or hit me. I just can't help it. I automatically just punch them."

Beyond these three references, pupils did not discuss the environment outside school as insufficient in any way. In fact, quite unlike the deficit model put forward by adults, Jeanne expressed hope that the outside environment would have a positive effect on pupils:

> I know someone who gets picked on by people at the school and my brother was saying that you're best just to leave it 'cause [the bullies] will probably leave in 4th year, 'cause knowing what they're like, they're just not wanting to come to school. And when they go out and start treating people like what they do at school, they'll get a big surprise, and hopefully change.

While adults in the school repeatedly suggested that Royal Mills was an "oasis of calm," none of the pupils explicitly stated that the school was a refuge from a difficult outside environment.

Pupils did, however, indicate that Royal Mills felt like a community or a family. Jemima thought the school was similar to a big family because "sometimes people talk to each other, like, bad, but sometimes we're really nice to each other." Georgia agreed with this, suggesting the school had a community feel since "you've got a load of people that you ken[1] and even if you're not pals with them, they're still there for you when you need them."

I discussed with the first-year pupils whether they felt that they had a voice at Royal Mills, as members of the Royal Mills family or community. A few pupils felt confident that they were listened to, with Nathalia highlighting the senior management team: "We do kind of have a say in decisions because [the headteacher] is that kind of guy where he, like, notices things and helps a wee bit." With a few caveats, Springer Spaniel concurred:

> Sometimes we'll get to make a decision, the teacher will give us choices. Or when we go into groups, sometimes they'll let us pick our own groups depending on how we've behaved. And, like they said with the [potential new school], [the headteacher] is letting us . . . he's seeing what we want to have, although we're not actually voting on it.

Uncertainty as to whether pupil voice made an actual difference was stated more strongly by other pupils. John cited a recent call for pupil opinions about a policy issue: "But you know on the sheets, like, our opinion, they willnae get registered as anything, they willnae get used. They'll just be chucked in the bin or something." Georgia echoed this cynicism: "No people can make a change. Not unless you're the queen." In the pupil questionnaire, 64% *agreed* or *strongly agreed* that it was easy for them to share their opinions with adults in the school. The number dropped to 51% when asked if pupils help to make decisions in the classroom; here, 21% of pupils either *disagreed* or *strongly disagreed.* These lukewarm numbers echoed the ambiguity in the learning circles. Although pupil opinion was requested, some pupils felt that adults determined the conditions, listening to them if they behaved well. Pupils were even less clear as to whether their opinions actually impacted the outcomes of decisions.

The everyday context experienced by pupils was one characterized by a sense of community, and a feeling of ambiguity as to whether their voice mattered within that community. Pupils did not make drastic distinctions between life outside school walls and that within, seeing positives and negatives in both. In this section, relationships are alluded to in the naming of Royal Mills as a family. The next theme explores relationships more explicitly.

The Daily Pupil Experience: "There's good people, popular people, mean people, bullies, smart people, dumb people, fit people, unfit people, healthy people, just like chubby-ish people."

The most discussed aspect of schooling amongst pupils was relationships. And within relationships, pupils emphasized those with other pupils. Pupils presented a mixed assessment of these relationships: Royal Mills felt like a big family but was also divided into cliques; most pupils in the school got along but also argued and fought a lot. The contradictions were first apparent in the pupil questionnaire. Thirty-two percent of respondents *agreed* that pupils in the school respected one another; no pupils *strongly agreed* with the statement; 23% *disagreed*; 2% *strongly disagreed*; and a full 43% *neither disagreed nor agreed.* The responses were slightly more positive for pupils feeling like they belonged: Thirteen percent *strongly agreed*; 28% *agreed*; 53% *neither agreed nor disagreed*; 4% *disagreed*; and 2% *strongly disagreed.* It is difficult to pinpoint the reason behind the large numbers of students who remained neutral for these two questions. The lack of strong agreement indicates an area ripe for more exploration.

Through the learning circles and co-researcher activities, specifics were revealed about how pupils experienced peer relationships. As mentioned, several pupils alluded to the feeling that the school was "like one big family" (Sheldon). Viewing Royal Mills as a family did not, of course, mean that all members got along at all times. There was some discussion about how Royal Mills was divided into "wee cliques" (Nathalia), depending, according to pupils, on the pupils' appearance, intelligence, personality, and a variety of other factors. In her co-researcher interview, Georgia illustrated both the range of groups and the importance of knowing your place in those groups, when talking about advice she would give to a new pupil:

> **Georgia:** I'd tell her it's a nice place, but people can be mean if you don't match with the right crowd. 'Cause there's definitely, like, crowds in this school. There's, like, good people, popular people, mean people, bullies, smart people, dumb people, fit people, unfit people, healthy people, just like chubby-ish people, ...
>
> **Me:** So what kind of group would you tell her to get herself into?
>
> **Georgia:** The nice one. And the smart one, if she was smart.
>
> **Me:** Are those the groups you're in?
>
> **Georgia:** Na. I'm in the angry group and the nice group. And a dumb group 'cause I'm dumb.

Although pupils warned against getting into groups that might get a pupil in trouble, there were also limits placed on mobility between such groups. Where a pupil fit within Royal Mills was often decided by factors deemed outside a pupil's control. One of the limiting factors which first year pupils spent much time discussing was age. There was a definite sense that there was a hierarchy of ages within the school in which all the older grades looked down upon the first years. The physical school was informally divided into sections where each year was allowed to sit, with no place left over for first years. First year pupils were quite discouraged by this, feeling the dominance of upper year pupils was supported by adults in Royal Mills. Although "pupils tend to be meaner if they're older" (Springer Spaniel), pupils felt adults viewed pupils as more important as they increased in age. As Awesome McAwesome put it: "And then there's the 6th years, no one really touches them. They're just the higher cause."

The language used between pupils—and in general—was a hot topic for pupils. Although all pupils in Royal Mills spoke English as their first language, on the questionnaire, in identifying languages they spoke, 30% wrote Scottish, 9% slang, 2% swag, 2% Glaswegian, and 2% United Kingdom. Language seemed to be an area where pupils could express aspects of their identity, whether regional or age-related. In the learning circles and co-researcher activities there was much discussion about the presence of "bad" language, swearing, and slang. Nathalia lamented in her co-researcher interview that "people swear in our school a lot. There's not at least one minute when you don't hear swearing." Sheldon explained the variety of language used: "We all talk, like, slang quite a lot. But, like, to each other, like a doormat or something. Or to each other like the best friends, like sisters or brothers. But depends on what mood they're in and who they are." Language was viewed as a way to connect with other pupils as well as to disrespect one another.

Like the language used, examples were given both of pupils getting along and of pupils fighting. Almost all pupils at some point in conversation gave an overall assessment of the pupils in Royal Mills as being friendly and mostly getting along. Yet these summaries glossed over other points pupils made about peer relationships. Jeanne, in her co-researcher interview, summed up the range of relationships pupils needed to navigate:

> Um, well, most of the pupils get along really well. That'd be nice if, like, everyone could get along. And some people, you're scared of 'cause you know that they'll hurt you that bad if you were . . . .'cause we got someone in our class that's quite noisy and that, and if you tell 'im to be quiet, he'll go mental and start picking on you. Start being nasty to you or something.

Although the summaries often painted Royal Mills as a friendly environment, the majority of examples given—either in the learning circles or through the co-researcher observations—were of pupils in conflict. Of the numerous examples given in co-researcher notebooks, here are two that occurred during the observation period: "A girl shoved a Jaffa Cake in a boys' face and the teacher didn't do anything about it" (Daisy); and "Somebody asked for a pencil, right, and she went, 'Nwa! You seen yourself, you're not gettin' my one!' And then she just starts being mean and cheeky and it's annoying" (Georgia). The responses in the learning circles and the co-researcher activities revealed how pupils daily navigated relationships with one another that were complex, varied and dependent on a large number of factors.

The Role of Adults in Royal Mills: "The only thing they can do, really, is shout, 'cause they don't have any way to take their anger out."

The other set of relationships that dominated pupil lives were adult–pupil relationships. Pupils named many adults within Royal Mills who treated them well, who were, in their words, "nice" or "friendly," spoke to them with respect, explained lessons carefully, and gave them room to make decisions. As John said in his co-researcher report, the friendly adults were "the good thing about this school." This positive feeling towards adults was reflected in the pupil questionnaire, as well. In contrast to the response to the statement about pupils respecting one another in which only 32% of pupils *agreed*, 87% of pupils felt that they were respected by adults. Thirteen percent were ambivalent; notably, not one pupil *disagreed* with this sentiment.

Of course, in reality, there were exceptions to adults respecting pupils, which became clear in the learning circles and co-researcher interviews. Buttercub raised a general complaint in her co-researcher interview: "Okay, so, like, some teachers don't listen to you. And some teachers just ignore you." Awesome McAwesome was more specific with his concerns, articulating an issue of fairness that resonated with many pupils: "A pupil will do something and the teachers will go, like, really mental at, like, the whole class and then everyone will get a row[2] and everyone will get the blame for it, and everyone will get a punishment. Which is annoying." Most of the comments about relationships with teachers took into account the context. Pupils were cognizant that teachers were not all the same ("Teachers talk to pupils like they're trying...like, some of them say it as if you're stupid. But some of them explain it, like, so you get it" [Eva]) and that even one teacher's response differed depending on the pupils he/she was dealing with ("And some teachers are nice to several kids, but they're not as nice to other children. Depending on the way that they're acting" [Springer Spaniel]) or other aspects of the situation ("'Cause if they keep repeating it to you and you just don't understand it, they kind of get, like, quite...not like rude but kinda like..." [Rose]). Despite understanding the contextual nature of relationships with adults, the one universal complaint from pupils concerned the amount of shouting that occurred at Royal Mills. Most pupils did not understand why adults shouted to the extent they did, feeling that "they shout too much. Way too much" (Awesome McAwesome). Although pupils were often baffled by the shouting, Jeanne offered this explanation: "If one of the pupils are winding up the teachers, the only thing they can do, really, is shout, 'cause they don't have any way to take their anger out...And they can't really do anything but shout, 'cause they're not...you can't really hurt people. Yeah, they're not allowed to hit pupils 'cause they'll get fired or anything." The emphasis that pupils gave to shouting stood in stark contrast to the insistence from educators that shouting was no longer prominent within Royal Mills and that RA had helped to produce a calm environment.

Despite being baffled about the amount of shouting, there were very few pupils who suggested that pupils treated adults well. Examples given in learning circles and through co-researcher observations usually placed blame on pupils for negative interactions with adults. Daisy found that "quite a lot of students talk back to the teacher when they're not meant to. 'Cause they're quite rude and, like, if you get in a row, then you get in a row and you've got to accept it and not shout back." Pupils discussed how adults were often justified in their responses, particularly if pupils were repeatedly disruptive. As Nathalia reported in her co-researcher interview, "Like, they're having to be told, like, three times to do something and they still didn't do it after the third time. And teachers kind of get frustrated and in a bad mood." Jeanne was sympathetic to teachers, seeing their choice to teach as a sacrifice and wishing that they received more respect since "they're sort of giving up their time to teach us 'cause they could be doing something—a proper job that they've always wanted to do—but instead they went and done teaching to help out or something. 'Cause there might not be enough teachers around." Pupils did believe that context played a role in how pupils treated teachers but, interestingly, did not give fellow pupils as much benefit of the doubt as they afforded teachers.

When discussing relationships with adults, one of the core ideas that surfaced was that of trust. Almost all pupils could name at least one adult in Royal Mills whom they felt comfortable approaching to discuss a major issue. Staff who worked in the Pupil Support department topped the list of trusted adults, followed closely by registration (or *reggie*) teachers.[3] As Awesome McAwesome confided, "And then something, like, something, like, sad happened to me out of school. And I was, like, I talked to my reggie teacher about it 'cause, like, we do see her everyday and there's not a teacher that we've got 5 days a week apart from our reggie teacher." Pupils did not seem shy about seeking support from the adults of Royal Mills. On the other hand, they wished that the trust was more mutual. Sheldon saw reciprocal benefits in this type of trust: "Like, for teachers to, like, trust pupils. 'Cause if they trust, then pupils would probably give them more respect." For several pupils, trust was best expressed in tangible ways, such as allowing pupils to sit with friends in class or relaxing various rules.

Although adult–pupil relationships were also complex, pupils tended to see them as more straightforward than pupil–pupil relationships. Examples were given of adults who did not treat pupils well and who shouted for perplexing reasons, yet pupils trusted adults more than they trusted other pupils and felt that pupils were largely to blame for bad relationships. Some pupils were interested in receiving more trust from adults, thinking this might be a way to create more mutually beneficial relationships.

▬▬▬▬▬

How Rule-Breaking is Handled: "Like, you would have to write, I won't swear at the teacher, like, 100 times or something."

Pupils were very aware of rules at Royal Mills and, for the most part, simply accepted the presence of rules, viewed them as fair, and could articulate the necessity of them. For example, Daisy named a rule she thought was necessary: "I think that walking out of class 'cause a lot of people do that and they're not meant to. 'Cause, like, if anyone did that then they'd think that no one's learning, they just walk out of class all the time." A few pupils mentioned rules that they did not understand, but were still willing to accept. "In a way, I think all the rules are fair, but, like, the thing about hoodies is it's not the school uniform so of course we can't wear them. So, if it was the school uniform we'd probably be allowed to wear them. But it's not so we've just got to put up with it and not wear hoodies" (Eve). The school uniform was one of the more contested rules. Although most pupils in the learning circles claimed to follow rules unconditionally, they were quick to point out that not all pupils were like them. Continuing with the school uniform theme, Eve said, "Some people don't like following the rules, they like trying to do their own thing. Most people, like, follow, they take off their hoodies in class and, like, behave pretty well. But some people don't." There was a mix of reasons given for pupils who did not follow rules, from disobeying rules such as the school uniform for practical reasons ("'Cause it is, like, really cold" [Didier]) to trying to get attention.

When rule-breaking occurred, pupils found that teachers had a variety of responses. A lack of consistency between teachers was noted: "Yeah, some teachers will, like, let you off with stuff if, like, if someone's wearing a hoodie in class and they're not supposed to. But some teachers will, like, tell them to take it off" (Emile). Observations in the co-researcher notebooks suggested that rule breaking was sometimes ignored ("A guy was, like, abusing this other guy in class, and the one teacher didn't do anything about it." [Eve]); sometimes confronted with shouting, threats, or exclusionary measures from the teacher ("And the person that wasn't doing anything got sent out. And then the teacher started shouting at them." [Sheldon]); sometimes discussed between adults and pupils ("The teachers just usually tell them to stop or, if they don't, they'll take them outside and talk to them" [Springer Spaniel]); and once, called out by other pupils ("A boy was chewing in class and he got told not to. A girl asked him why he was chewing" [Georgia]).

Shouting seemed to be one of the more common—and least understood—responses to pupil disruptions. Almost equally as common, however, were teachers who would discuss an issue with the pupil themselves or send pupil(s) to Pupil Support to have a discussion. As co-researcher, Buttercub, reported: "Well, the teacher and the pupils would talk; like, if they had a problem, they would talk about it." This discussion approach occurred most frequently in situations in which two or more pupils were having a conflict that disrupted the classroom. Jimmy voiced his appreciation for the role of adults in such situations: "[Teachers] would talk to them both. Then ask each side of the story. They wouldnae take sides on that."

Another common response to behavior issues at Royal Mills, however, was in the form of exclusion, either sending pupils into the hall or giving them detention. Detention was mentioned by a few pupils; many more gave examples of being sent to stand in the hall—for such issues as being rude or not getting on with work—sometimes for the whole period. Walking through the hallways, I noticed a few pupils on any given day, standing and waiting in the hallway. Almost as frequently mentioned as being sent to the hall was the assignment of punishment exercises (or a *punnie*), a practice that all educators named useless and infrequent. In his co-researcher interview, John explained his own experience with the practice: "You get a punnie, if you've been bad. It's a sheet like that, but it's green...no, yellow...and it's got lines on it you would write. Like, I once...like you would have to write, *I won't swear at the teacher*, like 100 times or something." Others, such as Eve, included punishment exercises in the list of usual responses to rule breaking: "Well, usually [pupils] would, like, get a detention slip. Or a punishment exercise. Or get sent to the headteacher. Or the head of department to come and like give them a row." Even if adults felt the use of punishment exercises were infrequent at Royal Mills, this was not the impression of the pupil participants.

When asked how pupils thought Royal Mills could better deal with issues of misbehavior, the responses were as individual as the pupils themselves. The following co-researchers offered these ideas: John suggested a "stronger approach" in which more pupils would be threatened with expulsion; Jeanne favored rewarding good behavior, "sort of like doggy treats if they sit down" and also thought that there needed to be more modeling from adults about how to "properly act"; and Eve made the suggestion that teachers get pupils more "involved, like, talking in group work" so as to build better relationships and cut down on peer conflicts. Pupils made these suggestions as they, too, grappled with the issue of a small group of pupils disrupting an otherwise enjoyable classroom environment, citing how a few pupils "ruin it" for the majority (Rose). Jeanne voiced it this way:

> I think when you're in your class and there's somebody disrupting—'cause we've got somebody, a couple of them are like that, they're, like, quite disruptive and the teachers are getting annoyed and stuff. Sometimes if everybody's shouting it just goes to your head and stuff. It's just sort of really annoying. I just wish it would stop.

Again, pupils were sympathetic toward adults in these situations and expressed much frustration toward the pupils themselves.

Pupil sympathy for adults, however, did have its limits. As frustrated as pupils might be toward chronically disruptive pupils, they did not dismiss them outright and were critical of adults seeming to do so. As Jemima explained:

> Sometimes the teacher's at fault, sometimes 'cause if someone's being quite nippy someday and they get sent out, the teacher wouldnae give them a second chance. Which they kinda should, 'cause they didn't mean it or anything. 'Cause some people actually have anger problems and that, so when they get sent out, they're like sent out for the rest of the class, so they don't really get a second chance. And maybe that makes them a bit more upset and angry.

Other pupils gave examples of pupils who made a bad first impression and then were unable to convince the teacher to view them differently. The main grievance, however, as mentioned earlier, related to teachers who reacted to one pupil's misbehavior by getting "angry at the whole class and we end up in trouble for doing nothing" (Daisy).

Overall, pupils understood the need for adults to respond to incidents of misbehavior or disruption and were well versed in the multiple options available to teachers at Royal Mills. Although discussion was a fairly common response by adults and was appreciated by pupils, discussion was part of a list of much more punitive responses. Pupils were sympathetic toward adults, as long as adults were seen to be responding in a manner that was fair to both individuals and to the class as a whole.

How Issues Are Solved at Royal Mills:
"If something goes wrong, they'll sort it. Definitely."

Beyond responding to behavior that breaks rules, is a response to harm, when a conflict or someone's action has caused another to be hurt in some manner, whether a rule is broken or not. When harm occurred, pupils had more trust in the ability of the adults of Royal Mills to help sort issues out than in their own ability to do so. Trust in adults, however, was not limitless with multiple examples given of teachers who dismissed pupil concerns, ignored issues, and refused to believe pupils. Left to their own devices, pupils expressed a variety of methods of sorting things out. For the most part, however, they did not feel they were equipped to adequately handle issues themselves.

In the pupil questionnaires, 75% of respondents exhibited confidence in the ability of adults to help them resolve conflicts. This confidence was reiterated in the learning circles and co-researcher activities. As an illustration of adults intervening in a positive manner, co-researcher Eve explained the following scenario that she had recorded in her notebook:

> One time two boys in my class were fighting and the teacher split them up and sent one of them outside and talked to the one to try and see what was happening between, trying to make things better. And I think it did work because they stopped fighting afterwards. They went back to just being boys.

As exceptions to this trust, pupils gave a few examples of being let down by the adults in Royal Mills. Most of these examples involved inaction on the part of the adults, such as Jemima's example in her co-researcher interview: "It was, ehm, somebody in first year, as well, stole my phone away from me and a teacher was talking to another teacher not that far away. And looked at them running away but, like, didn't really do anything about it." A few felt they had been wrongfully dismissed by adults, particularly when they were the pupil seen to be responsible for the conflict or harm. Respondents to the pupil questionnaire concurred, indicating a belief that pupils would be listened to more readily if they were the one hurt (80% agreed adults would want to hear his/her side of the story) rather than the person who had been seen to be misbehaving (64% *agreed* adults would want to hear his/her side of the story).

The place at Royal Mills where pupils were rarely let down was Pupil Support. Pupils had almost unanimous trust in the ability of the staff at Pupil Support to listen to their issues and assist in figuring out how to make things better. In his co-researcher report John told a story of a friend of his physically humiliating him, resulting in a visit by some adults from Pupil Support. He ended the conversation with an unconditional endorsement of Pupil Support: "If something goes wrong, they'll sort it. Definitely."

Pupils also provided anecdotes and examples of how they were able to sort out their own issues. Some pupils felt it best to ignore minor issues and a few others relied on discussion to deal with conflicts. Jemima offered a combination of these two strategies:

> I, like, get along with everyone in my class. And then, like, if we have a fall out, then we'll talk about it, and then hopefully, like, we sort it. But if not, then we'll, like, leave it for a little while. And it's, like, quite a lot of people argue, but then, like, they'll talk and just talk...Not realizing that it's just talking and, like, that fixes everything.

Pupils who mentioned walking away or discussion were, however, in the minority. Most of the pupils who indicated they would take care of issues themselves employed force, even if as a last resort or in self-defense.

Co-researcher John did not see himself as aggressive, but was willing to defend himself:

> Like, maybe four, like, three weeks ago. One of my pals was standing on a railing, and I was under him. And he jump off and land... grabbed onto me and smacked my head on the ground. But that was like... I was... so I just got up and whacked him. That stopped him. Ha.

Force did not seem limited by gender; co-researcher Georgia was also willing to defend herself physically:

> Last time I got in trouble by the police 'cause a guy was really annoying me—he was an older guy, he was about 15 or 16. He came up to me and he pushed me, so I punched him and I gave him a black eye and people that saw phoned the police.

These various strategies aside, most pupils at Royal Mills did not feel that they were equipped to deal with conflicts or issues of harm themselves. Awesome McAwesome could not imagine pupils resolving an issue without adult support: "It's always usually the teachers that, like, sort it out. Because if you've just had an argument with someone you wouldn't really want to talk to them about fixing it. So, it's always usually the teachers." The pupil questionnaires backed this sentiment up. In contrast to the 75% of pupils who believed adults would help them sort conflicts out, only 29% had confidence that pupils could do it themselves. Supported by adults, pupils exhibited trust in the ability to talk through issues and harm; left to themselves, most turned to force as an effective response.

Overall Assessment of Royal Mills: "I suppose if it were a perfect school, I'm pretty sure it'd be quite boring."

Replete with examples that pointed to a school in which peer and adult–pupil relationships were supportive and empowering on the one hand and controlling and undermining on the other, pupils insisted that, overall, their experience of Royal Mills was positive. Pupils expressed a sense of pride in Royal Mills, while at the same time identifying aspects that they would want to improve. Most of their recommendations had to do with the quality of relationships within the school. Their overall assessments were balanced, recognizing that schools are never perfect.

Pupils often compared Royal Mills to other schools, finding others lacking. Several pupils raised the issue of violence and physical fighting; Sheldon declared that "compared to other schools, it's hardly violent." Others pointed to various clubs, projects, or opportunities offered that were unique to the school. The male pupils were especially quick to acknowledge the football program as being superior to that in other jurisdictions. Finally, a few highlighted the support mechanisms that existed at the school, whether for academic or social issues. Springer Spaniel talked about such support:

> We have guidance and learning support which a lot of other schools might not have. They're very involved in what we do. Whereas in other schools, they might not be so involved. And we have the buddy room that we can go to if we want.

Pupils were content with many aspects of their school experience.

In the individual interviews, as in Canada, pupils were asked to offer an analysis of their school. They, too, were asked the question, "Of what you observed, what would you like less of?" Without exception, every response centered on relationship issues, either between peers or between pupils and adults. Georgia focused on peer relations, offering this list in her co-researcher interview: "Less shouting, less bullying, less picking on people, less . . . less screaming! Less picking on [a pupil] just because he's different." Others, including co-researcher Jemima, wanted relations between pupils and adults to be more respectful within the classroom wishing for less pupils "talking back and interrupting the class." On the flipside, pupils were asked to respond to the question of what they would like more of. Much of what was said in response articulated similar sentiments to the previous question, desiring better relationships and pupils to be more respectful in class. Nathalia gave her own wish list in her co-researcher interview: "More people to stop being annoying and disrespecting, and shouting out and being silly and being idiots." Students also voiced a desire to be given more choices by teachers—both in terms of academics and social situations—and to be awarded more trust.

As a final question in the individual co-researcher interviews, pupils were asked to provide advice to a pupil new to Royal Mills. Despite their observations containing many negative examples of pupil–pupil and pupil–teacher interactions, their final analysis was decidedly more balanced: "It gives you a lot of great opportunities to do stuff in life, they do lots of good shows and people are very talented. But I would say watch out for the bullies and people who are just annoying because they'll let you down" (Nathalia); and, "There could be like arguments and that, but no one would come up and just start stuff with you. And the teachers are very nice, too. They just need to explain it more, but if you ask for it, they'll tell you" (Rose). Jeanne summarized what seemed to be the feeling of many with her comment, "I suppose if it were a perfect school, I'm pretty sure it'd be quite boring. Just the same thing repeating itself. Quite boring." These co-researchers brought together peer discussions, individual observations, and their own analysis to present layer upon layer of the complexities of schooling at Royal Mills.

Conclusion

Taken together, the educator and pupil themes reveal how RA in Royal Mills is "attentive to the range of private and public relationships that support, or potentially thwart, human flourishing" (Llewellyn & Llewellyn, 2015). Relationships played a central role in educator comments and, especially, in the pupil experience. Relationships were used by educators to create connections and mutually respectful interactions as well as to subtly or explicitly enforce compliance with rules and order in the classroom. Evident in educator comments, in the connections between educator views and pupil views, as well as in the disconnection between those views, were discourses of transformation and affirmation. Pupils, in relating their general schooling experience, pointed to RA as an approach that engaged them, offering experiences of trusting relationships underpinned by mutual respect, concern, and dignity. They also described an environment in which adults fit RA in with rules, threats, and punishment in a quest for classroom order and control. Evidence of affirmation and social control sat, sometimes comfortably, sometimes uneasily, beside evidence of transformation and social engagement. A blending of social engagement and social control was how RA was understood and used by educators; a blending of social engagement and social control was how RA was experienced by pupils.

Notes

1. Scottish for "to know"
2. Scottish for "a reprimand"
3. Those teachers in charge of what in North America is often called *homeroom*

10

Holding the Studies Side by Side

Iembarked on this study with a largely idealized understanding of RJ in education as implicitly transformative. This view is not unlike that of many RJ advocates. The transformative understanding of RJ is that it is used to "address injustice and to improve the lives of the many" (Woolford, 2009, p. 17) and, in education, to transform schools to places "characterized by possibility, relationship, hope, and justice" (Vaandering, 2009, p. 39). This study, which examined the intersection between educator beliefs about RJ and how students actively experience RJ, challenged my beliefs and forced me to re-examine my thinking and ultimately change my views on RJ in education. While implementing RJ can achieve these objectives—to be transformative and foster social engagement—the evidence also suggests the opposite—that it can and is used as a tool, not unlike more overtly disciplinary approaches, to engender obedience and student compliance. The understandings that educators draw on when enacting RJ have significant impact on how students experience RJ.

Adult Intentions, Student Perceptions, pages 149–161
Copyright © 2019 by Information Age Publishing
149

Scottish Summary: The Reality of Both/And

The Scottish educator and pupil experience, as relayed by my participants, was layered and complex. It was a reality of *both/and*, as pupils encountered discourses of both transformation and affirmation: an educational system that was both cohesive and disjointed, staff that were both reflective and shortsighted, and relationships that were both empowering and controlling.

On the transformative side, Scottish culture as a whole prioritized critical reflection. This tendency toward reflection was evident in national, regional, and school contexts. As suggested in the brief historical overview of Scotland, the Scottish Enlightenment encouraged its citizens to "see the world as it really is" (Herman, 2001, p. 428). Contemporary critical reflection, an embodiment of the enlightenment, is undertaken not for its own sake, as a good in itself, but to engage and mobilize the values—wisdom, justice, compassion, and integrity—which Scots as a whole see as representative of themselves, the values engraved on the Scottish mace in the devolved Scottish Parliament.

In the education system, there was, as the data suggested, systemic cohesion: educational leaders, policy makers, and educators found common ground in focusing on professional educator autonomy and student-centered teaching, two themes prominent in the CfE. Within this systemic cohesion, RJ was implemented in a thoughtful, deliberate manner, introduced through a uniquely Scottish pilot project that considered regional contexts and focused on the complexities of schooling, not formulaic techniques. Although the initial impetus of RJ nationally and regionally was to improve exclusion rates, there was a more recent, intentional move beyond this metric to focus on the quality of relationships within schools and establishing a restorative ethos. Nationally and regionally, there was much evidence of discourses of transformation.

Within Royal Mills, itself, pupils were experiencing a transformed environment in which violence had been radically diminished since the arrival of the current headteacher who worked to build trust with staff, pupils, and families and bring order to chaos. Staff were empowered to deal with issues themselves and members of the senior management team were actively involved in pupils' lives and committed to their wellbeing. Most pupils trusted at least one adult in the school—particularly those adults in Pupil Support. Many pupils had faith that adults would help them sort issues in their lives, from conflicts with other pupils to life-altering issues such as pregnancies. Staff often dealt with pupils' interpersonal issues through restorative conversations; such impromptu conversations were visible throughout the school. Overall, pupils loved Royal Mills, equating the relationships of trust there to those of a family; pupils embraced the school in all its complexity. Royal Mills appeared, from the broader policy context and the elements of its everyday implementation and practice, to be a model of a transformative vision of RJ.

In the spirit of both/and, however, the Scottish reality of the national, regional, and school context brought with it cultural residue, the historic precedent of a long Calvinist tradition anchored in a moral system where redemption is achieved through punishment. Although current contexts are not direct replications of the past, historical contexts often reverberate in current ones. As an example of the reverberations of the Calvinist history, only recently had the Scottish educational system discontinued corporal punishment (embodied in the use of the strap), which had been supplanted by a reliance on punishment exercises and other punitive practices.

The national, regional, and school RJ documents reflected contradictory impulses along the transformative-affirmative continuum. Education Scotland website's page on RJ emphasized positive relationships, created within a supportive and fair ethos, concepts that tend toward the transformative end of the continuum; yet the videos featured on this website depicted RJ affirmatively, as "one of the latest behavior management tools available to teachers." RJ was frequently framed as part of a broader menu of behavior management options, backed up with the threat of punishment. In Royal Mills' staff handbook, the section following an explanation of RJ suggested the deployment of formal sanctions when RJ did not improve behavior. As several adult participants observed, the religious tradition of relying on punishment to alter behavior continues to echo in Scotland; and the echoes affected how RJ was understood and implemented among the school administrators, teachers, and pupils.

Within Royal Mills, educators hoped that RJ would help improve pupil behavior and would teach skills the adults thought absent from pupils' home environments. The educators, while caring about pupils, saw themselves as separate from the pupils and their social context, and saw RJ as primarily there to address pupil—not staff—behavior. RJ was described as being natural for adults ("just the way we are" [Heather]) and alien to pupils ("They're obviously not learning [restorative skills] from their home" [Sophie]). RJ was commonly used as a classroom management tool where staff remained the ultimate authority. Pupils, although feeling that they were listened to, were uncertain how much their opinions mattered. Pupils, in contrast to what adults said, felt that staff were quick to shout and blame pupils unfairly. While pupils empathized with the adults in stressful situations that precipitated shouting, they did not believe that their empathy was always reciprocated. Some pupils felt that teachers did not often give chronically disruptive pupils second chances. Pupils indicated an interest in more mutually empathetic and trusting relationships with adults.

In Scotland, I witnessed a centralized system pursuing a transformative agenda, embodied by a range of initiatives including RJ, supported by people in leadership positions nationally, regionally and within Royal Mills. The coherent national agenda, however, was only partially reflected in the school and its classrooms. Within teaching staff, there was a continuum of beliefs as staff members grappled openly with just how restorative and inclusive an effective school could or should be. For pupils, their experience was a mixture of transformative, mutually respectful relationships alongside authoritarian, punitive ones depending on the particular individuals involved and the particular situation. Educators who understood RJ as an approach to build relationships, primarily engaged with pupils in an exercise of mutual understanding; educators who understood RJ as an approach to manage behavior, primarily sought compliance from pupils.

The transformative agenda found roots in the Scottish values of the mace and in the Scottish critical and systematic approach to schooling; it also found inhospitable ground in the traditional religious focus on punishment and authority. The intentions of the educators who used RJ, informed by the historical and current context, ensured that pupils experienced the reality of *both* transformative *and* affirmative RJ.

Canadian Summary: Individual Commitment

In contrast to the Scottish education system's discourse of systemic cohesion, Alberta was characterized by systemic fragmentation. Albertan educational discourses eschewed talk of vision and instead focused on damage control in the midst of impending budget cuts. There was no provincial or even regional plan to implement RJ in a cohesive fashion; the few documents that did mention RJ mostly framed it as a criminal justice approach, rather than in education terms.

Lack of systemic cohesion, however, is traditionally seen in Alberta as more asset than hindrance. In the Canadian context, Albertans have a long history of seeing themselves and being seen as a maverick people who embrace contradictions and break rules. Albertans prioritize individual rights—especially the right to choose—in such areas as education. Consistent with this approach, Alberta's schools were free to choose how to best ensure their schools met safe and caring standards, as laid out in the provincial Accountability Pillar. Rocky Creek chose—independent of any provincial or regional encouragement—to focus on RJ and Rights Respecting Schools (RRS). They framed the two approaches as a combined effort to: ensure students felt safe and cared for, build relationships, and give students voice. While students experienced RJ in a school not connected to a systemic framework, it was carefully thought through at an individual school level.

Within Rocky Creek, itself, there were many social and pedagogic challenges. Students were at different developmental stages, there was poor staff communication, the Behaviour Learning Assistance (BLA) program was demanding, and many students came from cultures seen as non-supportive of restorative values. Students provided examples of bullying, racism, and sexism; all circumstances not easily dealt with through restorative or other processes. Some educators responded to the challenges in the school by, for example, exercising control on the leading of circles and, when deemed necessary, by the imposition of consequences (or punishments) as the outcome of circles. This school, with its challenges and without broader, institutionalized support, seemed positioned to allow discourses of control and compliance to thrive.

Yet, despite an environment ripe for affirmative RJ, signs of transformative RJ were everywhere: many educators openly confronted their own attitudes and behavior, holding each other to account in the same way they held their students to account; circles were used proactively to build community; and most educators hoped that RJ would empower students and give them voice in both the short- and long-term. Behavioral change, in this school, was not the primary focus. Students almost completely trusted that the adults would work with them, listen to them and support them. Importantly, most students felt decisions adults made—including the rules they enforced and how they enforced them—made sense.

The school leadership and staff, with almost complete freedom from an overarching authority and largely permitted to make independent choices, created their own interpretation of RJ to implement in Rocky Creek. The personal commitment that staff members had to RJ and RRS resulted in relatively consistent school-wide restorative practices that were mainly transformative. Although systemic support for RJ was lacking—and it is difficult to know how students fared after leaving this school—the experience of students while in Rocky Creek was predominantly transformative. The personal commitment of staff members, who interacted directly with students, ensured that the implementation of RJ was transformative. Transformative RJ was not diluted by the time it reached the students.

Holding the Studies Side by Side

Each school, individually, was complex; when held side by side, the complexity was multiplied. There are no simple explanations as to why and how discourses of affirmation emerged as dominant over transformation or vice versa. In Scotland, with its tradition of critical reflection and apparent systemic cohesion, Royal Mills appeared to have all the support needed to effectively apply transformative RJ; in contrast, Rocky Creek, set in an environment informed by individualism and in a context of systemic fragmentation and incoherence, with little broader leadership and even less institutional support, would appear to have been disposed toward affirmative RJ. In the study of these two schools, it becomes apparent that the most important determinant of RJ as experienced by students was not any broader systemic influence, but the understandings of RJ and education held by administrators and educators. Those understandings were informed by many contextual factors, all of which influenced the level of individual understandings of and commitment to transformative RJ. Stated otherwise, the evidence in these two schools suggests that the key factor is not whether there is broad institutional support—with all the right words and principles in place—or even if RJ is being systematically applied, but the purposes the educators are using RJ (or other ideas and tools) to achieve. Is there a desire (whether implicit or explicit) for social control or is there a desire for social engagement?

Intentions versus Perceptions

In this study, in order to understand the various ways that RJ can be conceptualized and experienced, I examined the overlap between adult intentions for the use of RJ and student experience of RJ. Intentions are difficult to determine—there are stated and unstated intentions, and there are implicit intentions where the intention remains obscure even to the actor, especially if there is little critical reflection. And, of course, within one group, there are at least as many distinct intentions as there are individuals. What I have done, in the previous summaries, is identify the trends and patterns of intentions within the educators as a group in each country. After exploring the national, local, and school documents, interviews, educator questionnaires, and educator learning circles, what seemed to be the overriding purposes for which educators and school leaders were implementing RJ in Royal Mills and Rocky Creek? And how did those purposes align with student experiences?

There were times when the intentions of the educators did not match the student perceptions and experience. For example, many Scottish educators felt they were using RJ to create a calm, quiet school environment; all Scottish students in my study remarked on an excessive amount of shouting to deal with disciplinary issues. In Canada, educators suggested that RJ was allowing students to deal with their own issues without adult support; instead Canadian students found it almost impossible to resolve issues without adult assistance.

For the most part, however, adult intentions—whether explicitly stated or implicitly expressed through actions—strongly aligned with student perceptions. In Royal Mills, most educators tended to understand and use RJ primarily as a behavior management tool and, as such, with its expedients of discipline and control, pupils were provided with fragmented support in the navigation of school life, and were unsure of the power of their own voice. In Rocky Creek, most educators tended to understand and use RJ primarily as a means of facilitating social engagement where, with its expedients of respect and empathy, students received constructive, cohesive, and empowering support in the navigation of school life. Clearly, the understandings that educators drew on when enacting RJ had significant impact on how students experienced school.

Could It All Come Down to Relationships?

As I attempted to make sense of the experience in these schools, my own thinking evolved. I began this research project with a transformative understanding of RJ and its role in education. With some caveats, I believed in RJ as an ideal that would naturally disrupt taken-for-granted assumptions, hierarchies, and behavioral approaches in school. I wanted to learn from students to what extent the practice and application of RJ embodied these transformative dynamics and/or might actually deviate from this ideal. To determine this, I created a continuum of the two conceptual extremes or ideals of RJ—affirmative RJ where the objective is student behavioral change and transformative RJ where the objectives are to facilitate student engagement, development, and critical reflection in all its complexity. I examined how student experiences along this affirmative-transformative continuum aligned or did not align with educator intentions. As I conducted my research, I realized the focus on RJ, even when expanded on the continuum, was too narrow for the complex realities of students and educators.

Directly and definitively, it quickly became obvious that students in both Scotland and Canada were completely unaware of the term *restorative*. That did not mean that they had not experienced or been impacted by

RJ as practiced or formulated by school staff; they were simply unaware of restorative terminology and therefore could not interpret their school's values and practices as being part of a restorative framework, and certainly could not understand nor answer questions about their perceptions using the terminology of RJ.

This conundrum of how to engage students about their perceptions of the RJ experience without them knowing the vocabulary of RJ required a conceptual shift. The objectives of transformative and affirmative RJ are quite clear. If successfully implemented in its idealized extreme, transformative RJ results in a learning environment of pupil engagement, participation, empowerment, and mutual respect, with flat social hierarchies between students, educators, and administrators in a web of mutually supportive interactions. In its extreme, affirmative RJ results in a stable learning environment where compliance and good behavior, as defined and implemented by administrators and educators from within strong social hierarchies, provide classrooms where knowledge can be imparted efficiently and with minimum social or intellectual disruption as pupils comply with the rules and conventions. While these descriptions are politically charged and can be used to make the case for ether kind of learning environment, they ultimately describe one constant: relationships. They describe a type or quality of relationship between the usual actors in schools—students, teachers, and administrators. And relationships are something that students spoke of in great nuance and length.

While it is obvious—bordering on tautology—that relationships, whatever their quality, are present in all classrooms, and, it follows, that examining relationships between the actors in the classroom will tell us about the dynamics in that classroom or school, I must admit a certain blindness to the importance of studying the quality of relationships to understand if the classrooms were environments where transformative or affirmative RJ prevailed. The primacy of relationships in classrooms eluded me.

Being unable to ask students explicitly about their experiences with RJ, however, required casting a wider and deeper net that reached beyond RJ as a phrase, a definition, or a concept. This took the research directly into the schooling experiences of students. The student co-researchers in this study shone the light of their experience, presenting evidence that relationships mediate and define essentially all of their schooling experience. The students ultimately helped guide this study beyond the conceptual limitations of RJ and even of the affirmative-transformative continuum to the place—most obvious to students, less so for educators—where education happens, in relationship. Bricks and mortar give us a physical space, where students and teachers may meet, and a curriculum gives teachers a learning guide to follow. Neither, though, give us a classroom until it is animated by relationship. The students made it clear that relationships are central, notwithstanding any other educational agenda, including RJ. Filtering the student experience through any agenda, including RJ, narrowed and limited the analysis of how students experience their schooling.

For the Students, It Is All About Relationships

At its core, Hendry (2009) says, RJ in schools is about building, maintaining, and repairing relationships. Although students were almost completely unaware of RJ as a term, students were acutely aware of the very relationships that RJ seeks to build, maintain, and repair. Students confirmed the significant position that relationships held in their lives; they provided mixed reports on whether the majority of relationships in their schools represented positive relationships—those that allowed for social transformation, engagement, and coherence—or negative ones—those that confused or sought to control and manage students.

In both Scotland and Canada, the student experience of school was best characterized as a constant navigation of relationships: with peers, teachers, and other adults. There was very little that mattered to students outside of relationships; everything else was framed as either an afterthought or byproduct. The learning circles, the co-researcher notebooks, and the co-researcher interviews all revolved around how staff members interacted with students and with other staff members, and the various relationship dynamics on display between students in classrooms, in the hallways, on the playground, and outside of school.

For pupils in Scotland, relationships fell firmly into the "both/and" category. Although Royal Mills was "like one big family" (Sheldon), pupils felt mostly unable to sort out issues with their peers without force and only one-third of the pupils felt that they respected one another. In contrast, most felt respected by adults and all participants could name one adult that he/she trusted and would approach if necessary. Yet, the actions of some adults in reference to behavior issues or conflicts baffled them.

Students in Canada, although naming such relational issues as racism, sexism, bullying, and fighting in their school as prevalent, had almost universal confidence in the ability of their peers—with adult help—to sort out issues in a satisfactory manner. As Code7 said, "And if anyone fights they would actually be solving it." Notably different from the Scottish experience, students in Rocky Creek thought that what adults did—whether in enforcing rules or supporting their needs—made sense. Students had what Antonovsky (1987) defined as a *sense of coherence,* in which they saw school life and the relationships in it as comprehensible, manageable, and meaningful.

For the Staff, It Is About More Than Just Relationships

In both Canada and Scotland, relationships were discussed and, in some ways, officially prioritized. In Canada, several members of the Rocky Creek staff raised the idea that relationships must be created in order for restorative circles to be successful. As Kirsten stated, "It's really hard to problem solve when [students] don't know who you are." Trust was closely tied to relationships. There was the feeling that RJ would be ineffectual if relationships did not already exist. Rocky Creek staff discussed this criterion as important for adults as well: Adults could not engage with one another restoratively if relationships of trust and support were not first present. Although important, educators also raised the notion that a focus on relationships was not sufficient, particularly when students were involved. There was a sense that students would not understand the impact of their actions—either for the specific incident in question or to deter future misbehavior—if there were no externally imposed consequences or punishments.

In Scotland, relationships came up repeatedly when discussing education in general. Members of Royal Mills' senior management team listed relationships in the school as a key priority. Positive relationships in Royal Mills were seen as crucial to helping pupils learn how to be active members of the broader community. Mutual respect and mutual trust were identified as important byproducts of the relationships—especially those that RJ helped to build. Yet there were a few disconnects to this relationship focus. Staff saw themselves and their culture as separate from that of pupils, caring for them though not necessarily identifying with them. Although most staff stated that they neither shouted nor gave punishment exercises, the majority of pupils countered this by reporting both shouting and punishment exercises as common responses to misbehavior. Additionally, some Royal Mills' staff did not recognize that other actions could also be construed as punishment, such as: sending pupils out of the room, using blaming language, or giving consequences.

Relationships were a stated priority for staff in both schools, yet, contrary to the students' all-encompassing focus, they were not the only—and often not the first—priority. Although many staff in the schools viewed relationships as important, they also valued—and/or were required to value—such things as order, academics, authority, tradition, discipline, safety, curricula, and consequences. As such, the schools in Scotland and Canada were cluttered with other agendas and discourses. Hoy and Weinstein (2006) point out that while students place primacy on relationships with teachers,

teachers commonly focus more on student behavior, seeking respect, cooperation, and compliance. Relationships are only one consideration—and often a time-consuming one—layered into many often contradictory values and agendas. Much of what happens in schools exists in what Bingham and Sidorkin (2004) call a "fog of forgetfulness" which, they write, clouds the simple idea that education is primarily about human beings meeting one another to learn. Relationships are such a constant that they often remain unexamined in schools.

For Me, It Is About Letting Go of Restorative

After casting my research net wide and paying close attention to my data, I then attempted to force all that I learned back into the box labeled *restorative*. It did not fit. I started this research journey generally convinced that RJ was the panacea that would transform conflict, people, schools, and societal conditions. Yet, students kept repeating a much simpler and more obvious message: It is all about relationships.

Since RJ attends to relationships, some of what they revealed can indeed be parsed and sorted as restorative. But the lines are not at all distinct between what can be called restorative and any or all of what can be called RRS, School of Football, circle time, Pupil Support, teachers who care, a headteacher that walks the corridors, reflective staff, pals that have your back, and any other of the less defined layers of student experience. RJ is enmeshed with all the other approaches and the inherent dynamics of schools. RJ, I learned, both reflects and affects—as do the other approaches—the real core of the school: relationships. Relationships are both the noun (the what) and the verb (the how) of schools.

This message might seem too obvious. Or, conversely, not obvious at all because it is so central to and implicit within all aspects of schooling. Teachers and administrators, faced with many competing agendas, each with their own imperatives, tend to lose focus on relationships, even when and if those agendas would be more successfully served by prioritizing relationships. This is not the case for students. They care about the centrality and quality of relationships. Period. Broad frameworks that shape school practices are mediated through relationships. When frameworks—whether RJ or otherwise—are grounded in public and private relationships, embodying "what is necessary to live collectively and as our 'best selves'" (Elliott, 2011, p. 5), they are more likely to be coherent, relevant, and potentially transformative to students. When frameworks prioritize one of the myriad of other agendas within schools, they may be narrowly effective by their own isolated matrix, but matter little to students and, more than likely, be of little long-term consequence. If educators wish school to be relevant to students, then it is the relationships to which they must attend.

The Real Question: Social Control or Social Engagement?

In *No Education without Relation*, the Manifesto of Relational Pedagogy states, "Human relationality is not an ethical value. Domination is as relational as love" (Bingham & Sidorkin, 2004, p. 7). Once the centrality of relationships is established, the question then becomes what sorts of relationships exist and what is the effect of being in relationship. Understanding the quality and effect of relationships necessitates a return to the concepts of social control and social engagement.

Although my data do indeed reveal the presence of both affirmative and transformative RJ, the focus is too narrow to be meaningful. Students experience social control and social engagement not only in RJ; regardless of the framework or approach used, students experience ideologies—restorative or otherwise—within relationship. Relationships are the baseline by which to understand the extent of transformation and affirmation.

Relationships as the milieu in which we as humans understand ourselves is both an ancient and continually evolving idea. Llewellyn and Llewellyn (2015) place RJ within relational theory which draws on such thinkers as Buber, Bakhtin, Dewey, Gadamer, Heidegger, Noddings, Gilligan, and Freire, among others (Bingham & Sidorkin, 2004; Llewellyn, 2011b; Llewellyn & Llewellyn, 2015). Other theories make similar claims about the centrality and primacy of relationships: attachment theory (Ainsworth, 1973; Bowlby, 1969); self-determination theory (Deci & Ryan, 2012); socioecological models (Berkes & Folke, 1998; Bookchin, 2007; Bronfenbrenner, 2005); and, in education, school climate research (Anderson, 1982; Cohen, 2006; Smith, 2008) and education for the common good (Dorn, 2017; Westheimer, 2017). My study confirms the significance of relationships in schools, exploring the quality of those relationships.

In my study, I build on Morrison and Vaandering's (2012) conceptualization of schools as institutions of social control and social engagement, but branch from their thinking in a number of ways. One, my research shows that a school that embraces RJ does not necessarily become an institution of social engagement; schools can continue to operate as agencies of social control while embracing RJ. In fact, RJ can become a tool of social control. Two, I disagree that schools that focus on social control are rule-based and those that focus on social engagement are relationship-based. As the students in my study reveal, schools simply are relational spheres and everything that happens in schools unfolds in this relational context. The difference is whether those school relationships are about control or engagement.

Despite these differences, I concur with Morrison and Vaandering (2012) that schools based on social engagement are better situated to support individual and communal well-being and development than those based on social control. This echoes Llewellyn and Llewellyn's (2015) assertion that relationships have the power to foster human flourishing (those based on social engagement) and hinder human flourishing (those based on social control).

The real question of RJ is ultimately not whether schools use RJ affirmatively or transformatively. The real question is about relationships. Are relationships in schools about social control? Or are they about social engagement? And what can be mobilized to ensure that relationships lean more toward social engagement in schools than control?

Conclusion: RJ as Window

Schools are constituted by relationships. Yet relationships are, to borrow from Marshall McLuhan's idea about culture, "as imperceptible to us as water is to fish" (McLuhan & Parker, 1969, p. 5). We simply exist in relationship. Relationships, however, as has been pointed out, are not innately good. They can both empower and dominate. They can be about both social control and social engagement.

Understanding RJ in schools is only meaningful if viewed as a window into the actual core of the school: relationships. RJ can be affirmative and used for the purpose of social control; RJ can also be transformative and used for the purpose of social engagement. RJ is used in the service of predominant relational objectives in the school. A school in which relationships are ones of social control—based on compliance, rules, behavior, punishment, and seeing students as isolated individuals—will utilize RJ to strengthen that control. A school in which relationships are ones of social engagement—based on relationships of equality and mutuality, with a broad focus on justice, empowerment and connection—will utilize RJ to strengthen that engagement.

The power in viewing RJ as a window into the character of school relationships is that it helps make relationships visible. It makes perceptible, going back to McLuhan (McLuhan & Parker, 1969), the water in which the students are swimming. It can be used to ask questions about those relationships and, if the intention exists, potentially assist in fostering a different relational context.

11

Restorative Justice as a Window Into Relationships

I began this book by suggesting that RJ was a concept whose time may have finally arrived (McCluskey, 2011). Attending to the increasing interest in RJ, I, along with other RJ advocates (including, Bargen, 2011; Elliott, 2011; Lockhart & Zammit, 2005; McCluskey et al., 2008a; Sullivan & Tifft, 2001; Vaandering, 2009; Woolford, 2009; Zehr & Toews, 2004) wondered whether the understanding of RJ being applied in mainstream society—including schools—was as transformative as we understood it to be. If RJ's time had, indeed, arrived, was RJ disrupting mainstream structures and systems, that is, being transformative; or, conversely, was RJ propagating the status quo, that is, being affirmative?

Summary of Study

So, in looking at this one study, how do students in Scotland (Royal Mills) and Canada (Rocky Creek) perceive RJ in schools? They experience RJ in

Adult Intentions, Student Perceptions, pages 163–171
Copyright © 2019 by Information Age Publishing
All rights of reproduction in any form reserved.

both affirmative and transformative ways, with contextual differences resulting in the Scottish experience leaning more toward affirmation and the Canadian experience leaning more toward transformation. Students revealed that it is not RJ, but relationships to which we must attend if we are to understand how schooling is both about engagement and control.

RJ can be a window into the character of these school relationships. A school in which relationships tend toward social control will utilize RJ to strengthen that control. A school in which relationships tend toward social engagement will utilize RJ to strengthen that engagement. Perhaps this is sufficient: for schools to recognize and name the relational objectives that exist within their body. I would assert, however, that schools genuinely interested in supporting *human flourishing* (Llewellyn and Llewellyn, 2015) would then seek to move beyond mere recognition of the character of school relationships to intentionally work toward relationships of social engagement, using RJ and/or other approaches as a framework to foster such a relational context.

RJ provides the ways and means to analyze the nature of relationships in a school environment. While RJ can be utilized to be transformative, RJ is neither necessary nor sufficient to achieve such an outcome. Such an outcome is instead dependent upon the quality of the relationships, those that foster engagement versus those of control.

The Lens and the Window

Howard Zehr's (1990) book *Changing Lenses* is one of the first articulations of a comprehensive RJ theory (Gavrielides, 2007; Vaandering, 2011; Van Ness & Strong, 2010). In it, Zehr suggests that a new lens is needed for viewing crime and justice; he advocates for a shift from a retributive lens to a restorative lens. Through the restorative lens, crime is viewed as a violation of people, relationships, and community, rather than as an individual offence against the state.

RJ, in its original articulation, was a lens through which one focused on the nature of relationships and, in so doing, reframed our perception of crime and justice issues. The metaphor was—and is—powerful. *Changing Lenses* suggests a radical paradigm shift; seeing crime and justice issues as rooted in relationships and community entirely changes the focus from individual retribution and punishment to restoring communal equanimity where, in the instance of crime, the victims, perpetrators, and community identify needs and find collective solutions.

Put in context beside this original, fundamental conception of RJ, I and, I believe, many others in the RJ field, are guilty of conceptual conflation. RJ has drifted from being a lens into the quality and character of relationships, where the object is the analysis of understanding and working with relationships, to becoming an object of its own, where it has become something we look *at* rather than *through*, where we assume it will foster quality relationships, where we have conflated the mechanisms of practicing RJ with the desired outcomes. It has become a practice, a technique, a method; a concrete object. In my study, I discovered that looking at RJ produced a limited view and did not allow for the complexity of the school experience. It was only when I took a step back and looked through RJ at the schools that the centrality, quality, and character of relationships came into focus.

My study, seen in this light, is a return to RJ as it was originally intended: something to look through. I describe RJ as a *window* in this study. In part, I shy away from using *lens* in deference to Zehr's original and groundbreaking use; in part, I believe that *window* more accurately describes the current state of RJ. Twenty-five years after first proposing a *restorative lens*, RJ has grown and morphed through theorizing, practice, and application. RJ, as it is understood and practiced, has expanded into many other relationship-based fields, including education. RJ is understood more broadly and has a greater reach than in its early days. The use of the continuum—from affirmative to transformative—is witness to this expansion. An RJ lens focuses attention within set parameters; an RJ window allows much broader panorama.

Parsing that which has been conceptually and in practice conflated, RJ, as a window, becomes a powerful way to identify or isolate what might otherwise remain implicit and unexamined. By itself, RJ does not guarantee certain qualities of relationship, but it does allow us to examine those qualities. It bounds and brings rigor to understanding relationships. If I were to have set out to directly study relationships in schools—the water, as I have described, in which members of the school community swim—it would have been too amorphous and all-encompassing to grasp. RJ provided focused space to attend to relationships. RJ in my study is a window through which to view the quality and character of relationships.

Implications

Listening to the students in my study, in both Scotland and Canada, brought me back to first principles. School, for students, is constituted of relationships and equated with relationships. They intimately understand Bingham and Sidorkin's (2004) assertion that education is primarily about humans who are in relation with one another, that "meeting and learning are inseparable" (p. 5). The focus my student co-researchers placed on relationships provided clear evidence of the ultimate centrality of relationships, not only for RJ, but also for education in general. Relationships are the essence of education. They mediate and animate any and all other curricular objectives (Bingham & Sidorkin, 2004; Cavanagh, 2011). By using RJ as a window to make school relationships explicit, we are able to examine the quality and character of relationships and, with this, ask questions of how they are used to control and/or engage.

Implications for Education

My study, in making relationships explicit, calls for a return to first principles, in schools and in teacher education.

Return to First Principles in Schools

It is easy to lose sight of that in which we are immersed. This is, I believe, the case of schools and relationships. My study sheds light on the essence of schools—relationships—serving as a reminder of that to which we must attend if schools wish to be relevant, engaging, and meaningful to students. It is a call to focus on what Westheimer (2017) names education for the common good.

This is where the idea becomes both simple and profound. Most humans can relate to the simple fact that we exist in relation. Systems, structures, and institutions—governments, justice system, and schools, to name a few—were organized by humans to attend to human needs, for the common good. Yet, as those systems become entrenched, the simple and essential focus on people and relationships becomes obscured. "The needs of these institutions," Elliott (2011) charges, "are viewed as more important than the needs of the people they were meant to serve" (p. 169). Sullivan and Tifft (2001) go further, referencing the taken-for-granted structural violence that occurs when, to meet systems' needs, systems are organized to deny the voice and active participation of some (p. 120). When this occurs—when the needs of the school, for instance, are deemed more important than the needs of the student, or when school is organized to deny student voice—relationships do not cease to exist; they simply become relationships of social control rather than social engagement, with largely unexamined consequences for other objectives, pedagogic, curricular, social, or cultural. They work against the common good.

A return to first principles in schools calls, first, for recognition that relationships are the essence of schools and, second, for an examination of the character of those relationships. I would suggest that schools interested in attending to relationships conduct a form of *relationship audit*, honestly assessing the nature of existing relationships. While the term *audit* should be used with great care because it is fraught with connotations of faux accountability, where measurement is mistaken with accountability, it would focus attention on relationships and their primacy in our societal interactions. A relationship audit in schools, undertaken to maximize engagement potential, could utilize the identified components of social control and social engagement to genuinely assess the relational health of schools. Importantly, the student point of view would need to be given equal or even more weight than the views of adults in the school for the audit to be effective and complete.

Return to First Principles in Teacher Education

As evidenced in my study, personal commitment on the part of educators to relationships of equality and mutuality is immensely influential on the student experience of school. Students in Rocky Creek and Royal Mills referenced teachers whom they trusted, and named such teachers as part of their positive assessments of school. Students in both sites also wished for more relationships with educators based on mutual trust.

Although all educators in the study expressed feelings of care toward their students, it was clear that many educators—in both schools—did not identify with students and their social contexts. This was evidenced in how educators from both sites lamented how, in their view, restorative values were alien to students, their families, and cultures. Teaching is often described as a helping profession and good teachers are described as ones who care about children (Brown, Morehead, & Smith, 2008). Yet McCuaig (2012), in identifying a proliferation of discourses of care in education, suggests that the notion of *caring teachers* needs to be deconstructed. Moving beyond care to identification is crucial. One of the components of social engagement is mutuality, or, what Llewellyn (2011b) terms "equality of relationships" (p. 91), which is not relational "sameness" but are relationships characterized by mutual respect, concern, and dignity. In schools, equality of relationships is experienced when adults view students as humans to be engaged with rather than as objects to be controlled (Morrison & Vaandering, 2012).

How do teachers learn to engage with students as humans, through relationships of equality? As Garvis (2012) observes, care and relationality rarely appear in teacher education outcomes, professional standards for teachers, or assessment criteria. Although teacher candidates may hold the mainstream view that teaching is a caring profession, teacher education does little to interrogate this view or to offer insight into the character of student-teacher relationships. Although it surely happens, it is difficult to know how often teacher educators in universities raise the topic of relationships in particular courses; what is clear is that there are few courses offered in teacher education programs that focus specifically on relationships. Western University Centre for School-Based Mental Health conducted a study in 2014 for Physical and Health Education (PHE) Canada that scanned all courses available to pre-service teachers enrolled in Bachelor's of Education programs in Canada to identify classes that taught mental health. One of the four elements they used as criteria for such courses was a focus on relationships. The scan found that teacher education programs provide "very little" in the way of mental-health related courses (Teach Resiliency, n.d., para. 1). In terms of relationships specifically, the study found that while most programs offer courses on classroom management, those courses routinely discuss using behavioral techniques to increase student motivation rather than other aspects of relationships.

In order for schools to be places characterized by relationships of equality, such relationships need to be at the forefront of teacher education. My study shows that teacher candidates need to be engaged in an exploration of student–teacher and student–student relationships, moving beyond a notion of caring to one of mutuality and equality. Vaandering (2014) describes a professional development program on a relational understanding of RJ, designed so that participants both learn about RJ and experience it. In this case, RJ was both the window and the object. The program began with the concept of relationship to self and rippled outwards. Although the course was centered on RJ, such a relational approach could be applied to any teacher education course, or to a course specifically on fostering relationships of equality. Teacher candidates must both discuss and experience mutuality if they are to engage their students similarly.

Implications for RJ in Schools

This study utilized RJ as a window into relationships. Yet RJ in schools is both window and object; we need to think through both what RJ shows us about schools (the character of relationships) and how RJ is being used in schools (affirmatively or transformatively) to control and/or engage. Making school relationships explicit in my study allows for the identification of three lessons in terms of RJ in schools: continual reflection, school cohesion, and building on natural inclinations.

Continual Reflection

Transformative RJ, as outlined in this study, insists that school relationships are grounded in mutuality, encompass all aspects of schooling, and attend to structural and power imbalances. Transformative RJ seeks to disrupt the usual discourses that value individuals, order, compliance, rules, behavior, and social control. Disrupting these discourses is much more difficult than aligning oneself with them, as affirmative RJ often does. Thus, perhaps, transformative RJ advocates will need to be content with, as Mc-Cluskey (2013) writes, continually insisting that the system or the school is not restorative enough, seeing this as a sign that transformative RJ is beginning to, or might eventually, take root.

Such continual insistence requires continual reflection. This study reveals that if RJ is to be brought into a school in a transformative manner, reflection is required both before RJ is implemented and throughout its use. Royal Mills showed the importance of reflecting prior to bringing RJ into a school. Nationally and regionally, in particular, the application of RJ was part of a broader conversation where there was reflection about how RJ aligned with systemic priorities. The region assessed schools as to how prepared they were to implement RJ, based on adherence to restorative values. Although there was discussion of initial commitment to school-wide reflection, many admitted that the current state of RJ in the school teetered between being embedded and being lost. Most participants were not sure which it was. Although the senior management team and those in Pupil Support were committed to RJ and were open to reflection, this was not representative of the staff as a whole. In Rocky Creek, staff also went through a reflective process before selecting RJ as an approach, albeit less systematically than in Scotland. During the maintenance stage, staff as a whole exhibited an openness to honest reflection on the state of RJ in the school. In some ways, staff were leading the school leadership team in this conversation, as reflected in the request that I run a staff circle. Building on the strengths exhibited in both cases, I believe that reflection conducted both before implementation—to determine if values are in place to bring about relationships of mutuality and equality—and during all stages of implementation and maintenance—to continually be insisting the school work harder on those relationships—is crucial to ensuring that such an approach leans more toward transformation than affirmation.

School Cohesion

This study reveals that implementing RJ does not ensure that schools will be based on relationships of social engagement. The evidence suggests that RJ is only one piece of the puzzle. RJ both reflects and affects the character of relationships in schools, but it is neither necessary nor sufficient for relationships of social engagement. In both Royal Mills and Rocky Creek, there were other approaches that worked together with RJ to cohesively bring about relationships of engagement. In Royal Mills, Pupil Support, the senior management team and, to a lesser extent, RRS, combined with RJ to ensure that students felt that there was at least one adult they could trust; students characterized the school as family. In Rocky Creek, the frequent use of circles—either restorative or other—and the all-encompassing focus on RRS, combined with RJ to ensure that most students felt listened to, safe, and respected. Strengthening the links between these approaches could make for more consistent experiences of social engagement. On the other hand, linking RJ more with the idea of punishment, consequences, and affirmative understandings of rights (as something to be lost if responsibilities are not upheld) makes for more consistent experiences of social control.

Building on Natural Inclinations

RJ is, as Hendry (2009) writes, about building, maintaining, and repairing relationships. Since relationships are, in the eyes of students, the essence of education, an approach such as RJ that attends to relationships makes sense to students. Despite students' intimate knowledge of the core of RJ—relationships—if not its terminology, adults in both schools felt that restorative values were remote to students, concepts that were difficult to impart. This is, I believe, an example of adults complicating, as Bingham and Sidorkin (2004) write, simple, straightforward ideas. If students' natural interest in and inclination toward relationship were to be built upon, within the framework of RJ, relationships of equality and mutuality would be better placed to flourish in schools.

Final Words

The students in this study were generous, open, and complex, revealing—through their words and observations—layers of experiences, wisdom, dynamics, and relationships. The adults in this study were sincere, nuanced, and professional, providing insight into the complicated nature of being committed, supportive, and effective educators. Both schools in the study, in many ways, had evolved from punishment-based institutions to ones characterized by trusting relationships. I am grateful to all participants for what they taught me.

Using RJ as a window into the experience of students in the Scottish and Canadian school clarified the centrality of relationships in their classrooms. The RJ window also explained how those relationships were used to control students and how they were used to engage students. Relationships are the essence of schools. If RJ brings those relationships to light, allowing us to view their character, then, indeed, RJ is an idea whose time has finally arrived. RJ's time, however, has not arrived for its own sake, to promulgate expressions of RJ, whether affirmative or transformative; RJ's time has arrived to mobilize relationships of social engagement—however they are labelled—in schools and in society at large.

References

Aertsen, I., Parmentier, S., Vanfraechem, I., Walgrave, L., & Zinsstag, E. (2013). An adventure is taking off: Why Restorative Justice: An International Journal? *Restorative Justice: An International Journal, 1*(1), 1–14.

Ainsworth, M. D. S. (1973). The development of infant-mother attachment. In B. Cardwell & H. Ricciuti (Eds.), *Review of child development research* (Vol. 3, pp. 1–94) Chicago, IL: University of Chicago Press.

Alberta Catholic School Trustees' Association. (2010). ACSTA history. Retrieved from https://www.acsta.ab.ca/about-us/acsta-history

Alberta City. (2012). Municipal census.

Alberta Conflict Transformation Society. (2012). Annual Report, 2012.

Alberta Education. (n.d.a). *Caring, respectful and safe learning environments history.* Retrieved from https://education.alberta.ca/safe-and-caring-schools/safe-and-caring-schools/

Alberta Education. (n.d.b). Curriculum redesign: What will change?

Alberta Education. (2005a). *The heart of the matter: Character and citizenship education in Alberta schools.* Edmonton, Canada: Alberta Government. Retrieved from https://education.alberta.ca/media/142774/the_heart_of_the_matter_character_education_and_citizenship_in_alberta_schools.pdf

Alberta Education. (2005b). *Our words, our ways: Teaching First Nations, Métis and Inuit learners.* Edmonton, Canada: Aboriginal Services and Learning and Teaching Resources Branch. Retrieved from https://education.alberta.ca/media/307199/words.pdf

Alberta Education. (2008). *First Nations, Métis, and Inuit education policy framework progress report 2008.* Edmonton, Canada: Aboriginal Policy Branch. Retrieved from https://files.eric.ed.gov/fulltext/ED506114.pdf

Adult Intentions, Student Perceptions, pages 173–187
Copyright © 2019 by Information Age Publishing

Alberta Education. (2012a, January 20). *Education: Business plan, 2012–15.* Retrieved from http://www.finance.alberta.ca/publications/budget/budget2012/education.pdf

Alberta Education. (2012b). *Education funding in Alberta: Kindergarten to grade 12, 2011/2012 school year.* Edmonton, Canada: Alberta Government.

Alberta Education. (2013). *Guide to education: ECS to grade 12, 2013–2014.* Edmonton, Canada: Alberta Government.

Alberta Education. (2015). *How the accountability pillar works.* Retrieved from https://education.alberta.ca/accountability-pillar/how-the-pillar-works/everyone/evaluation-information/

Alberta Education—Cross-Ministry Services Branch. (2013). *A guide to effective collaboration between school administrators and police working in Alberta's schools.* Edmonton, Canada: Author. Retrieved from https://open.alberta.ca/dataset/754ad763-8a44-495a-b61f-a5b209af718b/resource/69182447-24b6-49e2-82dd-993f66d47fa3/download/policeschoolsprint.pdf

Alberta Government. (2011, January). *Background information. Action on research and innovation: The future of charter schools in Alberta.* Edmonton, Canada: Author.

Alberta Government. (2013). *Aboriginal peoples of Alberta: Yesterday, today, and tomorrow.* Edmonton, Canada: Author.

Alberta Government. (2014). *Alberta's occupational supply outlook, 2013–2023: Visible minorities, Aboriginals, and people with disabilities.* Edmonton, Cananda: Author.

Alberta School Board. (n.d.a). Behaviour and learning assistance program [Brochure].

Alberta School Board. (2013). *Find a school.*

Alberta School Board. (2014). *Three year education plan, 2013–2016; annual education results report, 2012–2013.*

Alberta Teaching Association Staff. (2013, March 12). Provincial budget fails to protect public education. *ATA News, 47*(13).

Amstutz, L. S., & Mullet, J. H. (2005). *The little book of restorative discipline for schools: Teaching responsibility; creating caring climates.* Intercourse, PA: Good Books.

Anderson, C. (1982). The search for school climate: A review of the research. *Review of Educational Research, 52*(3), 368–420.

Antonovsky, A. (1987). *Unravelling the mystery of health.* San Francisco, CA: Jossey-Bass.

Arnott, K. (2007). Restorative justice: Making brand-new endings. *Education Today, 19*(2), 22–23.

Bakhtin, M. (1992). *The dialogic imagination: Four essays.* Austin: University of Texas Press.

Bargen, C. (2010). *Educating for peacebuilding: Implementing restorative justice principles and practices in a school system.* Langley, Canada: Community Justice Initiatives.

Bargen, C. (2011). Transforming power: The key to justice? In *Re-visioning justice: Restorative justice week 2011.* Ottawa, Canada: Restorative Justice Division, Correctional Service of Canada.

BBC History. (2014). *20th Century Scotland–An introduction.* Retrieved from http://www.bbc.co.uk/history/scottishhistory/modern/intro_modern3.shtml

BBC News, Scotland. (2011, October 23). *Scotland could be sixth richest in world, says Swinney.* Retrieved from https://www.bbc.com/news/uk-scotland-scotland-politics-15423494

BBC News, Scotland. (2014a, September 12). *Scottish independence: World media suggests 'domino effect.'* Retrieved from http://www.bbc.com/news/uk-scotland-29178438

BBC News Scotland. (2014b, September 19). *Scottish referendum: Scotland votes 'No' to independence.* Retrieved from http://www.bbc.com/news/uk-scotland-29270441

Berkes, F., & Folke, C. (Eds.). (1998). *Linking social and ecological systems: Management practices and social mechanisms for building resilience.* Cambridge, England: Cambridge University Press.

Bickmore, K. (1998). Teacher development for conflict resolution [Maple Elementary School]. *Alberta Journal of Educational Research, 44*(1), 53–69.

Bingham, C., & Sidorkin, A. M. (Eds.). (2004). *No education without relation (Counterpoints: Studies in the postmodern theory of education, 259).* J. L. Kincheloe & S. R. Steinberg (General Editors), Vol. 259, New York, NY: Peter Lang.

Bishop, R., Ladwig, J., & Berryman, M. (2014). The centrality of relationships for pedagogy: The Whanaungatanga thesis. *American Educational Research Journal, 51*(1), 184–214.

Black, A. (2014, October 6). Scotland votes 'no': What happens now? *BBC Scotland.* Retrieved from http://www.bbc.com/news/uk-scotland-scotland-politics-29252899

Black, C., Chamberlain, V., Murray, L., Sewel, K., & Skelton, J. (2012, October 2). *Behaviour in Scottish schools 2012: Final report.* Edinburgh, Scotland: Scottish Government.

Bookchin, M. (2007). *Social ecology and communalism.* Edinburgh, Scotland: AK Press.

Bourdieu, P., & Passeron, J. (1990). *Reproduction in education, society and culture* (2nd ed.). Thousand Oaks, CA: SAGE.

Bourgon, L. (2017, April 20). Brexit has brought the idea of Scottish independence back from the dead. *The Atlantic.* Retrieved from https://www.theatlantic.com/international/archive/2017/04/scotland-sturgeon-may-brexit-britain-independence/523623/

Bowlby J. (1969). *Attachment and loss, Volume 1: Attachment.* New York, NY: Basic Books.

Boyes-Watson, C., & Pranis, K. (2014). *Circle forward: Building a restorative school community.* St. Paul, MN: Living Justice Press.

Bronfenbrenner, U. (2005). *Making human beings human: Bioecological perspectives on human development.* London, England: SAGE.

Brown, N., Morehead, P., & Smith, J. B. (2008) . . . . But I love children: Changing elementary teacher candidates' conceptions of the qualities of effective teachers. *Teacher Education Quarterly, 35*(1), 169–184.

Burns, H. (March, 2013). "Transforming Scotland: Lecture by Sir Harry Burns" presented by Howard League Scotland. Edinburgh, Scotland.

Camara, H. (1971). Spiral of violence. London, England: Sheed and Ward. Retrieved from http://www.alastairmcintosh.com/general/spiral-of-violence.htm

The Canadian Press. (2014, March 22). Alison Redford resignation: Did sexism play a role in her demise? *CBC News.* Retrieved from http://www.cbc.ca/news/canada/alison-redford-resignation- did-sexism-play-a-role-in-her-demise-1.2582789

Cavanagh, T. (2010). Restorative practices in schools: Breaking the cycle of student involvement in child welfare and legal systems. *Protecting Children, 24*(4), 53–60.

Cavanagh, T. (2011). Creating a culture of care in schools: A New Zealand perspective on using restorative practices. In A. Charlton, S. Pavelka, & P. J. Verrecchia (Eds.), *International perspectives on restorative justice in education* (pp. 136–159). Kanata, ON: J. Charlton.

Cavanagh, T., Vigil, P., & Garcia, E. (2014). A story legitimating the voices of Latino/Hispanic students and their parents: Creating a restorative justice response to wrongdoing and conflict in schools. *Equity & Excellence in Education, 47*(4), 565–579.

CBC. (2001). *Canada: A People's history, Social Credit Party.* Retrieved from http://www.cbc.ca/history/EPISCONTENTSE1EP13CH3PA2LE.html

CBC. (2015). *Tories at 40, 1971–2011: Alberta and the national energy program.* Retrieved from http://www.cbc.ca/alberta/features/tories40/nep.html

Chmelynski, C. (2005). Restorative justice for discipline with respect. *The Education Digest, 71*(1), 17–20.

Clamp, K. (2016). *Restorative justice in transitional settings.* Abingdon, England: Taylor & Francis.

Cohen, J. (2006). Social, emotional, ethical and academic education: Creating a climate for learning, participation in democracy and well-being. *Harvard Educational Review, 76*(2), 201–237.

Communities Analytical Services. (2014b, December). *Scottish poverty statistics briefing.* Retrieved from http://www.gov.scot/Topics/Statistics/Browse/Social-Welfare/IncomePoverty/povertybrief

Conrad, D., & Unger, D. (2011). Violence at school, the violence of schooling: Restorative alternatives. In A. Charlton, S. Pavelka, & P. J. Verrecchia (Eds.), *International perspectives on restorative justice in education* (pp. 30–68). Kanata, ON: J. Charlton.

Cook-Sather, A. (2006). Sound, presence, and power: "Student voice" in educational research and reform. *Curriculum Inquiry, 36*(4), 359–390.

Cosh, C. (2012, April 30). One wild rise. *Maclean's, 125*(16), 16–20.

Cotter, J. (2014, March 28). Alberta students to be taught legacy of Indian residential schools. *CTV News.* Retrieved from http://www.ctvnews. ca/canada/alberta-students-to-be-taught-   legacy-of-indian-residential-schools-1.1750176

Cronin-Lampe, K., & Cronin-Lampe, R. (2010). Developing a restorative school culture: The blending of a personal and professional 'pilgrimage.' *Explorations: An E-Journal of Narrative Practice, 1,* 14–33.

Cunneen, C. (2012). Restorative justice, globalisation, and the logic of the empire. In J. McCulloch & S. Pickering (Eds.), *Borders and transnational crime: Pre-crime, mobility and serious harm in an age of globalisation* (pp. 99–113). Basington, England: Palgrave Macmillan.

Daily Record (2013, April 9). Hundreds of Scots mark Margaret Thatcher's death in Glasgow's George Square. *Daily Record.* Retrieved from http://www.dailyrecord.co.uk/news/scottish-news/scots-celebrate-margaret-thatchers-death-1819505

Daly, K. (2000). Revisiting the relationship between retributive and restorative justice. In H. Strang & J. Braithwaite (Eds.), *Restorative justice: Philosophy to practice* (pp. 33–54). Farnham, England: Ashgate.

Daly, K. (2002). Restorative justice: The real story. *Punishment Society, 4,* 55–79.

Deci, R., & Ryan, R. (2012). Motivation, personality, and development within embedded social contexts: An overview of self-determination theory. In R. M. Ryan (Ed.), *Oxford handbook of human motivation* (pp. 85–107). Oxford, England: Oxford University Press.

Donaldson, G. (2010, December). *Teaching Scotland's future: Report of a review of teacher education in Scotland.* Edinburgh, Scotland: Scottish Government.

Dorn, C. (2017). *For the common good: A new history of higher education in America.* Ithaca, New York, NY: Cornell University Press.

Drewery, W. (2004). Conferencing in schools: Punishment, restorative justice, and the productive importance of the process of conversation. *Journal of Community and Applied Social Psychology, 14,* 332–344.

Drewery, W., & Winslade, J. (2003, December). *Developing restorative practices in schools: Flavour of the month or saviour of the system?* Paper presented at the Australian Association for Research in Education/New Zealand Association for Research in Education Conference, Auckland, New Zealand. Retrieved from https://www.researchgate.net/publication/228537725_Developing_Restorative_Practices_in_Schools_Flavour_of_the_month_or_saviour_of_the_system

Duff, R. A. (2001) *Punishment, communication and community.* New York, NY: Oxford University Press.

Duff, R. A. (2003). Probation, punishment and restorative justice: Should altruism be engaged in punishment? *Howard Journal of Criminal Justice, 42*(2), 181–197.

Duncan, C. (2015). Education and social innovation: The youth uncensored project—A case study of youth participatory research and cultural democracy in action. *Canadian Journal of Education, 38*(1), 1–25.

Eagle, H. (2011). *Re-visioning the restorative justice movement: Getting to the soul of justice.* In Re-visioning justice: Restorative justice week 2011. Ottawa, Canada: Restorative Justice Division, Correctional Service of Canada.

Education and Learning Directorate. (2012). Relationships and behaviour in Scottish Local Authority [brochure].

Education Scotland. (n.d.a). About positive relationships and behaviour.

Education Scotland. (n.d.b). Additional support needs. Retrieved from https://education.gov.scot/parentzone/additional-support/What%20are%20additional%20support%20needs?

Education Scotland. (2011, September). Scottish schools online. Retrieved from http://www.educationscotland.gov.uk/scottishschoolsonline/schools/xxxx

Education Scotland. (2012). Find a school. Retrieved from http://www.education-scotland.gov.uk/parentzone/myschool/findaschool/schools/xxxx.asp

Education Scotland (2013). Free meal entitlement. Retrieved from http://www.educationscotland.gov.uk/scottishschoolsonline/schools/freemeal-entitlement.asp xxxx

Elliott, E. M. (2011). *Security with care: Restorative justice and healthy societies.* Nova Scotia, Canada: Fernwood.

Ellis, J., Hetherington, R., Lovell, M., McConaghy, J., & Viczko, M. (2013). Draw me a picture, tell me a story: Evoking memory and supporting analysis through pre-interview drawing activities. *Alberta Journal of Educational Research, 58*(4), 488–508.

Enns, E., & Myers, C. (2009). Ambassadors of reconciliation: Diverse Christian practices of restorative justice and peacemaking (Vol. 2). Maryknoll, NY: Orbis Books.

Evans, K., & Vaandering, D. (2016). *The little book of restorative justice in education: Fostering responsibility, healing and hope in schools.* Lancaster, PA: Good Books.

Famous Five Foundation. (2012). *The "persons" case.* Retrieved from http://www.famou5.ca/the-persons-case/

Finch, D., Varella, P., & Deephouse, D. (2012, March 8). Making the oil sands personal. *The Globe and Mail.* Retrieved from http://www.theglobeand-mail.com/globe-debate/making-the-oil-sands-personal/article551987/

Foucault, M. (1979). *Discipline and punish.* New York, NY: Vintage.

Foucault, M. (1991). Politics and the study of discourse. In G. Burchell, C. Gordon, & P. Miller (Eds.), *The Foucault effect: Studies in governmentality* (pp. 53–72). Chicago, IL: University of Chicago Press.

Fraser, N. (1997). *Justice interruptus: Critical reflections on the "postsocialist condition."* New York, NY: Routledge.

Fraser, N. (2000). Rethinking recognition. *New Left Review, 3,* 107–120.

Freire, P. (2002). *Education for critical consciousness.* New York, NY: Continuum.

Fronius, T., Persson, H., Guckenburg, S., Hurley, N., & Petrosino, A. (February 2016). *Restorative justice in U.S. schools: A research review.* Retrieved from http://jprc.wested.org/new-report-restorative-justice-in-u-s-schools-review-of-research/

Garvis, S. (2012). Examining the impact of the author's pedagogy on developing relationality and care in pre-service early childhood teachers. *US-China Education Review A, 4*, 431–441.

Gavrielides, T. (2007). *Restorative justice theory and practice: Addressing the discrepancy.*

Helsinki, Finland: European Institute for Crime Prevention and Control.

General Teaching Council for Scotland. (2013, January/February). Resetting the standards. *Teaching Scotland, 48*, 18–19.

Goldi Productions. (2007). *The Hudson's Bay Company and the North West Company.* Retrieved from http://firstpeoplesofcanada.com/fp_furtrade/fp_furtrade3.html

Goodman, J. F. (2006). School discipline in moral disarray. *Journal of Moral Education, 35*(2), 213–230.

Graham, G. (2000). Behaviorism. In E. N. Zalta (Ed.), *The Stanford encyclopedia of philosophy.* Retrieved from http://plato.stanford.edu/entries/behaviorism/

Grant, G. (1993). Discovering how you really teach. In K. A. Strike & P. L. Ternasky (Eds.), *Ethics for professionals in education: Perspectives for preparation and practice* (pp. 135–147). New York, NY: Teachers College Press.

Haraway, D. (1990). A manifesto for cyborgs: Science, technology, and socialist feminism in the 1980s. In L. J. Nicholson (Ed.), *Feminism/Postmodernism,* New York, NY: Routledge.

Harber, C., & Sakade, N. (2009). Schooling for violence and peace: How does peace education differ from 'normal' schooling? *Journal of Peace Education, 6*, 171–187.

Helbig, L. (2014). *Beautiful destruction.* Vancouver, Canada: Rocky Mountain Books.

Hendry, R. (2009). *Building and restoring respectful relationships in schools: A guide to using restorative practice.* New York, NY: Routledge.

Herman, A. (2001). *How the Scots invented the modern world: The true story of how Western Europe's poorest nation created our world and everything in it.* New York, NY: Crown.

Herr, K., & Anderson, G. L. (2003). Violent youth or violent schools? A critical incident analysis of symbolic violence. *The International Journal of Leadership in Education, 6*(4), 415–433.

Hopgood, S., & Missal, C. (2013, November). *Building a restorative culture* [Webinar]. Retrieved from http://resources.safeandcaring.ca/resource-students/restorative-practices/

Hopkins, B. (2011). *The restorative classroom: Using restorative approaches to foster effective learning.* London, England: Teach to Inspire, Optimus Education.

Hoy, A. W., & Weinstein, C. S. (2006). Student and teacher perspectives on classroom management. In C. M. Evertson & C. S. Weinstein (Eds.), *Handbook of classroom management: Research, practice and contemporary issues* (pp. 181–219). Mahwah, NJ: Lawrence Erlbaum.

Illich, I. (1983). *Deschooling society*. New York, NY: Harper & Row. (Original work published 1971).

International Institute for Restorative Practices. (2013). *IIRP Factbook 2013: July 1, 2012–June 30, 2013*. Retrieved from http://www.iirp.edu/pdf/IIRP-Factbook_2013.pdf

Jain, S., Bassey, H., Brown, M. A., & Kalra, P. (2014). *Restorative justice in Oakland schools: Implementation and impacts*. Report prepared for the Office of Civil Rights, U.S. Department of Education. Retrieved from http://www.ousd.org/cms/lib07/CA01001176/Centricity/Domain/134/OUSD-RJ%20Report%20revised%20Final.pdf

Johnson, J. C., Avenarius, C., & Weatherford, J. (2006) The active participant-observer: Applying social role analysis to participant observation. *Field Methods, 18,*(2), 111–134.

Johnstone, G., & Van Ness, D. W. (2007). The meaning of restorative justice. In G. Johnstone & D. W. Van Ness (Eds.), *Handbook of restorative justice* (pp. 5–23). Portland, OR: Willan.

Kane, J., Lloyd, G., McCluskey, G., Riddell, S., Stead, J., & Weedon, E. (2007). *Restorative practices in three Scottish councils: Final report of the evaluation of the first two years of the pilot projects 2004–2006*. Edinburgh, Scotland: Scottish Government.

Karp, D. R., & Breslin, B. (2001). Restorative justice in school communities. *Youth & Society, 33*, 249–272.

Kecskemeti, M., & Winslade, J. (2016). *Better classroom relationships*. Wellington, NZ: New Zealand Council for Educational Research Press.

Kidner, C. (2010, February 3). Scottish Parliament Information Centre briefing: Curriculum for excellence. Edinburgh, Scotland: Scottish Parliament.

Kitzinger, J. (1994). The methodology of focus groups: The importance of interaction between research participants. *Sociology of Health and Illness, 16*, 103–121.

Kohn, A. (1996, November). Beyond discipline. *Education Week*. Retrieved from http://www.edweek.org/ew/articles/1996/11/20/12kohn.h16.html

Lewis, S. (2009). *Findings from schools implementing restorative practices*. Bethlehem, PA: International Institute of Restorative Practice Graduate School.

Llewellyn, J. (2011a). A relational vision of justice. In *Re-visioning justice: Restorative justice week 2011*. Ottawa, Canada: Restorative Justice Division, Correctional Service of Canada.

Llewellyn, J. (2011b). Restorative justice: Thinking relationally about justice. In J. Downie & J. J. Llewellyn (Eds.), *Being relational: Reflections on relational theory and health law* (pp. 89– 108). Vancouver, Canada: UBC Press.

Llewellyn, K. R., & Llewellyn, J. J. (2015). A restorative approach to learning: Relational theory as feminist pedagogy in universities. In T. Penny Light, J. Nicholas, & R. Bondy (Eds.), *Feminist pedagogy in higher education: Critical theory and practice*. Waterloo, ON: Wilfrid Laurier University Press.

Lloyd, G., & McCluskey, G. (2009). *Restorative practice pilots and approaches in Scotland: Follow up*. Edinburgh, Scotland: Scottish Government.

Lloyd-Smith, M., & Tarr, J. (2000). Researching children's perspectives: A socio-logical dimension. In A. Lewis & G. Lindsay (Eds.), *Researching children's perspectives* (pp. 59–70). Buckingham, England: Open University Press.

Lockhart, A., & Zammit, L. (2005). *Restorative justice: Transforming society.* Toronto, Canada: Inclusion Press.

London, R. (2011). *Crime, punishment and restorative justice: From the margins to the mainstream.* Boulder, CO: First Forum Press.

Lyubansky, M., & Shpungin, E. (2016). Challenging power dynamics in restor-ative justice. In T. Gavrielides (Ed.,) *The psychology of restorative justice: Managing the power within* (pp. 183–201). Abingdon, England: Routledge.

MacAllister, J. (2013). Restorative, transformation or education? A philosophi-cal critique of restorative approaches in schools. In E. Sellman, H. Cr-emin, & G. McCluskey (Eds.), *Restorative approaches to conflict in schools: Interdisciplinary perspectives on whole school approaches to managing relation-ships* (pp. 97–110). London, England: Routledge.

MacDonald, A. (2013). *Considerations of identity in teachers' attitudes toward teach-ing controversial issues under conditions of globalization: A critical democratic perspective from Canada* (Doctoral thesis). Ontario Institute for Studies in Education, Toronto, Canada.

Manitoba Government. (n.d.). Hudson's Bay Company history. Retrieved from https://www.collectionscanada.gc.ca/confederation/023001-3040-e.html

Mayworm, A. M., Sharkey, J. D., Hunnicutt, K. L., & Schiedel, K. C. (2016). Teacher consultation to enhance implementation of school-based restor-ative justice. *Journal of Educational and Psychological Consultation, 26*(4) 1–28. doi:10.1080/10474412.2016.1196364

McCluskey, G. (2011, February). *Swimming pools, flash mobs and disruption in schools: False hopes or promising futures?* Paper presented at the ESRC-funded seminar series on Restorative Approaches to Conflict in Schools, Edinburgh, Scotland. Paper retrieved from http://www.educ.cam.ac.uk/research/projects/restorativeapproaches/seminarfour/

McCluskey, G. (2013). Challenges to education: Restorative practice as a radi-cal demand on conservative structures of schooling. In E. Sellman, H. Cremin, & G. McCluskey (Eds.), *Restorative approaches to conflict in schools: Interdisciplinary perspectives on whole school approaches to managing relation-ships* (pp. 132–141). London, England: Routledge.

McCluskey, G., Kane, J., Lloyd, G., Riddell, S., Stead, J., & Weedon, E. (2013). Effective evaluation of restorative approaches. In E. Sellman, H. Cremin, & G. McCluskey (Eds.), *Restorative approaches to conflict in schools: Inter-disciplinary perspectives on whole school approaches to managing relationships* (pp. 142–156). London, England: Routledge.

McCluskey, G., Lloyd, G., Kane, J., Riddell, S., Stead, J., & Weedon, E. (2008a). Can restorative practices in schools make a difference? *Educational Re-view, 60*(4), 405–417.

McCluskey, G., Lloyd, G., Kane, J., Riddell, S., Stead, J., & Weedon, E. (2008b). "I was dead restorative today": From restorative justice to restorative approaches in school. *Cambridge Journal of Education, 38*(2), 199–216.

McCold, P. (2000). Toward a mid-range theory of restorative criminal justice: A reply to the maximalist model. *Contemporary Justice Review, 3*(4), 357–414.

McCold, P., & Wachtel, T. (2003). In pursuit of paradigm: A theory of restorative justice. *Restorative Practices E-Forum.* Retrieved from www.iirp.edu/article_detail.php?article_id=NDI0

McCuaig, L. A. (2012). Dangerous carers: Pastoral power and the caring teacher of contemporary Australian schooling. *Educational Philosophy and Theory, 44*(8), 862–877.

McLuhan, M., & Parker, H. (1969). *Counterblast.* Berkeley, CA: Gingko Press.

Meyers, D. T., (1997). Introduction. In D. T. Meyers, (Ed.), *Feminists rethink the self.* Boulder, CO: Westview Press.

Morgan, E. (2004). Open the doors. Scottish Parliamentary Corporate Body.

Morris, E. W. (2005). 'Tuck in that shirt!' Race, class, gender and discipline in an urban school. *Sociological Perspectives, 48*(1), 25–48.

Morrison, B. E. (2007a). *Restoring safe school communities: A whole school response to bullying, violence and alienation.* Leichhardt, Australia: Federation Press.

Morrison, B. E. (2007b). Schools and restorative justice. In G. Johnstone & D. W. Van Ness (Eds.), *Handbook of restorative justice* (pp. 325–350). Portland, OR: Willan.

Morrison, B. E. (2011). From social control to social engagement: Enabling the "time and space" to talk through restorative justice and responsive regulation. In R. Rosenfeld, K. Quinet, & C. Garcia (Eds.), *Contemporary issues in criminology theory and research* (pp. 97–106). Belmont, CA: Wadsworth.

Morrison, B. E. (2015). Restorative justice in education: Changing lenses on education's three Rs. *Restorative Justice, 3*(3), 445–452. doi:10.1080/2050 4721.2015.1109367

Morrison, B. E., & Vaandering, D. (2012). Restorative justice: Pedagogy, praxis, and discipline. *Journal of School Violence, 11*(2), 138–155.

National Records of Scotland. (2013). Table 2: Ethnic groups, Scotland, 2001 and 2011 (Data file). Retrieved from http://www.scotlandscensus.gov. uk/documents/censusresults/release2a/rel2asbtable2.pdf

Natural Resources Canada. GeoAccess Division. (2005). Land and freshwater area, by province and territory. Retrieved from https://www150.statcan .gc.ca/n1/pub/11-402-x/2010000/chap/geo/tbl/tbl07-eng.htm

Noddings, N. (2004). Foreword. In C. Bingham & A. M. Sidorkin (Eds.), *No education without relation* (pp. vii-viii). New York, NY: Peter Lang.

Nucci, L. P. (2001). *Education in the moral domain.* Cambridge, England: Cambridge University Press.

Orum, A. M., Feagin, J. R., & Sjoberg, G. (1991). Introduction: The nature of the case study. In J. R. Feagin, A. M. Orum, & G. Sjoberg (Eds.), *A case for the case study* (pp. 1–26). Chapel Hill: University of North Carolina Press.

Pakan, N., & Society for Safe and Caring Schools and Communities. (2007). Restorative justice community/classroom conferencing: A guide for parents and teachers. Edmonton, Canada: Society for Safe and Caring Schools and Communities.

Palmer, H., & Palmer, T. (1990). *Alberta: A new history.* Edmonton, Canada: Hurtig.

Parliament of Canada. (2014). Women's right to vote in Canada. Retrieved from https://lop.parl.ca/sites/ParlInfo/default/en_CA/ElectionsRidings/womenVote

Pawlychka, C. (2012). Punishment or logical consequences: A response to the punishment debate within restorative justice. *Alaska Journal of Dispute Resolution, 2012*(1), 95–118.

Porter, A.J. (2007, June). Restorative practices in schools: Research reveals power of restorative approach, part II. *Restorative Practices EForum.* Retrieved July 20, 2009, from http://www.safersanerschools.org/library/school research2.html

Porter, L. (1996). *Student behaviour: Theory and practice for teachers.* St. Leonards, Australia: Allen & Unwin.

Priestley, M., & Minty, S. (2013). Curriculum for Excellence: 'A brilliant idea, but...' *Scottish Educational Review, 45*(1), 39–52.

Raby, R. (2012). *School rules: Obedience, discipline and elusive democracy.* Toronto, Canada: University of Toronto Press.

Reimer, K. (2009). Teachers, administrators and gatekeepers of change: A case study of the implementation of restorative justice in one Ontario public school (Master's thesis). University of Ottawa, Ottawa, Canada.

Richards, S. (2013, August 23). Scotland is going it alone—regardless of the referendum. *The Guardian.* Retrieved from https://www.theguardian.com/commentisfree/2013/aug/23/scotland-referendum-devolution-separate-directions

Riestenberg, N. (2003). *Restorative schools grants final report, January 2002–June 2003: A summary of the grantees' evaluation.* Minnesota Department of Education. Retrieved July 22, 2009 from http://education.state.mn.us/MDE/Learning_Support/Safe_and_Healthy_Learners/Safe_Learners/Violence_Prevention_Restorative_Measures/index.html

Riestenberg, N. (2012). *Circle in the square: Building community and repairing harm in school.* St Paul, MN: Living Justice Press.

Rowe, D. (2006). Taking responsibility: School behaviour policies in England, moral development and implications for citizenship education. *Journal of Moral Education, 35*(4), 519–531.

Saul, J. R. (2008). *A fair country: Telling truths about Canada.* Toronto, Canada: Viking Canada.

Sawatsky, J. (2001). A shared justpeace ethic: Uncovering restorative values. *Conciliation Quarterly, 20*(3), 2–4.

Scottish Executive. (2001). *Better behaviour—Better learning: Report of the discipline task group.* Edinburgh, Scotland: Her Majesty's Stationery Office.

Scottish Executive. (2003). *Circular 8/03 guidance on exclusion from school.* Edinburgh, Scotland: Scottish Executive Education Department.

Scottish Government. (n.d.). *Curriculum for Excellence.* Retrieved from http://www.gov.scot/Topics/Education/Schools/curriculum

Scottish Government. (n.d.). *What is GIRFEC?* Retrieved from http://www.gov.scot/Topics/People/Young-People/gettingitright/background

Scottish Government. (2010, August). *Relative poverty across Scottish local authorities.* Retrieved from http://www.gov.scot/Publications/2010/08/26155956/0

Scottish Government. (2013a). *Demographics.* Retrieved from http://www.gov.scot/Topics/People/Equality/Equalities/PopulationMigration

Scottish Government. (2013b). *The key to life: Improving quality of life for people with learning disabilities.* Retrieved from http://www.gov.scot/Publications/2013/06/1123/10

Scottish Government. (2013c). *Schools: Frequently asked questions.* Retrieved from http://www.gov.scot/Topics/Education/Schools/FAQs

Scottish National Party. (n.d.a.). *About us.* Retrieved from http://www.snp.org/about

Scottish National Party. (n.d.b.). *The new Scotland.* Retrieved from http://www.snp.org/referendum/the-new-scotland

Scottish National Statistics. (2012, December 11). *Statistical bulletin, education series: Summary statistics for schools in Scotland, No.3. Scottish Government.* Retrieved from http://www.gov.scot/Resource/0041/00410232.pdf.

Scottish Parliament. (2012a). *How the Scottish Parliament works,* (3rd ed.) [Brochure]. Scotland, United Kingdom: Scottish Parliamentary Corporate Body.

Scottish Parliament. (2012b). What happens in the Debating Chamber. [Brochure]. Scotland, United Kingdom: Scottish Parliamentary Corporate Body.

Smith, J. D. (2006). Solutions for bullying: Restorative practices for classrooms and schools. *Contact—TESL Ontario Newsletter, 32*(2), 42–51.

Smith, J. D. (2008). Promoting a positive school climate: Restorative practices for the classroom. In D. Pepler & W. Craig (Eds.), *An international perspective on understanding and addressing bullying,* (PREVNet Series, Vol. 1, pp. 132–143). Toronto, Canada: PREVNet.

Statistics Canada. (2008). *Population reporting an Aboriginal identity, by age group, by province and territory, 2006 Census.* Retrieved from https://www150.statcan.gc.ca/n1/en/catalogue/98-510-X#tables

Statistics Canada. (2009). *Visible minority population, by province and territory, 2006 Census.* Retrieved from http://www.statcan.gc.ca/tables-tableaux/sum-som/l01/cst01/demo52c- eng.htm

Statistics Canada. (2011). Focus on geography series, 2011 Census. Census metropolitan area of Alberta. Retrieved from https://www12.statcan.gc.ca/census-recensement/2011/as-sa/fogs-spg/Facts-cma-eng.cfm?LANG=Eng&GK=CMA&GC=825

Statistics Canada. (2013). Population projections by Aboriginal identity in Canada, 2006 to 2031, analysis of results. Retrieved from http://www.statcan.gc.ca/pub/91-552- x/2011001/ana-eng.htm#a_1

Statistics Canada. (2014a). CANSIM Table 051-0001, population by year, by province, by territory. Retrieved from http://www.statcan.gc.ca/tables-tableaux/sum- som/l01/cst01/demo02a-eng.htm

Stinchcomb, J. B., Bazemore, G., & Riestenberg, N. (2006). Beyond zero tolerance: Restoring justice in secondary schools. *Youth Violence and Juvenile Justice, 4,* 123–147.

Sullivan, D., & Tifft, L. (2001). Restorative justice: Healing the foundations of our everyday lives. Monsey, NY: Willow Tree.

Teach Resiliency. (n.d.). *Mental health education did not come to school today.* Retrieved from http://www.teachresiliency.ca/#section-4

Thorsborne, M. (2013). A story of the emergence of restorative practice in schools in Australia and New Zealand: Reflect, repair, reconnect. In K. S. van Wormer & L. Walker (Eds.), *Restorative justice today: Practical applications* (pp. 43–51). Thousand Oaks, CA: SAGE.

Tomkins, G. (1986). A common countenance: Stability and change in the Canadian curriculum. Scarborough, Canada: Prentice-Hall Canada.

Tomporowski, B., Buck, M., Bargen, C., & Binder, V. (2011). Reflections on the past, present and future of restorative justice in Canada. *Alberta Law Review, 48*(4), 815–829.

Tonry, M. (Ed.). (2011). *Why punish? How much? A reader on punishment.* New York, NY: Oxford University Press.

Truth and Reconciliation Commission of Canada. (n.d.). *Residential school locations.* Retrieved from http://www.trc.ca/websites/trcinstitution/index.php?p=12

Umbreit, M., & Armour, M. P. (2010). *Restorative justice dialogue: An essential guide for research and practice.* New York, NY: Springer.

UNICEF. (n.d.). *Rights respecting schools award.* Retrieved from http://www.unicef.org.uk/rrsa

United Kingdom Office for National Statistics. (2013). *Population.* Retrieved from http://www.ons.gov.uk/ons/taxonomy/index.html?nscl=Population

Vaandering, D. (2009). *Towards effective implementation and sustainability of restorative justice in Ontario Public Schools: A critical case study* (Doctoral dissertation). University of Western Ontario, London, Canada.

Vaandering, D. (2011). A faithful compass: Rethinking the term restorative justice to find clarity. *Contemporary Justice Review, 14*(3), 307–328.

Vaandering, D. (2013). A window on relationships: Reflecting critically on a current restorative justice theory. *Restorative Justice: An International Journal, 1*(3), 311–333.

Vaandering, D. (2014). Relational restorative justice pedagogy in educator professional development. *Curriculum Inquiry, 44*(4), 508–530.

Van Herk, A. (2001). *Mavericks: An incorrigible history of Alberta.* Toronto, Canada: Penguin.

Van Ness, D. W., & Strong, K. H. (2010). *Restoring justice: An introduction to restorative justice* (4th ed.). New Province, NJ: Matthew Bender & Co., Inc.

Von Heyking, A. (2006). Fostering a provincial identity: Two eras in Alberta schooling. *Canadian Journal of Education, 29*(4), 1127–1156.

Von Heyking, A. (2013). *Aberhart, Manning and religion in the public schools of Alberta.* Retrieved from http://www.thefreelibrary.com/Aberhart,+Manni ng+and+religion+in+the+public+schools+o f+Alberta.-a0349221830

Wachtel, J. (2012, December 18). *Restorative practices data from Hampstead Hill implementation.* Restorative Practices eForum. Retrieved from http://restorativeworks.net/2012/12/restorative-practices-data-from -hampstead-hill-implementation/

Wagner, M. (1999). Charter schools in Alberta: Change or continuity in progressive conservative education policy? *Alberta Journal of Educational Research, 45*(1), 52–66.

Wearmouth, J., McKinney, R., & Glynn, T. (2007). Restorative justice: Two examples from New Zealand schools. *British Journal of Special Education, 34*(4), 196–203.

Western University Centre for School-Based Mental Health. (2014). *Mental health education in Canada: An analysis of teacher education and provincial/territorial curricula.* Physical and Health Education Canada. Retrieved from https://phecanada.ca/sites/default/files/content/docs/resources/ mentalhealtheducationincanada.pdf

Westheimer, J. (2017). Education that matters. *Canadian Journal of Education, 40*(2), 1–15.

Wheeldon, J. (2009). Finding common ground: Restorative justice and its theoretical construction(s). *Contemporary Justice Review, 12*(1), 91–100.

Wilkinson, S. (1998). Focus groups in health research: Exploring the meanings of health and illness. *Journal of Health Psychology, 3*, 329–338.

Woolford, A. (2009). *The politics of restorative justice: A critical introduction.* Nova Scotia, Canada: Fernwood.

Yes Scotland. (n.d.). *What independent Scotland can mean.* Retrieved from http:// www.yesscotland.net/news/what-independent-scotland-can-mean-you

Youth Justice Board for England and Wales. (2004). *National Evaluation of the Restorative Justice in Schools Programme.* London, England: Author.

Zehr, H. (1990). *Changing lenses: A new focus for crime and justice.* Scottdale, PA: Herald Press.

Zehr, H. (2002). *The little book of restorative justice.* Intercourse, PA: Good Books.

Zehr, H. (2005). Evaluation and restorative justice principles. In E. Elliot & R. M. Gordon (Eds.), *New directions in restorative justice: Issues, practice, evaluation* (pp. 296–303). London, England: Routledge.

Zehr, H. (2006, April). Values and principles in the practice of restorative justice. Paper presented at the International Conference on the Introduction of Restorative Justice in Ukraine: Results and Perspectives, Kyiv, Ukraine. Retrieved from http://restorativejustice.org/rj-library/values -and-principles-in-the-practice-of-restorative-justice/8799/#sthash.ulK0 W0CI.dpbs

Zehr, H. (2010). Foreword. In M. Umbreit & M. P. Armour, *Restorative justice dialogue: An essential guide for research and practice* (pp. vii–viii). New York, NY: Springer.

Zehr, H. & Toews, B. (Eds.). (2004). *Critical issues in restorative justice.* Monsey, NY: Criminal Justice Press.

Zulfa, M. (2015). *A case study examining the restorative justice practices implemented in three California high schools* (Doctoral dissertation). Liberty University, Lynchburg, Virginia.

Lightning Source UK Ltd.
Milton Keynes UK
UKHW011813050219
336792UK00003B/154/P